A PATRI...
FOR TODAY

*Love of country
in dialogue with the
witness of Dietrich Bonhoeffer*

KEITH W. CLEMENTS

Foreword by Eberhard Bethge

COLLINS

For my parents
In love of home, the love of country has its rise   *Charles Dickens*

Collins Liturgical Publications
8 Grafton Street, London W1X 3LA

Distributed in Ireland by
Educational Company of Ireland
21 Talbot St, Dublin 1

Collins Liturgical Australia
PO Box 316, Blackburn, Victoria 3130

First published 1984 by Bristol Baptist College
Published in Collins Flame, 1986

© 1984 and 1986 Keith W. Clements

ISBN 0 00 599956 1

Grateful acknowledgment is made to the following for permission to use passages from the English translations of the works of Dietrich Bonhoeffer: SCM Press Ltd; Collins Publishers; Fortress Press; Edwin H. Robertson.

Typeset by Dorchester Typesetting (Bristol)
Printed in Great Britain by Bell and Bain Ltd., Glasgow

Contents

Foreword

by Eberhard Bethge

I have taken up this book with the most contradictory feelings: with intense curiosity and with certain touches of anxiety.

The curiosity is due to the place and time of this reception of Bonhoeffer. In the 1950s, all over the world, theologians and churchmen concerned that faith in Christ should still be capable of presentation, discovered the author of *Cost of Discipleship* and accordingly drew for themselves a picture of the martyr for such a faith. In the 1960s, it was the author of the letters from Tegel Prison who was discussed, who finally acknowledged the irreversibility of the Enlightenment, and, so that Christ and his body might not be robbed of an effective, contemporary presence, assimilated its philosophical, cultural and technological consequences. But what now, when this book by a western theologian seeks to investigate the particular 'patriotism' for which Bonhoeffer actually went to the gallows? When Keith Clements traces the way taken by that devoutly praying and radically theologizing thinker – a way which he found to lead from his vision of suffering for the international, universal church to the ambiguous death of a conspirator, ending in total *incognito*? And who, moreover, did this for his country at the moment when it was destroying itself? What might have opened the English author's eyes to this? What brought him to this level of the history of Bonhoeffer's influence? As a matter of fact, today we are in a period when Bonhoeffer's *Ethics* has shifted to the centre of interest. This is as true in Japan and the United States as in Germany itself. Hence the curiosity, as to why now an English writer is stepping this way, and doing so by directing questions at the fate of patriotism in his own country in recent times, and linking them with the role, as vital as it was critical, which Bonhoeffer played in this area – biographically, ecclesiastically and theologically – in the Nazi period. And *intense* curiosity, as to how fruitful this could well be. For the purpose of making a competent judgment I certainly cannot make myself into an Englishman; but the tension holds to the last page. What a Bonhoeffer steps into the light here!

And now, those touches of anxiety! While the theme did not first suggest itself to the author with the Falklands crisis, this event has nevertheless retained for him and the reader – the German reader above all – an uncanny note. Quite unexpectedly and overpoweringly there was a strident reawakening of feelings, aspirations and commitments believed to have been long dead. What was true and genuine in this, what was propaganda, what was merely an interlude? What subterranean interests or equally hidden nerves of identity were emerging into the light of day and demanding their rights? Then came the surprising reports of the controversies surrounding the Thanksgiving Service in St Paul's Cathedral: was this the church reacting critically and ecumenically against the declared will of the government? How does this case compare with Bonhoeffer's patriotic pride and national shame? This is how it seemed to one in Germany, where as yet there has been scarcely any comprehension either of the British patriotic renaissance occasioned by the Falklands War, or of Bonhoeffer's penitent 'patriotism' which took the way of conspiring – against his own government – for the Jews.

In Germany, there has recently entered into public life at many levels a contrived form of national speech. Wherever possible, government representatives are using the term 'Fatherland' again. But it is clear that this attempt is being met by an overwhelming wave of new and bitter contempt, both intended and expressed. The destruction of all authentically felt responses during the Hitler period has not been repaired. On the other hand, there is but little readiness to accept that one can only be German today if one knows Germany as the country of Goethe *and* of Hitler.

But now, what excitement – and incitement – will this book by Keith Clements stimulate? If its time has come on the English side of the Channel, is the time ripe on this side? Is it not indeed high time?

My curiosity mingled with anxiety is answered in these pages by a treatment of this exciting and vitally important topic, which is admirable in its analysis, presentation and structure. As far as the Bonhoeffer theme is concerned, I wholly commend the sensitive selection of facts and writings which in my view have for decades received far too little attention in the ecumenical world. A full and true picture is presented here. Regarding the treatment of the British scene, some passages make my anglophile German heart leap almost too much (all I miss is the Choir of King's College, Cambridge!); but correction is also experienced, together with some violent jolts concerning the urgent issues facing the British in their identity today. At any rate the picture of the situation seems wholly plausible and enlightening to the German observer.

This work impresses me as a pioneering contribution to the Bonhoeffer phenomenon and to the contemporary issue of national identity. It calls for follow-up in other contexts, and, in due course, further discussion. I believe that maybe Japanese Christians could be the next to communicate their insights, as the turns of their country's home and foreign policies give occasion for high sensitivity as to how their patriotism is to be expressed and tested. This might also apply to Christians in the United States, who have already lived several years with the Jerry Falwell phenomenon – Jerry Falwell of Lynchburg, the founder of the moral majority for Ronald Reagan, who to quite some effect has promoted the sticking of the two symbolic badges on the lapels of his countrymen as they go into church: on the left 'Jesus first' and on the right the American flag.

Preface to the Second Edition

The reception given to the first appearance of this book was very encouraging to an author who had argued the need for 'much more serious and constructive thought to be given, not least by the churches, to what "loving our country" means today'. The responses have come not only from Britain, but from contexts as various as Ireland, the United States, the Netherlands, West Germany, East Germany, South Africa and Argentina. The last-named post-mark was especially significant in view of the attention given in this book to the Falklands War and the resurgence of 'patriotism' which it engendered both in Britain and in Argentina. But to repeat what was said in prefacing the first edition, work on this study began a year before the outbreak of the South Atlantic conflict. The political exploitation of the crisis, the crude slogans of the 'Gotcha' mentality emanating from some parts of Fleet Street and the reactions from certain quarters to the churches' refusal to provide a liturgy of national self-glorification in St Paul's Cathedral – these were but symptoms of a long-term British crisis of identity and purpose in the modern world. What is more, it appears that to discuss the particularity of the British problem, especially in dialogue with such a pertinent figure as Dietrich Bonhoeffer, far from limiting the interest of the theme, has prompted those readers elsewhere to reflect on the parallels and contrasts in their own countries.

Over the last two years several events and developments in British affairs have conspired to ensure that the subject of national loyalty has been well publicized, and continually so, in ways that could not have been wholly foreseen. On the one hand controversy surrounding certain aspects of the Falklands War, especially the circumstances of the sinking of the *Belgrano*, has not been as ephemeral as some predicted. Then came the anniversaries of D-Day and VE-Day which provoked not only nostalgia for the war-time spirit but also a wondering concern as to how the stated ideals of the war against fascism are faring today. Civil servants, too, have made their contribution, as represented by individuals who in celebrated court cases have testified to the claims of conscience, as well as the claims of the state or simply the government of the day, in defining their 'duty'. Meanwhile the debate on nuclear weapons continues, and as before assumptions about national loyalty are important

factors in the stances taken in that debate, not least in the matter of
'civil disobedience' in the strategy of opposing what is seen as moral
evil. One could even mention the Church of England report *Faith in
the City* as illustrating what Chapter 8 in this book calls for, namely,
a critical examination of how responsible we are as a nation to the
total community of 'the people'.

There is one particular factor in the political scene, however,
which has recently caused a shift in the perspective on Britain's role
in the world at large. This is the increasingly close and overt
identification of Britain with the foreign policies of the United
States, of which the British assistance in the air-strike against Libya
has been the most controversial example to date. Some would argue
that latent British desires after a leading world-role are now being
met by riding upon the messianic patriotism of the White House. Be
that as it may, the British and American scenes are now being
presented with very similar questions. Eberhard Bethge's remarks in
his Foreword concerning the relevance of this study to the religious
patriotism of the American right have proved to be more timely, for
all of us, than we realized.

All such issues, however, still need to be set within a larger frame
of reference than the immediate present. This book tries to set the
historical discussion in the context of the whole British experience
over the past century, and at times, however sketchily, on the canvas
of the whole Christian west. Above all, the treatment is theological,
that is, it attempts to assess the meaning of 'love of country' in the
light of Christian beliefs concerning humankind as the creature of
God, and of human society as standing under the judgment and
grace of God.

To many readers, the reasons for choosing Dietrich Bonhoeffer as
a partner in dialogue on this theme will be self-evident. If not, those
reasons should emerge in the following pages. It may of course be
thought that to limit the theological input mainly to a single figure,
however illustrious his record and however significant his contribution, will produce a certain narrowing of perspective. On the
other hand, the complaint is frequently voiced these days, that where
two or three theologians are gathered together they talk only to each
other. This is as likely to happen in the pages of a book as in a
refectory. I judge that it is more fruitful to allow someone like
Bonhoeffer to engage directly with our contemporary scene,
without him having to talk with too many other theologians on the
way.

Beyond studying his works, the nearest that one can come to
actual conversation with Dietrich Bonhoeffer today is by talking
with Eberhard Bethge, Bonhoeffer's closest friend, recipient of the

prison letters and biographer, and with his wife Renate, a niece of Bonhoeffer. Like others who have tried to study Bonhoeffer in some depth, I have found such conversations with them an immense stimulus and encouragement. In relation to this particular study I was especially grateful to Eberhard Bethge for pointing out to me the great significance of the fiction which Bonhoeffer tried to write during his first few months in prison. The whole of this material has only recently become available in an English translation, and it is becoming clearer that, far from being incidental to the 'radical break-through' which Bonhoeffer made from the end of April 1944, such writings were an important intellectual and psychological prelude to it. They reveal, among other things, an attempt to grapple with a wider consciousness of society, which evidently contributed a good deal to his growing sense of need for a radical re-interpretation of traditional Christian concepts. This needs saying here, for the reader may be surprised that the 'radical' prison theology receives relatively little mention in this book. This is not to minimize in any way the importance of the later prison material for modern theology, but rather to emphasize the breadth and depth of the context of thought out of which that bold new venture arose. For, as will emerge in this study, Bonhoeffer was as much gripped by the question of what it meant to be *German*, as by what it meant to be Christian.

This book is written out of the conviction that the question of what it means to be British, and to love Britain, is no less vital for us today, and that Dietrich Bonhoeffer more than most can keep that question alive for us, and indicate the lines along which, in Christian perspective, the answers will lie.

Bristol Baptist College
Pentecost 1986

1
An Age of Patriotism?

It is tempting to begin any book dealing with Britain today by declaring yet again that the nation is facing a 'crisis'. The trouble is that so many of the 'crises' affecting us have continued for so long that it would be more appropriate to speak of chronic rather than acute disorders. The decline in industrial performance, the rise in unemployment, the decay of the inner cities and the hostilities in Northern Ireland all contribute to the 'malaise', to use yet another favourite term of commentators. This book is not directly about any of these problems, but about another kind of disorder in national life, working at a different level but highly relevant to the way we face such issues. It has to do with how we value and esteem ourselves as a nation, and of how we conceive of loyalty to Britain today; in short, what 'patriotism' means for contemporary Britain.

On St George's Day 1982 the *Guardian* carried a feature, 'It's the age of patriotism':

Working class and lower middle class youngsters, who are pretty disgruntled with Mrs Thatcher's Britain, are nevertheless ready to fight for it. While their notions of patriotism are confused, they strongly support the hardline policy towards Argentina and, if the worst came to the worst, would favour a military call-up to win a war against it.[1]

The writers of the article had studied the attitudes of a group of men and women in their early twenties during the mounting tension of the Falklands crisis. The 'confusion' in their attitudes was shown in the first place by a marked reluctance, even embarrassment, at speaking about what patriotism meant to them (in spite of their willingness to fight), and secondly by the fact that when invited to select pictures which they thought symbolized 'the values for which Britain stood' they chose an array of traditional images remote from their immediate, everyday concerns: royalty, stately homes, beautiful landscapes and opulent possessions. If such a sample of interviewees is typical of their contemporaries, then there is indeed a confusion and unease on which we ought to reflect, a serious disorder of mind in the public consciousness of our time.

An individual person may at any time suffer one or more crises in the shape of 'things that happen to him': a fractured ankle, loss of his job, bereavement. How he will react to such situations, however, depends on something vital but less readily observable, deep within him. To cope with them and eventually overcome them, he needs a belief that while life may not be a bed of roses it is worth living, and that he has a place in it. This requires that in some sense he has a commitment to himself, a positive estimation of his worth as a person, a belief that *his* life is worth living. He needs to know himself and own himself so that with integrity and responsibility he may take himself into the future. In this respect, it is not wrong to speak of his need to love himself. Fracture, loss of work, bereavement – it does not take much imagination to see how these can be images of various aspects of British experience this century. The question is whether Britain, in the attitudes of its people, has enough of the right kind of loyalty to itself to cope with them and to meet the future; or whether it is in process of giving up living except in a dream world of its own making.

Of course the British often take pride in their art of understatement and this alone may partly account for a certain inhibition in declaring one's patriotism. 'Are you patriotic?' often receives a non-commital answer, yet no-one likes to be accused of being *un*-patriotic. 'Who is here so vile that will not love his country?' asks Brutus, and to a man all reply 'None.' In fact the British literary tradition is well aware of the ambiguity of the term 'patriotism' or its equivalents. Dr Johnson in a famous remark called patriotism 'the last refuge of a scoundrel', implying that it can be a cover for otherwise naked self-interest, while Alexander Pope declared 'Never was patriot yet, but was a fool.' Indeed, if patriotism means making high-flown claims about the rights, virtues and greatness of one's country compared with all others, is not this foolishness all too obvious? George Bernard Shaw confessed: 'I never was a good son or a good brother or a good patriot in the sense of thinking that my mother and my sister and my native country were better than other people's, because I happened to belong to them.' C. S. Lewis tells of the old clergyman, to whom he remarked that every people thinks its own men the bravest and its women the fairest in the world, and who solemnly replied 'Yes, but in England it's true.'[2]

Already it has become obvious that 'patriotism', 'love of country', are terms laden with a variety of possible meanings and nuances. Shaw's remark, for instance, at once raises the question of whether love of one's country has to mean making comparative claims at the expense of other countries. On a psychological level, as in any other type of affective relationship, we must expect to find it a much more complex affair than one single emotion or attitude. Historically it has taken very different forms in the life of the same nation at different periods. The focus of this book will be the particular situation of Great Britain in the late twentieth century, and its frame of reference a Christian theology of man and creation, together with the ethical implications of this, and drawing upon one recent theologian in particular. Such a study should be highly relevant to the process of self-examination in Britain today. For such a process demands that we both know and love the country, and therefore we must explore what loving the country – and this country in particular – will entail. Part of the agenda of Christian theology is to reflect on human relationships, especially those claiming the name of love, in the light of *the* love, God's love for his world.

Love of country is therefore a proper matter for theological reflection. But for the moment we need to explore a little further some of the factors involved in the confusion and unease which surround 'patriotism' in Britain today, and which form part of the context of our study. Four main factors may be recognized.

1. Pressures from within: regionalism

It is not wholly surprising that there should be a certain hesitation in expressions of loyalty to Britain, since the nature of Britain as a single entity is in some dispute. The growth or re-birth of regional self-consciousness is challenging an overall 'British' identity. In fact there has always been a certain ambivalence in the use of 'British', especially in England. For the English, Britain is essentially England, with the celtic communities attached somewhere on the fringe. That they are attached at all is a fact for which they ought to be more grateful than they often are, in the English view. Englishness supplies the norm for political, social and cultural life, but the Celts are allowed such variations as lend colour to the scene. Life would be duller without tartan and Eisteddfods. But the uncertainty which even the English feel about national identity surfaces at a number of symbolic points. For instance, while most of them will not bat an eyelid at having their nationality recorded as 'British' on their passports, once abroad they tend to identify themselves as 'English' or 'from England'. Perhaps still more significant is the rarity with which any of us call ourselves 'Britons' unless we are deliberately trying to be quaint, or to invoke some supposed genius of the pre-Roman past. Indeed the term is used more often by foreigners, in friendly fashion or otherwise. On the whole then, the English prefer not to be too specific as to what constitutes either British or English identity. To be English means to be part of the dominant British group, and to be British means to be led by England.

It is this equation of an assumed English dominance with British identity which has been increasingly challenged by Scottish and Welsh nationalism, and by events in Northern Ireland. Some have even warned darkly of the 'disintegration' of the United Kingdom.

Whether or not some form of devolution will finally emerge acceptable to the majorities of Scotland and Wales, it seems clear that greater recognition will have to be paid to the diversity of the peoples of the United Kingdom and to the political expression of this diversity. Of course we must beware of generalizing, for Scotland and Wales as regions are very different and so are their nationalist movements. Scottish nationalism strongly reflects Scotland's previous history as a self-governing entity. It can build upon much in the administrative and legal structure which has continued independently of the English since 'union' early in the eighteenth century. Not just the feelings, but much of the actual apparatus, of separate identity thus undergirds Scottish nationalism, and the arrival of North Sea oil and its allied industries simply added economic weight to what many already felt was socially and politically a very strong case. Wales, on the other hand, never was a political entity independent of England as was Scotland. It cannot draw on either a history or a folk-memory of national parity with England, as do the Scots. Welsh nationalism is obviously a political force, and it too draws on a sense of economic exploitation (from reservoirs to weekend cottages). But as compared with Scotland its inspiration is much more cultural. A way of life is felt to be under threat, and undervalued even by many within the Principality itself. The most obvious sign of this is the concern for the Welsh language, seen here, as in other contexts where a people's identity is felt to be at stake, as both the symbol and vehicle of all that is distinctive and precious in a people's life.

But it is across the Irish Sea that the severest testings of a sense of corporate British identity are being applied. To those on the 'mainland', Northern Ireland is by turns a nagging, tedious, baffling and horrifying problem. There seems to be no parallel there with any other situation in the United Kingdom. Those who call themselves Loyalists do not, to many English eyes, appear to be loyal to much that seems relevant to a modern democratic state in western Europe. They appear as alien as their republican enemies who of course *are* alien to the continuance of any part of Ireland in the United Kingdom. The fact is that in Belfast class and religion combine in a formula almost unique in Britain, in the shape of a solid working-class Protestantism. Like it or not, it is there, a further denial of the homogeneity of the British.

In face of all this regional diversity and the movements for its political expression, can 'Britain' as a whole be an object of loyalty today? Such a question is likely to cause more anxieties to the English than to the others, because there is so much more at stake for the English in the maintenance of the United Kingdom as it is. There is no English nationalist movement corresponding to those in the regions for the obvious reason that these movements are against the English hegemony or (as in Ulster) against another perceived threat. Regional nationalism grows from a sense of subjection and aspires to a status not yet acquired. In present circumstances, English nationalism exists only in the sense of the desire to maintain English supremacy in the United Kingdom; and to many outside England, utterances from London calling for the unity of Britain are a scarcely-disguised plea for just that. It is difficult to envisage the future, but it may well be that the future 'Britain' will be more clearly an aggregate of peoples and that 'patriotism' may take on a yet more sharply defined regional focus. But it is equally hard to imagine that these peoples would be without some overall sense of identity, a feeling that they had more in common with each other than with the rest of the world. Indeed it might be that, meeting more as equals, there could be a more genuine sense of unity than before. For the moment, it can be conceded that regionalism introduces uncertainties into the idea of national loyalty in Britain, but that an overall loyalty to 'Britain' need not be an obsolete affair.

2. Pressures from without: the transnational world

Patriotism seems to imply that one's country is as distinct and separate from other countries, as an individual is from other individuals. Both as an article of belief and as a political reality the sovereign nation-state has taken a very long time to evolve. But scarcely has it arrived, and it seems to be crumbling at many points under the pressures of a world whose concerns and lines of communication pay scant heed to national boundaries. National sovereignty, in any case, can never mean national self-sufficiency in everything. And it may be felt that while political leaders often talk of 'managing the nation's affairs', in reality they have far less control than appears. We know that economics is of necessity an international and global affair, that cycles of trade and recession flow like tidal movements around the world, with individual countries helpless to do much except take advantage of the boom years and mitigate the worst effects of the lean years. Or the analogy may be used of 'good housekeeping' and squaring the family budget. But government policy is often accused of paying as much heed to the views of Zürich bankers as to the wishes of any at home.

Then there are the transnational companies, some of them immensely powerful corporations, virtually nations unto themselves, which can shift capital, exploit labour and create markets wherever and however it suits them in the world. Hard work has often been promulgated as a patriotic duty. But if the result of one's labour is a profit which the company proceeds to invest in a plant on the other side of the world, what price patriotism then? Or, what does 'buying British' mean if the car I purchase from a British firm in fact has a good many of its components made abroad? Loyalty to nation and commitment to capital do not require each other, and may prove to be quite divergent interests. Two centuries ago no less a person than Adam Smith could write:

A merchant, it has been said very properly, is not necessarily the citizen of any particular country. It is in a great measure indifferent to him from what place he carries on his trade; and a very trifling disgust will make him remove his capital, and together with it all the industry which it supports, from one country to another. No part of it can be said to belong to any particular country, till it has been spread as it were over the face of that country, either in buildings or in the lasting improvement of lands.[3]

All this would have been true had Britain not joined the European Economic Community, and would still be true if Britain withdrew from it. But it may be felt that membership of the EEC piles up the questions even higher against the reality of 'nationhood'. Have we not surrendered vital aspects of our national sovereignty in acceding to the Treaty of Rome? Are we not on the way to becoming just one element in a European super-state? Does not the Brussels bureaucracy now have the final say in how we are taxed, in what we can grow in our fields and how we package our goods on the shelves? If this is the reality of our time, then patriotism can appear to be sheer romanticism, attaching itself to a separate and distinctive nation existing only in the mind. True, there are those who would not only advocate withdrawal from the EEC but call for the erection of tariff walls and import controls to safeguard the manufacturing base at home. Even if that were to happen, however, the transnational world could not be kept at bay on other levels. There is a fast-growing common culture spreading across the world at the level of sport and popular entertainment, for example. Very soon, through satellite television, viewers in Britain will have a far greater choice of American than British channels to tune into.

In such a world, the means by which we earn a living, the source of the goods we buy, the pop-stars we most admire and the footballers we most enjoy watching, may have very little to do with the country we happen to live in. There are indeed immense pressures from outside, threatening to crush the instinct of loyalty to one's own country. What is surprising is the extent to which the sense of national loyalty does survive. That is at least one of the lessons of the Falklands war. The transnational world seems to be producing its own counter-reactions. As for Britain, the sheer physical fact of being a group of islands still counts for much. The old joke about the

London newspaper headline 'Fog in the Channel – continent cut off' still raises a laugh, for the old sensibilities remain.

3. A question of ethics: patriotism good?

Whether or not it is realistic to see one's nation as a fit object of one's affections, *ought* we to be particularly concerned for our own nation these days? Is there not a profoundly moral case against anything savouring of nationalism when what the world needs above all is a new *international* consciousness? The words of Edith Cavell, the British nurse executed by the Germans in 1915, made a profound impression in a Britain till then largely lost in war-hysteria: 'I realize that patriotism is not enough. I must have no hatred or bitterness towards anyone.' To the liberal conscience of today, this assumes too much. Patriotism 'not enough'? Is it not altogether too much in a world overladen with capacities for mutually assured destruction? Patriotism, in short, would appear to mean national egoism and even megalomania.

In fact the vocabulary of national sentiment has been extended to cater for a range of its manifestations, noble and less noble. We use *jingoism* to describe the attitude of cocksure bellicosity towards other nations. It originated in the music hall song dating from the eve of the Crimean War:

> We don't want to fight,
>   But, by Jingo, if we do,
> We've got the ships, we've got the men,
>   We've got the money too.

Chauvinism denotes a similar feeling, although perhaps because of its French derivation we tend to use it more of foreigners, or of social groups other than our own, to label *their* jingoism. (Nicholas Chauvin was a sergeant in Napolean's army, and inordinately patriotic.) Then there is *nationalism*. Rather than a sentiment of loyalty, nationalism generally denotes a certain political belief about the independence, rights and sovereignty of one's country vis-à-vis other nations. The minimal content of nationalist belief is crisply stated by A. H. Birch: 'In my view, a nationalist is best defined as a person who believes that the nation to which he belongs ought to govern itself (or to continue doing so); and that a debate about whether it would do so (or does so) efficiently is unnecessary because self-government is more important than efficient government. He may harbour other beliefs, ranging from the importance of sporting victories over other nations to the desirability of territorial expansion, but these are extensions of the doctrine rather than an essential part of it.'[4]

Put like this, there can be hardly anyone who is not a 'nationalist' of some sort in Britain today. It is in what Birch calls extension of the doctrine that nationalism appears in a problematic light, if it means deprecation of other nationalities, or encroachments on their rights, especially the minimal right to self-government. But there is no inherent contradiction between minimal, basic nationalism on the one hand, and a concern for international justice and peace on the other. Internationalism does not mean non-nationalism, any more than a stress on the inter-personal nature of human community means a belief in non-personhood. The nationalist who believes in self-government for his country can equally well be an internationalist also, in believing that in their self-government nations must not be wholly motivated by self-interest and disregard of the rights, needs and sovereignty of other nations. Of course it may well be asked whether the very notion of 'sovereignty' is inimical to true internationalism, if it means that a nation can act without reference to other nations or to the world community as a whole. But limitations on national *sovereignty* will not mean the end of the *nation*. This fact is liable to be overlooked by the idealist pressing the case for 'one world'. To return again to the personal analogy, community is possible only if there is due recognition *both* of the dependence of members upon each other, and of their individuality. Real life is meeting, as Martin Buber insisted. But meeting requires actual persons with something to give each other. People become true persons in relationship, but relationships require actual people. If stable and creative relationships between individuals require individuals who have a measure of self-awareness and security within themselves, it is no less true that harmonious international relationships will require peoples who have a real sense of who they are, what their histories have taught them, and something of their own strengths and weaknesses. Indeed a nation that has no sense of its distinctiveness and worth is hardly likely to be able to appreciate what moves other nations – and what seems to make them behave irrationally at times. National loyalty is not a contradiction to internationalism, but one of its presuppositions. Patriotism and nationalism have to be viewed with discrimination, which certainly means a suspicion about their seemier manifestations, but also a realism about the deep human instinct to identify with others in a recognizable group. Alan Booth writes:

Nationalisms old and new lift up their heads, sometimes enlarged to continental proportions, and claim an ardent loyalty that seeks appropriate expression. Cultural, ethnic and linguistic cohesions claim and receive allegiance to provide men with a sense of their significance in time and space; and each of them proliferates a myth of its own importance. Such myths and assertions of value usually contain a strong element of glorification, an expression of the desire to affirm that human life is not merely nasty, brutish and short, which it sometimes appears to be. But often also there is a more precise claim for justice, freedom and the right to be one's original self.[5]

4. A question of worth: Britain in decline

This is the most serious of the factors which are confusing the issue of national loyalty in Britain today. At its root lie two presuppositions: patriotism means *pride* in one's country and its achievements, and Britain is in *decline*. The question therefore raises itself as to whether Britain today is worth our loyalty and devotion. As a stage and screen star living in semi-retirement on the Isle of Man puts it: 'I like the island. I like the country away from strikes, burglaries, muggings, vandalism, greed and lack of discipline. I love Britain but I love it the way it should be, the way it used to be, the way the Isle of Man still is.'[6] Not all who might wish to do so, can emigrate like that. What has happened, however, is a large-scale spiritual emigration away from Britain as it is to 'the way it used to be'. Now this attitude is no new phenomenon. I have open in front of me a book of essays lamenting Britain's poor industrial performance relative to other countries, the laziness of British workmen, the apathy of our young people, the lack of discipline in the home and the generally indulgent manner of parents – a pleasure-seeking, frivolous society neglecting God and duty. '"You *were* a very great nation", acknowledged a foreigner the other day.' The most interesting thing about this book is that it appeared in 1913.[7]

Every age, it would appear, is capable of feeling itself to be in 'decline'. There are always some grounds for being dissatisfied with the present state of affairs, and deep within the human psyche lies a belief in an original paradise, an ideal world, the age of gold. The noisy, dusty present is thus always liable to be interpreted as the result of a fall from former splendour. But the view that in many respects Britain is in decline has to be taken seriously, because there are clear and objective facts on the historical record of change, such as Britain's declining industrial output relative to other countries since the turn of this century. More emotive, however, is the matter of Britain as a 'world power'. Dean Acheson's remark about Britain losing an empire and having yet to find a role has been quoted almost to excess, yet it does state part of the problem facing Britain since the Second World War. It can of course be debated just how far 'empire' entered into the picture that ordinary British people had of themselves. Bernard Nossiter argues that there is no way of measuring changes in national psyche from one generation to another.

It is quite true that immediately after World War II Britain ruled over about 550 million of the world's population of 2,225 million; today [1978] British rule is limited to about 55 million in a world nearly twice as populous. Does the proverbial man on the Clapham omnibus feel dispirited at the thought? Was his father or grandfather a happier, more energetic, more purposeful man because he was alive when most of the globe was coloured red?[8]

The question is well taken, but it is not wholly fair. Some of the most important elements in human self-awareness are too subtle for easy description. No, our grandparents may not have been more happy, energetic or purposeful because of the empire. But they probably did carry with them some feeling approaching *importance* as a result of being citizens of a country on whose empire the sun never set. Carrying with them as part of their mental apparatus a view of the world in which white, English-speaking people were obviously cleverer, braver and more industrious than other peoples, they were a people who knew their place in the total scheme of things. A people so effective must be deserving of applause, even if only from themselves. Alternatively, the pride might find religious expression:

> Praise to our God, Whose bounteous hand
> Prepared of old our glorious land, –
> A garden fenced with silver sea,
> A people prosperous, strong and free!
>
> Praise to our God! the vine He set
> Within our coasts is fruitful yet;
> On many a shore her seedlings grow;
> 'Neath many a sun her clusters glow.[9]

This imperial frame of reference is no longer available to us. On the whole the shedding of the white man's burden took place without trauma or tears – doubtless because deep down it *was* felt to a be a burden. But so much of the language and imagery of patriotism which we have inherited, and which is regarded as the true expression of devotion to Britain, originated in the imperial chapter of our history, and was designed for its service. The language and imagery no longer fit the reality. But they are still there, like a love-song looking for a lovely enough figure to be sung to. Hence the feeling that Britain today is not really worthy of devotion. There is less to be proud of in her. Britain is not worthy to be loved by us, as our grandparents loved her. *Then* 'Rule, Britannia!' and 'Land of Hope and Glory' really meant something. Today, they can only be sung nostalgically – unless an episode like the Falklands conflict offers a chance of a replay of 'greatness' in the old style.

Spiritual emigration out of the present can only be reversed by a loyalty to Britain as it is, without the clogging sense of inferiority compared with the imperial, expansionist age. But even when their attention is confined to this side of the white cliffs of Dover, many people find their country a place they can scarcely be proud of. 'To think that this is England!' screamed newspaper headlines over pictures of the inner-city riots in the summer of 1981. Both in Fleet Street and Downing Street there was a failure to grasp that many unemployed, frustrated and harassed people had been saying just that about their surroundings for months and years already. Not that Britain as a whole is a terrible place in which to live. It is terrible for some people in certain places, and for the nearly four million unemployed life is bleak. Britain is not doing as well as it should. But neither is it performing appallingly badly. The general picture is mediocre, and that is what is so inhibiting. It is difficult to raise any kind of strong feelings, for or against, about a country which is neither doing brilliantly, nor is a heap of ruins, nor languishing under the heel of an oppressor. Resignation, detachment or boredom would seem to be the order of the day in such a 'nation in retirement'.

The importance of patriotism: Enoch Powell

We have looked at four factors which in various ways and for different types of people make any straightforward assertion of patriotic loyalty difficult in Britain today. As far as the first three are concerned, it does not appear that any of them, taken in itself, makes a convincing case for dropping the idea of 'loving one's country'. The fourth simply raises the question of whether one loves only what is immediately lovable, or whether there is a deeper love which does not wait upon the attractiveness of its object, a subject to which we shall return several times in this book. But the four factors do create an atmosphere of doubt as to whether it is realistic, ethical or worthwhile to expend much concern on Britain. Certain observers of the British scene in recent years claim to have detected a sense of drift, an inability to look away from the past and to grasp the challenges and opportunities of the present. Over a decade ago, the Australian writer Donald Horne scathingly described the British problem as a peculiar failure to 'find consolation for fallen pride'.

A people once poised and assured have become socially awkward. They have not yet learned how to talk in a new way about their past, their present, and their future. Their traditional idea of their past is so irrelevant to their present that, except to those who are lost in nostalgia, it seems merely absurd; and there has not yet begun that critically important task of writing an interpretation of their past that would make their present and their future understandable and invigorating. Their future is a blank, and their present a series of unlikely, disconnected events. It is as if they had been ordered both to break step and mark time.[10]

Or if one prefers to hear a similar note sounded with archiepiscopal authority, and more recently:

An historian told me the other day that we had somehow lost confidence in the story of England. There was no national story of destiny to sustain us.[11]

Not that there has been a complete lack of volunteers to remedy this defect, as is shown by the case of Mr Enoch Powell.

In any discussion, on whatever level, about patriotism in Britain today, the name of Enoch Powell will come up sooner rather than later. The fact that politically he may not now be the force he was during the late sixties and early seventies, matters less than that for many people he is still seen as the one who 'spoke up for Britain'. For the moment, I consider it more important to focus attention on *why* many of his speeches over the past fifteen years have received such a wide hearing in this country. For it is important not only that his views on such matters as race and immigration should be countered, but that they should be met on the right level. As early as 1963 – fully five years before his controversial Wolverhampton speech on immigration – he stated: 'Every nation, to live healthily and to live happily, needs a patriotism. Britain today, after all the changes of the last decades, needs a new kind of patriotism and is feeling its way towards it . . .'[12] The most important questions, he decided, were not economic but political, and the most fundamental of all was 'Who are we? What *is* this nation?' Powell was therefore extremely perceptive among his contemporaries in recognizing that such questions were indeed waiting, beneath the surface of British life, and he shrewdly realized that whoever grasped this issue and offered some straightforward answers, would gain a ready hearing – especially among those affected by the 'decline' syndrome. When eventually he came to speak about race in 1968, it was therefore in the context of this wider and more basic issue, of national identity and self-esteem which he had earlier seen to be crucial in contemporary Britain. By raising the racial issue, he was laying bare a vacuum in modern British self-awareness, and offering to fill that vacuum with a racially-based identity: Britain is racially and culturally white.

There is of course no more effective way of raising some kind of national consciousness, than by speaking of threats to the country from 'alien' forces, especially if appeal is made to the subterranean fears and fantasies about race. Britain is especially susceptible here, not least because some compensation is sought for the esteem enjoyed during the imperial era. Then, we showed our superiority over blacks and Asians by ruling them in their own countries. Now we can show our superiority by ensuring they are not welcome in our own. But in face of Powell's potent brew, much of the liberal reaction (including liberal Christian reaction) has been totally vapid. It has presented itself in moralizing abstractions and generalizations about love of one's neighbour. Those who respond positively to Powell do so because they say he has expressed what they *feel* deep down. Moralizers who tell them what they *ought* to be feeling stand little chance. It must be recognized that the common thread linking Powell's views on a whole variety of issues is that of patriotism and national identity. The response to him indicates that he has found and exploited an emptiness, yearning to be filled, in the modern British soul. He has offered a way of being patriotic again. If he is to be adequately challenged, it must not be on the abstract moralistic base, but on this issue of being a nation with which one identifies. We may reject his answers, but he has been right to raise the question.

It is Powell's constant use of the *alien* concept and the *threat* imagery which reveals the basis of his peculiar 'patriotism'. Britain, it is implied, is never so British as when it has its back to the wall: 'Britain at this moment is under attack . . . The future of Britain is as much at risk now as in the years when Imperial Germany was building dreadnoughts, or Nazism rearming. Indeed, the danger is greater today, just because the enemy is invisible or disguised, so that his preparations and advances go on hardly observed.'[13] To this, it can only be said that a 'patriotism' which is based so largely on its emotive appeal to fear at the supposed threat, is utterly hollow at the centre. If we can feel what it means to be British only when an enemy is posited against us, if indeed we *need* an enemy to boost our identity, this merely shows how empty of real identity and selfhood we actually are. A true patriotism will speak first of what it believes the people to be. The patriotism which consists only of rejecting the 'alien' is spurious. Powell's tragedy is that, having rightly raised the question 'Who are we? What *is* this nation?' he never in fact answered it beyond saying, in effect, 'not black'.

The consequences of relying upon negations are still more evident in the extreme right-wing and fascist movements which base themselves on a racist ideology and, as is well-known, exploit the grievances of deprived sections of the white population, especially among the young. 'The growth of a far right axed on questions of race and immigration is in fact a comment on the absence of a normal nationalist sentiment, rather than an expression of nationalism' (Tom Nairn).[14] The inner vacuity is shown precisely by what is, according to traditional British standards, an exaggerated symbolism of national identity. British people have not normally found it necessary to form up in ranks behind the Union Jack and march in solemn procession after it. Trades union banners, regimental colours, mothers' union banners and the like, yes – for there are occasions on which it is proper to say by such means 'This is who we are.' But their Britishness is not something they have ever felt it necessary to go out of their way to assert, simply because they take it for granted. To treat the flag with such contrived and militant solemnity as does

the National Front, betrays the fact that its members, far from being
sure of being British, are in fact very unclear on what being British is
all about.

The Christian response

If views such as those of Enoch Powell are to be countered, they
must be challenged on the ground which they occupy, which is that
of national identity and patriotism. It is this ground from which
much of the mainstream Christian response has shied away. There is
a kind of prudery which fears that any talk of love of nation indicates
an incipient fascism, just as, at the other extreme, one sometimes
hears the call for social justice condemned as instigated by the
Kremlin. But being British and loving Britain need not and cannot
be left to the political right. A true British identity needs to be
recovered and carried forward, based on a patriotism of positive
affirmations about Britain and its people, and not on fears and
negations.

There has been a certain reluctance – in England at any rate – for
the churches to look seriously at these questions in recent years. Just
before, during and after the Second World War – the era of William
Temple, J. H. Oldham and T. S. Eliot – there was a very great deal of
Christian reflection on just what Britain was supposed to be fighting
for in the conflict with Nazism. And there has been no shortage of
Christian thinking and comment on specific social and political
problems ever since. But the matter of the total life and future of the
country, and of the commitment of individual citizens to it, is one in
which Christian interest is extraordinarily hard to sustain. For a brief
period in the 1970s it looked as if a revival of this interest might take
place. In 1975 Dr Donald Coggan, then Archbishop of Canterbury,
and Dr Stuart Blanch, Archbishop of York, issued their 'Call to the
Nation', inviting the public to respond to the questions 'What sort of
a society do we want?' and 'What sort of people do we need to be in
order to achieve it?' About the same time, the British Council of
Churches launched the 'Britain Today and Tomorrow' project. Ten
subjects covering the whole range of issues in British life, from local
to national and international affairs, from family life to education,
from work to defence, were to be dealt with by working parties and
study-groups all over the country. The results were miraculously
summarized and condensed in a compact paperback by Trevor
Beeson.[15] No-one can complain about 'lack of Christian comment'
on many of the vital issues affecting Britain today.

And yet . . . it seems to have been immensely hard work to engage
the churches as a whole in this kind of exercise. No doubt this was
always the case. But one fears that the churches are becoming

increasingly concerned with their life within the nation ('church growth', 'renewal') than with the life of the nation as a whole. Christians no less than others are confused about national identity and loyalty, in terms of the four inhibiting factors considered earlier. But Christianity is supposed to have some vital insights about relationships, and if so, included in these insights should be some understanding of the true relating of ourselves to our country as a whole. It is here that the weak point exists in much of the effort to engage Christians in concern for society. Until we know more of what it means to love our country, we shall not be able to engage effectively with many of our problems on the social and political level. We need a love which comprises both passion and clarity. Passion without clarity breeds not real love, but infatuation. Clarity without passion produces mere acquaintance, observation, analysis. We need to find our way to a love which can be both affectionate and critical, devoted and honest, avoiding equally a cynical indifference to our future, and the fantasies of archaic, imperialistic or racist patriotism. One of the few contemporary Christian writers to have raised the question of British identity and national sentiments, Daniel Jenkins, comments that while we need to take a fresh look at our communal life and institutions, 'it is one of the symptoms of our sickness that we are extremely reluctant to take it. We are not sure any more who we are, and, therefore, our relationship to what helped our predecessors to reach self-definition is embarrassed and reluctant. This partly accounts for the feverish hedonism and the related obsession with economic matters which are a feature of the public scene.'[16]

Again, I would simply affirm that to take a proper look at our country means an experiment in loving that country, with all the elements of gratitude, honesty, acceptance and possibly painful criticism, which love may include. To quote Jenkins again:

Patriotism as a slogan may be the last refuge of a scoundrel, but genuine love of those who are nearest to one and share one's life, whether in the national family or in the wider community, is the very basis of civilised responsibility. If a man cannot love his own kith and kin whom he sees, how can he love the international community, or for that matter the universal church, whom he does not see?[17]

Genuine love, says Jenkins. That is quickly said, but therein a whole universe of meaning requires to be explored. Something of that exploration is the aim of the rest of this book. There are numerous ways in which the theme could be tackled from a Christian perspective. But what I intend to attempt is a kind of dialogue with one twentieth-century figure in particular, whose story has more than once been summed up as 'true patriotism'. The context of Nazi Germany is vastly different from our own, and we do Dietrich

Bonhoeffer no honour by turning him into an oracle to answer all our questions. But few people in the modern world have shown so powerfully the profound implications of loving one's country. If ours is indeed to be an age of patriotism, he of all people should have much to teach us.

2
True Patriot

When, on Low Sunday 1945, Dietrich Bonhoeffer was called away from his fellow-prisoners to face the final and fateful court-martial, his parting words were to an Englishman. 'This is the end,' he told Captain Payne Best, 'for me the beginning of life.' He asked Best to pass on a message to another Englishman, his close friend the Bishop of Chichester, Dr George Bell: 'Tell him . . . with him I believe in the principle of our universal Christian brotherhood which rises above all national interests, and that our victory is certain.' Ever since, Bonhoeffer has continued to speak to the English, as to so many other nationalities. But what, particularly, has he to say to us in Britain today?

Dietrich Bonhoeffer's relations with Britain were close and important at a number of levels. His first real involvement with the ecumenical scene took place at Cambridge. For over a year he was pastor of the German congregation in Sydenham, south London, during which time that most significant friendship with George Bell was cemented. His twin-sister and her family came to England as refugees shortly before the war, and lived in Oxford. There was much in the traditional English scene that he relished, from the large breakfast to the quality of English choral music (although, as most continentals, he found the standard of heating in English houses insufferable). We find him in prison reading 'a gigantic English novel which goes from 1500 to today, by Hugh Walpole, written in 1909'.[1] Indeed, it was the sense of broad, centuries-old continuity and development, breeding an unpretentious confidence in social values and institutions, which appealed to him as one of the strongest features of British life. In the spring of 1939, while visiting London and Oxford, he saw the film *Queen Victoria*. 'He confessed that when he saw that continuous history of the country that was now threatened, he could not keep back tears of anger.'[2] In contrast to German 'honesty', he was even prepared to defend English so-called hypocrisy as a necessary reserve in speaking of certain things directly. 'I believe we Germans have never properly grasped the meaning of "concealment" . . .'[3]

Although Bonhoeffer felt himself at home with the British, at the time of his death he was known to only a handful of folk in this country. George Bell, his ecumenical confidante and counsellor in life, became in death the herald of his significance as a martyr. It was

Bell who organized the memorial service for Bonhoeffer in London on 27th July 1945, which was broadcast by the BBC to Germany, and heard by Bonhoeffer's parents in Berlin. In the immediate post-war years, with Hitler and Nazism synonymous with evil, there was an instinctive response to any figure who represented resistance – as the case of the imprisoned Martin Niemöller before and during the war had shown. Perhaps the life and death of Bonhoeffer even offered some further psychological assurance that the war against Nazi Germany had been justified, if any further justification was needed. There had even been Germans, *good* Germans, who had opposed Hitler to the point of ultimate sacrifice. And of course the martyr-figure has a powerful appeal. As yet, the political and ethical complications of the conspiracy against Hitler still lay hidden under the simple, heroic concept of 'resistance'. Bonhoeffer's standing as a Christian martyr was immeasurably increased in the English-speaking world with the publication of his *Cost of Discipleship* in 1948. 'When Christ calls a man, he bids him come and die.'[4] The book was read as a commentary on the martyrdom, and Bonhoeffer's death was seen as a straightforward fulfilment of the theme of the book. The very title of the English edition indicates the influence of this perspective, for the German original is simply *Nachfolge*, 'Discipleship'. Bonhoeffer himself would have looked askance at any undue emphasis on the costliness, in human terms, of obedience to Christ: discipleship focusses on the one who leads, rather than the experiences of those who follow.

In 1953 the first English edition of the prison writings, *Letters and Papers from Prison*, appeared. They were quickly recognized as a spiritual classic, for their unassuming testimony to courage and faith in the face of suffering and death, for their remarkable spiritual freshness and intellectual alertness in the grey confines of a prison cell, and for their venturesome thoughts on the prospects for Christianity in a world 'come of age'. But it was some time before the 'radical' letters (i.e. those dating from the end of April 1944 onwards) began to take on a particular significance of their own. The first British utilization of them in a new theological direction was by Ronald Gregor Smith, in the final chapter of his book *The New Man* (1956). It was Gregor Smith who, as editor of the SCM Press, had been instrumental in getting the prison writings into English as soon as possible.

Bonhoeffer was steadily acquiring greater status among such theologians, especially in ecumenical circles concerned with the nature of Christian mission in a 'secular' age. But it was in 1963 – a full ten years after the prison writings first appeared in Britain – that Bonhoeffer suddenly made headline news by being put alongside

Rudolf Bultmann and Paul Tillich in John Robinson's *Honest to God*. However questionable that book may appear to the theologically informed, and however selective its use of Bonhoeffer, the fact is that the public career of Bonhoeffer in Britain now really began in earnest. Bonhoeffer's role in the radical theology movements of the 1960s – that 'decade of fermentation'[5] – was psychological as much as intellectual. For his appeal was probably greatest among those who were themselves literally coming of age just then, especially in universities and theological colleges, who felt the need to submit Christian faith and practice to ordeal by questioning, and yet to remain identified with the Christian tradition. Bonhoeffer articulated the questions and, with an integrity sealed by his blood, demonstrated that being a Christian believer and a fully twentieth-century man were not incompatible. Meanwhile, the entire range of Bonhoeffer's earlier works was coming into print. But significantly, while references to Bonhoeffer abound in works by British theologians from the early 1960s onwards, no theological study of Bonhoeffer has ever appeared in print from a British author, to compare in weight and substance with works on him by continental and American scholars.[6]

At last, in 1970, Bonhoeffer the martyr and Bonhoeffer the radical theologian were joined by Bonhoeffer the conspirator, with the appearance of the English edition of Eberhard Bethge's definitive biography. Here was disclosed the full extent of what was meant by 'resistance': not a saintly refusal to bow the knee, like a modern Polycarp, but an involvement in the great 'masquerade of evil' which, to remove Hitler, entailed complicity in violence and all the moral ambiguities of working as an under-cover agent. The popular image of a man standing erect and defiant before his interrogators was now replaced by something less than glamorous – a man laying false trails, deliberately lying about his actions and motives to protect his accomplices and to preserve the chances of a successful overthrow. But even this picture has yet to make its full impact. In fact the more closely one examines Bonhoeffer, one meets theological and ethical complexities which one is tempted to dismiss as the inevitable features of a commitment shaped in such an abnormal context as the Third Reich, and limited in relevance to such an extremity. That this is not my own judgment is the presupposition of the rest of this book, as is my belief that there is an element in Bonhoeffer which has not yet fully challenged British thought. This latter element is his understanding of what it means to belong to, to love and to serve, one's country.

'A man suffered shipwreck in, with, and because of his country.'[7] So Eberhard Bethge describes his friend's fate. Among the last

fragments which Bethge received from Tegel prison, and not long
before his own arrest, was a poem 'The Death of Moses', which
concludes:

> To punish sin and to forgiveness you are moved,
> God, this people I have loved.
> That I bore its shame and sacrifices
> And saw its salvation – that suffices.[8]

Bethge points out that by 'this people' Bonhoeffer did not mean the
church, but Germany. The title 'True Patriot' has more than once
been accorded to Bonhoeffer,[9] but in Britain at any rate Bonhoeffer's
relationship to his country has not been fully used as an interpretative
framework for his career and theology. This is all the more unfortunate if, as was argued in the previous chapter, our attachment to our
country is a matter of confusion today. Perhaps we imagine that it is
only Germans who ought to be made to face Bonhoeffer at this point
(and as a matter of honesty it has to be said that nearly forty years
after the Second World War, it is not difficult to resurrect traces of
Germanophobia in Britain). True, there are still many in the German
Federal Republic who are embarrassed by Bonhoeffer and the whole
conspiracy, who still cannot conceive that there might come a point
where patriotic morality demands action of a kind normally thought
treasonable. But subsequent chapters will argue that there is much in
Bonhoeffer that calls us in Britain, too, to re-examine the ways in
which we relate to our country. Nor shall we fix our attention solely
on the paradox that, out of love for country, Bonhoeffer committed
himself to the overthrow of the state of the day. Bonhoeffer's 'true
patriotism' led to this ultimate decision, a remarkable one in any
context and an extraordinary one for a German Lutheran. But there
is a lifelong complexity and richness in Bonhoeffer's attachment to
his country which has to be appreciated if that final act of his drama is
to be understood, and which is highly educative in itself. Confused
and uncertain as we are about our 'patriotism', we should attend to
the wholeness of this man who inherited and appreciated so much of
the good in his country's tradition; who saw more clearly than most,
and more quickly than most, the ugly developments on its scene;
who had every reason, and every opportunity, to escape from his
country, sharing its fate, and taking part in an action aimed at
retrieving some of that country's honour, and preserving a remnant
of responsibility for its future. '*Es lebe unser Heiliges Deutschland!*' –
'Long live our sacred Germany!' – shouted Claus von Stauffenberg
as he faced the firing-squad on the evening of 20th July 1944, after the
failure of the bomb-plot earlier that day. Bonhoeffer could not have
said that. As we have seen, his own parting cry was more like 'Long

live our universal Christian brotherhood!' But he did wish to be in solidarity with such men.

For the rest of this chapter, therefore, we shall look at six main elements and developments in Bonhoeffer's life, which gave his attachment to his country such a distinctive shape. In other words, we shall try to see what it meant for Bonhoeffer to be German. We shall then have in clearer focus the one with whom, in subsequent chapters, we wish to discuss the question 'What does loving our country mean, especially for us in Britain today?'

1. Family and upbringing

'For what I have I thank this nation, through this nation I became what I am.'[10] Dietrich Bonhoeffer said this at the age of twenty-two. Later, and in a political context where such words could be interpreted in a sinister direction, he might not have phrased it quite so innocently. But Bonhoeffer never disowned his Germanness, and to the end he rejoiced in all the positive benefits he inherited through his nation. As so often happens, it was via his parental home that this national heritage was passed to him, and loyalty to it was fostered. One of the most striking things about Bonhoeffer – and never more so than in the prison writings – is his intense devotion to his family and above all to his parents.

The home in Breslau into which Dietrich and his twin-sister Sabine were born in February 1906 seems to have been the embodiment of all that was most aspired after in liberal, upper middle-class German life at the turn of the century. The father, Karl Bonhoeffer, was an eminent neurologist and psychiatrist. Agnostic in outlook, he was as respectful of the rights of others to their convictions, as he was cautious in stating his own. The mother, Paula (née von Hase), brought a combination of lively, independent spirit and traditional Lutheran devotion onto the domestic scene. Her own antecedents read like a *Who's Who* of nineteenth-century academic and artistic life, including theologians, philosophers, musicians and painters. 'The fullness of his forbears' lives set Dietrich Bonhoeffer the standards of his own. To it he owed an assurance of judgment and of manner that cannot be derived in a single generation. He grew up in a family that derived its real education, not from school, but from a deeply-rooted sense of being guardians of a great historical heritage and intellectual tradition.'[11]

If, as Charles Dickens stated, it is in love of home that love of country has its rise, then there is no finer illustration of this than the accounts of life in the Bonhoeffer household, which moved to Berlin in 1912 when Karl Bonhoeffer was appointed to a chair in the university there. And if it was through their family life that the Bonhoeffer

children imbibed their national heritage of life and thought, literature and science, music and history, then through the same medium
they learnt of simpler but no less important things. Accounts of
holidays in the family cottage in the Harz mountains seem quin-
tessentially German in their record of love of nature:

> At dusk we all sat in the living-room and played guessing-games or sang folk-songs,
> and watched the mists from the meadows waft and rise along the fir-trees. When the
> moon appeared, we remembered 'Oh look, the moon has risen', and sang it. My
> father did not have electric light installed in this house, perhaps so that we might be
> better able to watch the coming of the dusk, the night and the stars.[12]

Dietrich, while still a young boy, showed a marked aptitude for one
of Germany's greatest gifts to the world, namely music. Indeed at
one stage his parents seriously considered him being taught for a
professional career and it is intriguing to imagine Dietrich
Bonhoeffer the concert pianist instead of the theologian.

Karl Bonhoeffer counted among his forbears some representatives
of nineteenth-century revolutionary liberalism, and even some who
had actually been imprisoned for their political beliefs. On the other
hand, the von Hase family had been firmly committed to traditional
monarchist society. The result was a family with a strong sense of
tradition, yet a tradition which could only be maintained by a continual striving after the highest humanistic standards on the part of
its members. There was a loyalty to the existing order, but not a
blind one, no 'Prussian' worship of order for order's sake. It was a
belief in order, not in contradiction of liberal values, but for the sake
of maintaining those values. Significantly, one saying in the
Bonhoeffer household was that German sons had their backs broken
twice, first at school and then in the army. The family did not
hesitate to suport their country's cause in the First World War. The
two oldest sons, Karl-Friedrich and Walter, were conscripted into
the army in 1917. Refusing help to obtain commissions, they insisted
on serving in the infantry. Walter was killed during the final great
German offensive on the western front in April 1918. The news
shattered the Bonhoeffer household, and Dietrich never forgot his
mother's grief which made her ill for many weeks. Remembrance
Day always remained a deeply solemn occasion for him, even when,
as during the Nazi period, it was exploited for perverse ideological
ends.

Dietrich was twelve when the war ended, and so grew up during
the confusions and troubles of the socialist revolution and the
ensuing Weimar Republic. The Bonhoeffers accepted the Weimar
Republic with equanimity. They did not regard it, as did many of
their compatriots, as a hopeless experiment in woolly democracy,
a come-down from the good old days of the empire. Equally,

however, the Bonhoeffers shared the almost universal German feeling that the terms of the Versailles peace were grossly unjust, not only in the imposition of economic reparations but even more in the imputation to Germany of the sole guilt for the war. Meanwhile, the older Bonhoeffer sons and daughters were, by career or marriage, moving into some of the most responsible areas of post-war German life. Karl-Friedrich began an outstanding career in atomic physics. Klaus, the third son, graduated in law and went to work first with the League of Nations. Ursula, the eldest daughter, married a lawyer in the Transport Ministry, Rüdiger Schleicher. The second daughter, Christine, married another lawyer, Hans von Dohnanyi, whose civil service career was to take him along some of the highest corridors of government power. Sabine married yet another lawyer, Gerhard Leibholz, an academic specializing in constitutional questions. Such a network of connexions, some in very high places, was to prove of enormous significance in the resistance. As yet it simply represented a circle of highly gifted younger people putting their abilities, as a matter of course, into the rebuilding of their country.

Dietrich, the youngest boy, appeared to break step with this pattern when he decided, in his early teens, to become a theologian. It was characteristic of the family that they supported and encouraged him in his choice. So in 1923 Dietrich embarked on his studies, in true German fashion pursuing his course at more than one university. He began at Tübingen where his father and brothers had also studied. There he appeared to become a typical German student – in fact more so than Karl-Friedrich and Klaus had been, for he joined the *Igel* student fraternity which his brothers had eschewed because of its nationalist leanings. He even took part in a fortnight's military exercise in Ulm with the so-called Black Reichswehr. Bethge comments:

Bonhoeffer's Ulm interlude was certainly not based on any secret radical right-wing impulses. By nature and family tradition he had as little sympathy with this as he had with the flag-consecrating pastors of whom there were not a few in the Evangelical Church at the time. On the contrary, during the university vacation in the autumn of 1923 he and his brother ordered *Vorwärts*, the principal Berlin Social Democratic newspaper, to be sent to them at Friedrichsbrunn. But his letters to his parents show how important to him was the feeling of solidarity with his fellows, from whom he did not wish to cut himself off. He believed he was acting in the service of a state of which he approved, and he was not motivated by a vision of the German people in arms. This military interlude very soon faded from his mind.[13]

'The feeling of solidarity with his fellows': we meet this repeatedly in Bonhoeffer. Here, in his student days, it meant a natural, instinctive loyalty to his country and its defence. Grateful to his country for all its nurture of him, he felt it was worth protecting. It was as simple as that.

2. Experiences abroad

By birth, upbringing and education, Dietrich Bonhoeffer was privileged to know just how much there was to admire and cherish in the past and present life of his own country. But, more than most, he also received the privilege of experiences of the world outside Germany – at a time when many of his fellow-countrymen were denied it, or denied it to themselves. By the age of twenty-five, by any standards he was an unusually well-travelled man, but especially for a German of that time. After his year at Tübingen, in 1924 he had spent a term studying in Rome, during which he and Klaus also travelled south and across to Libya. Then, after completing his doctoral dissertation in Berlin, he had gone to Spain to work as assistant pastor with the expatriate German congregation in Barcelona, for a year (and again Klaus joined him for a trip to North Africa). Then in 1930, having qualified as a university teacher in Berlin, he spent a year as an exchange student at Union Theological Seminary, New York. During that year he characteristically travelled as widely as he could, not only through the United States, but also to Mexico and Cuba. It was not simply that, to use the cliché, travel broadened his mind. He found a compelling interest in cultures and styles other than his own, but he never simply rhapsodized over the exotic, or used the excitement of being abroad as an escape from the supposedly more mundane home scene. Rather, his foreign encounters became the means of reflecting critically on his previous experiences and assumptions, and of providing new insights to be considered and possibly adapted for application at home.

The time in Italy – a country for which he acquired an undying affection – shows how this was so at the very start of his theological development. In Rome, as well as attending theological lectures, he had expected to meet the wonders of classical antiquity, and was not disappointed. But what most impressed him – and unexpectedly in view of his native Lutheranism – was the sight of Roman Catholicism on full display in St Peter's. For Lutheran Bonhoeffer, 'church' had hitherto simply been part of the German Protestant scene, the place where one might go from time to time to hear the Sunday sermon, or on major festivals; but hardly of the essence of Christianity, which was mainly a matter of individual faith and morality. Here in Rome, however, was a Christianity which was essentially communal, a universal fellowship as evidenced by the gathering in St Peter's for the Easter liturgies. Bonhoeffer was given profound cause for reflection on the inadequacies of German 'culture

Protestantism', and it was here that the nature of the church as community began to present itself to him as the first major theme of his own constructive theology.

The year in Spain – another Latin and Catholic country yet so different from Italy – gave Bonhoeffer much food for thought on differences in European cultures and national temperaments. His letters home show how he was becoming aware of what we now call 'cultural relativity', with important things to be learnt by the Germans themselves. Thus:

> To Italy humanism and the classical period represented the solution of all problems, while in Spain there is a resistance to this which, I think, is also to a certain extent discernible in the Germans. Common to both Spaniards and Germans, I think, is the fact that neither completely exposed themselves to the impact of humanism, but always held something back.[14]

Some of his judgments on Spain surprised his relatives and friends, such as his stout defence of the bullfight as an antidote to the gloomy liturgy of Spanish Catholicism. Bonhoeffer was showing himself to be a master of empathy, as far as possible seeing a strange situation from within, and only then making judgments. The same approach made bearable his work with the German congregation in Barcelona, for the atmosphere of this community of small business people was almost as new to him as the native Spanish, coming as he did from the academic upper class of Berlin.

As for the United States (1930–31), Bonhoeffer was not at all certain whether to expect anything worthwhile there. He was dubious as to whether it had any theology to teach him, especially as he had by then become a committed disciple of Karl Barth, of whom very little had been heard in America till then. Moreover, Bonhoeffer expected to find here, as elsewhere in the Anglo-Saxon world, a continuing resentment against Germany. He went prepared to state Germany's case against the Versailles Treaty, and to parry accusations of German war-mongering and militarism. In fact this year was to affect him even more deeply and permanently than his visits to Italy and Spain. For one thing, he was gratified to find that in contrast to many of his own countrymen, Americans no longer seemed interested in re-living the war and debating its causes, though he did address several groups of young people on the subject. Much of the theology taught at Union Seminary fell to the standard he expected. American liberal and pragmatic theology appeared to him as little more than naive humanism with a religious gloss. But not all. Even here there were surprises. Above all, Reinhold Niebuhr's classes on social ethics for the first time brought him face to face with the need to analyse social issues theologically, and with the need for active Christian involvement in them. He was impressed with the intense social activism of many churches in New York, displaying a degree of practical Christianity unknown to him in Berlin. Above all he became absorbed in the black situation, sharing in the life of negro churches in Harlem. This interest was stimulated by his friendship with a black student at Union, Frank Fisher. A relationship of even more enduring significance was struck up with a French student, Jean Lasserre. A friendship between a Frenchman and a German at that time still made demands on both sides. What is more, Lasserre was a pacifist, which Bonhoeffer up to that time certainly was not. It was Lasserre who first prompted Bonhoeffer to take seriously the Sermon on the Mount as a concrete command for the Christian life – a line which was eventually to bear fruit in *Cost of Discipleship*. So once again we find Bonhoeffer open to what was new and at first sight alien, accepting people and situations as far as possible on their own terms, and always seeking to adjust his understanding to the new horizons. In the words of Paul Lehmann, then a young teacher at Union and with whom Bonhoeffer became a close friend, he 'focussed upon what was most remote from his previous experience', as shown most clearly in his black interest.[15]

Bonhoeffer, then, steadily widened his knowledge of the world while still a student, and this widening was to continue throughout his career. One cherished dream was never realized, that of visiting India and drawing from eastern spirituality some of the resources which he felt were lacking in the inwardly improverished west. But it is noteworthy that he did dream the dream. Only someone who was deeply secure within his own nation's inheritance could have been so open to the world outside, for what he saw of the wider world did not lead him to despise his own tradition, or play the part of the superior man who has seen the world and thereafter speaks patronisingly to those who have never left home. Continually, he sought to relate what he learnt of the world abroad to the life of his own people, and regarded foreign experience as educative for ful-filling his own responsibilities at home. Most clearly, he was free from any nationalist paranoia about the world outside his own country, deeply though he felt the injustice of Versailles. He saw himself as a citizen of Germany, a country to which he owed love and gratitude, and equally he saw Germany as but one of many peoples sharing the same earth.

3. Belief in the universal church

In Rome, as we have seen, the significance of the church dawned on Bonhoeffer for the first time. Shortly after returning to Germany to continue his studies in Berlin, Bonhoeffer came under the influence of the theology of Karl Barth, the Swiss Reformed theologian whose commentary on *Romans* had been the talking point of continental theology since the end of the First World War. The theological approaches of the Berlin school and of Barth seemed to be diametrically opposed to each other. In fact there took place an acrimonious correspondence between Barth and Berlin's most illustrious theologian, Adolf von Harnack. The Berlin school, since its origins in the early nineteenth century, had taken as its main object the study of religion as a human phenomenon – its history, social manifestations and psychological features. Harnack's own speciality was the history of the early church, but in particular he had achieved widespread international fame for his 'liberal' understanding of the historical Jesus: an inspired teacher who taught the fatherhood of God, and the spiritual and moral ennobling of the human soul in order to unite with the Father. The kingdom of God was the progressive upward movement of civilization imbued with the moral and spiritual ideals proclaimed by Jesus. Barth, in contrast, had called for an about-turn in this whole liberal approach. Theology had to be about *God*, what God thought about man, not what man thought about God; not about man's upward moral and religious struggle, but about God's wrathful judgment on all self-assertive human endeavour, including – and especially – the 'religious' endeavour; about God's total transcendence, the holiness of the 'Wholly Other'; about God's own revelation of himself to man, in the one person of Jesus Christ in whom alone heaven and earth intersect.

Dietrich Bonhoeffer read Barth's works intensely during the winter of 1924–25 and became a firm disciple, although over seven years were to pass before they met personally. But despite the revolutionary impact of this rigorously 'God-centred' theology, Bonhoeffer did not overthrow all that his Berlin teachers had to say. Far from it – in fact he saw a need to bring the two approaches together, and this he tried to do in his doctoral thesis *Sanctorum Communio*. The church, he insisted here, has to be understood both sociologically and theologically. It is a concrete human community, and precisely in this concreteness, it is divine revelation. It is 'Christ existing as community'. This is true whatever its failures and excesses may be in human terms, for the very essence of the church is its being the body of Christ on earth, Christ present with and for sinners, and therefore the community of the forgiveness of sins.

Consequently, Bonhoeffer held that wherever the church existed in some form of community, it had to understand itself in the highest possible theological terms, and behave accordingly. It was this which determined his view of the ecumenical movement in which he became involved soon after his return from the United States in

1931. In the late summer of that year he went as a German youth
delegate to the conference of the World Alliance for International
Friendship through the Churches, at Cambridge. Its main ethos was
an American, and to some extent British, pragmatism: *how* to
prevent war. Bonhoeffer was at first somewhat dubious. Both his
native Lutheranism and his recently acquired Barthianism made him
suspicious of what appeared to be a naive and pretentious effort to
'build the kingdom of God on earth'. On the other hand, his
American experience of practical church activity in the world did not
count for nothing. Above all, thanks to Jean Lasserre, the question of
peace had become crucial to him, and he was moving in a pacifist
direction.

While he found the Cambridge conference lacking in theological
content, Bonhoeffer nevertheless threw himself wholeheartedly into
the work of the Alliance, and was in fact appointed a travelling youth
secretary for Germany and central Europe. Much of his time during
the next two years, in addition to his academic duties in Berlin, was
spent organizing conferences in Germany and elsewhere on behalf of
the churches' peace movement. The high point was the conference
arranged jointed by the World Alliance and 'Life and Work' on Fanö
Island, Denmark, in the summer of 1934, when Bonhoeffer gave a
paper and preached a sermon, both uncompromising, on the
requirement of the church to proclaim peace as a concrete command
of God. It was while relaxing on the beach at Fanö that Bonhoeffer
was asked what he would do if war broke out, and replied 'I pray that
God will give me the strength not to take up arms.' At Fanö, too,
Bonhoeffer was elected to the council of Life and Work, which kept
him in touch with the centre of the ecumenical movement just when
the work of the World Alliance in Germany was in a state of dissolution owing to the Nazi regime. The chairman of Life and Work
was George Bell, the person to whom Bonhoeffer was closest in the
ecumenical movement, and who more than anyone else trusted
Bonhoeffer's integrity, and relied upon him for much of the information about church affairs in Nazi Germany.

For Bonhoeffer, then, the ecumenical movement and the peace
question were intrinsic to each other. This had vital implications for
his attitude towards his own country. Even before Hitler came to
power early in 1933, there was widespread opposition in Germany
to anything savouring of 'internationalism', and even German
church involvement on the wider ecumenical scene was held to be
unpatriotic and un-German in sentiment. Even prominent theologians like D. P. Althaus and D. E. Hirsch stated that 'all artificial
semblance of cooperation should be broken and . . . it should be unreservedly recognized that Christian and churchly understanding

and cooperation on questions of *rapprochement* between the nations is impossible so long as the others conduct a policy lethal to our nation'.[16] By his ecumenical involvement Bonhoeffer was thus even then incurring the odium of betraying his country's cause in the world. Certainly he knew that consciously belonging to the universal church was bound to qualify one's 'patriotism'. But he saw the ecumenical movement as an *opportunity* for his country's case to be heard on such questions as the Versailles Treaty, and he rejoiced at every sign of deepening sensitivity to German feelings by those from other countries. Ecumenism for Bonhoeffer therefore did not in the least mean any lessening of regard for his own country. The ecumenical movement was the meeting of representatives of the church of Jesus Christ from various lands, meeting *as* the church, to discover the truth with and for each other. It was therefore a mutual exercise in communication. For instance, Bonhoeffer insisted that not only should Christians abroad express their repugnance at Nazism, but should also recognize the part which post-war allied policies had played in justifying Nazi aspirations to the German people. Equally, he saw the ecumenical movement as having a positive part to play in the life of the German churches under Nazism, and to this area we now turn.

4. The German Church Struggle

When Hitler came to power in January 1933, there were widespread demands that the German Evangelical (i.e. Protestant) Church should actively support and reflect the nature of the new regime. In fact the Evangelical Church comprised a number of separate *Land* or regional churches, of the Lutheran, Reformed or United traditions. Many churchmen clamoured for there to be one Reich Church and, corresponding to the Reich Führer, one Reich Bishop. This was a relatively moderate demand. More sinister was the call by the so-called 'German Christians' for the imposition of an Aryan clause upon the church constitution, i.e. the barring from church office of any persons of Jewish or partly Jewish descent.

Most churchmen – even including such as Martin Niemöller who later became the great symbol of opposition through his imprisonment – had welcomed the Nazi revolution,[17] believing that at last the revival of German greatness had begun; the threat from 'bolshevism' had been removed; disorder was banished from the streets; the tiresome wheeling and dealing of parliamentary 'democracy' was past. Days of order, national pride and prestige had returned. Moreover, had not Hitler promised a firm place for 'positive Christianity' in the new Germany? Nevertheless there was alarm in Evangelical circles over the excessively anti-semitic outpourings of the 'German

Christians', and the crude and high-handed ways in which state-appointed officials were now handling affairs in certain of the *Land* churches. Through the summer the furore in the churches grew. In the autumn the Pastors' Emergency League, led by Martin Niemöller, was formed and provided the focus of opposition to Ludwig Müller, a former naval chaplain who was now Reich Bishop.

For Dietrich Bonhoeffer the issues were clear from the start. The church of Jesus Christ, to be true to itself, could not have a racial basis of membership or office. As with his view of the ecumenical movement, so in his view of the Evangelical Church, the actual nature of the human community in all its concreteness and visibility, was a theological issue. What had been explored in abstruse theological fashion in his doctoral thesis now became a matter of urgent struggle and decision.

At the end of May 1934, pastors and leading lay people opposed to the attempts to subject the church to state control and aryanization met at Barmen. Under Karl Barth's direction they drew up the now famous 'Barmen Statement'. Its opening paragraph simply quoted what had hitherto been accepted by all, including the government, as the basis of the Evangelical Church in Germany: 'The impregnable foundation of the German Evangelical Church is the Gospel of Jesus Christ, as it is revealed in Holy Scripture and came again to light in the creeds of the Reformation.' After expressing concern at the divisive policies of the 'German Christians', the rest of the declaration went on to spell out what that agreed basis of belief must *now* clearly mean as articles of belief. The first clause rang loud and clear: 'Jesus Christ, as he is testified to us in Holy Scripture, is the one Word of God which we are to hear, which we are to trust and obey in life and in death. We repudiate the false teachings that the church can and must recognize yet other happenings and powers, personalities and truths as divine revelation alongside this one Word of God, as a source of her preaching.'[18] Thus was laid the theological foundation of the 'Confessing Church', i.e. those who rejected state interference and aryanization in the church as theologically incompatible with the nature of the Evangelical Church.

For such as Dietrich Bonhoeffer, it was adherence to the Barmen Statement which determined whether one was truly part of the German Evangelical Church, and in accepting this as its basis the Confessing Church was laying claim to being that true Church. It was quite simply a matter of who now constituted the Evangelical Church of Germany. But if it was not a matter of forming a *new* church, a new consciousness of what it meant to be Christian inside Germany now arose. The church was not to be perverted for nationalistic or racist ends. The Word of Jesus Christ had to be sharply distinguished from all calls for 'national renewal' however high-sounding and uplifting. One had now as never before to decide whether the Bible was to remain the church's souce of revelation, or whether Hitler was also an oracle of ultimate truth; whether the swastika could replace the altar cross. It was in the Church Struggle, therefore, that Bonhoeffer felt most keenly the tension between himself and his people, between being Christian and being German. Loyalty to Christ and loyalty to country became sharply polarized. Could one maintain one's Christian identity other than by distancing oneself from the rest of the people and indeed much of the church? For it was not just the threat from the fanaticism of the 'German Christians' that had to be countered. The soft-centredness of many leading churchmen, who felt that the Confessing Church was as bigoted and fanatical as the German Christians at the other extreme, blurred the issues. Was the Aryan issue really worth so much pro-test, they asked, seeing that it affected relatively few in the church?

By the autumn of 1933, Bonhoeffer was somewhat weary and dis-illusioned with the ecclesiastical in-fighting, and did literally distance himself from Germany. Despite the protests of Karl Barth, he left Germany for his most extended stay in England, in charge of the German congregation at Sydenham, south London. If it was an attempt to escape, from the conflict, Elijah-fashion, it failed. For one thing, the German congregations abroad were being drawn into the Church Struggle and were being asked to take sides. Naturally Bonhoeffer did his utmost to win the support of the emigré churches in Britain for the Confessing Church – and was reasonably success-ful. Moreover he was now in regular contact with George Bell, supplying him with much first-hand information, and interpreting the news that was now coming from Germany almost daily. In all this there was continued ecumenical work, and constant travelling back and forth between London and Berlin to keep in touch with developments.

Bonhoeffer returned to Germany in 1935, in response to a call to take charge of the Confessing Church seminary at Finkenwalde on the Baltic coast. Though he returned, in some vital respects the distance remained. The security and status of a university lecturer were now denied him. His existence was now an isolated one, in a community of men who had chosen an unpopular path for their ministries. Again, the emphasis on the church as community emerged. Study, meditation, common worship, mutual confession and relaxation together formed the life of this seminary and its adjoining 'House of Brethren'. Here, Bonhoeffer was able to realize something of his long-held dream of deepening Protestantism's

sense of community and discipline. It was here that he gave the
lectures which formed the backbone of *Cost of Discipleship*, and also
put into practice what he later wrote up as *Life Together*. It has often
been pointed out that while *Cost of Discipleship* is undeniably a
moving book, it also seems extremely narrow in scope, viewing the
Christian life as a separation from the world for the sake of an
exclusive attachment to Christ. Bonhoeffer was certainly expounding the narrow way, but one must not overlook the book's
references to a humanity wider than the specifically Christian
sphere. Jesus, says Bonhoeffer, gives his blessing to *all* who suffer in
a righteous and just cause. Further, the focus of the book is
ultimately on the Christ who is followed, and becoming like him
through his grace. For that reason, although the way appears to be
narrow, it opens out again in limitless scope. That is clear in a
passage almost at the end of the book:

Christ took upon himself this human form of ours. He became Man even as we are
men . . . And in the incarnation the whole human race recovers the dignity of the
image of God. Henceforth, *any attack on the least of men is an attack on Christ who took the
form of men*, and in his own Person restored the image of God in all that bears a human
form. Through fellowship and communion with the incarnate Lord, we recover our
true humanity, and at the same time *we are delivered from that individualism which is the
consequence of sin, and retrieve our solidarity with the whole human race*.[19]

(Emphases mine.)

Thus the way of discipleship was exceedingly narrow: away from
the nationalist tribalism of the Third Reich, away from the seduc-
tions of secure employ in the ministry of the 'official' church, away
from the world to Christ. But the Christ who is followed is the one
who is incarnate and crucified for all men. The way to Christ leads
back, with him, to the world as God loves it. To Bonhoeffer's
sorrow, the Confessing Church took only the outward journey,
away from the paganism of the time. It did not return in solidarity
with those whose oppression was an affront to Christ. It did not cry
out for the Jews at large. It did not officially speak out against war (in
fact most pastors supported the Second World War as a fight against
communism). As Bonhoeffer wrote sadly in prison, the Confessing
Church simply protected itself, and exhausted itself in maintaining
the great Christian doctrines without interpreting them for the
time.[20]

Typical of Bonhoeffer is this paradox, that while no-one was
more committed to the cause of the Confessing Church, in the end
no one was more critical of that Church than he. The key to the
paradox is his theological approach, a ceaseless reference of all
human understanding and action to Jesus Christ as the one great
truth to be obeyed. Because the church is the church of Jesus Christ,
it must be distinguished from the world, including the world as

manifestated in the nation. But because Jesus Christ is God in the flesh, made man for man, it is not enough for the church to identify itself as 'not the world'. It has to return with a new solidarity inspired and shaped by Christ's own solidarity with sinful mankind. With the 'no' to the patriotism being proclaimed in flags and parades, came the 'yes' to the possibility of another kind of love of country.

5. Total identification with Germany's fate

Bonhoeffer knew that a solidarity with all men, to be more than an abstract ideal, had to begin with a solidarity with his own people. This was the basis for the most remarkable and fateful decision of his life, in 1939.

The Finkenwalde seminary had been closed by the Gestapo in 1937. The work of ministerial training had continued surreptitiously in 'collective pastorates' in Further Pomerania, where the students were stationed in outlying parishes and met together at intervals for joint study. Imprisonment was a frequent fact of life for many of the former students, and by 1939 Bonhoeffer's own circumstances were becoming exceedingly difficult. Pressing in on him was the likelihood of his military call-up. He could not see himself taking up arms for an aggressive war under Hitler, but neither did he wish to embarrass the Confessing Church as a whole by conscientious objection. Once again the sensible solution seemed to lie in going abroad. Reinhold Niebuhr facilitated an invitation from the United States for Bonhoeffer to undertake a lecture tour and perhaps act in some pastoral capacity among German refugees. He left for New York at the beginning of June, was warmly welcomed and was glad to renew old friendships. But within days he felt he had made a mistake in coming. He could not tear his thoughts away from family, friends and church in Germany, and so decided he must return, tendering his regrets to a bewildered and hurt Henry Leiper. But his letter of explanation ro Reinhold Niebuhr has become one of the classic statements of Christian commitment in the twentieth century. It embodies what Bonhoeffer meant by 'solidarity' and further comment upon it is superfluous:

I have come to the conclusion that I have made a mistake in coming to America. I must live through this difficult period of our national history with the Christian people of Germany. I will have no right to participate in the reconstruction of Christian life in Germany after the war if I do not share the trials of this time with my people. My brethren in the Confessing Synod wanted me to go. They may have been right in urging me to do so; but I was wrong in going. Such a decision each man must make for himself. Christians in Germany will face the terrible alternative of either willing the defeat of their nation in order that Christian civilization may survive, or willing the victory of their nation and thereby destroying our civilization. I know which of these alternatives I must choose; but I cannot make that choice in security . . .[21]

In a diary note, Bonhoeffer wrote: 'I cannot stay out here alone; I am quite clear about this, for, after all, over there is where I live.'[22] So Bonhoeffer stepped back onto German soil just before the gates of war closed upon it.

6. Involvement in the conspiracy

It has been said often enough that the greatest paradox of Bonhoeffer's life was that out of love for his country he was prepared to betray its leaders politically, and share in the scheme for the over-throw and assassination of Hitler. It is important, however, neither to exaggerate Bonhoeffer's role in the plot, nor to glamourize it. By the very nature of the conspiracy, no rigid line could be drawn between simply knowing with approval of what was going on (many were executed for just that after July 1944) and actively par-ticipating in it. But a definite stage can be identified when Bonhoeffer moved beyond sympathy to active conspiracy. This was in the autumn of 1940.

After his return from the United States, Bonhoeffer continued with the clandestine work of training pastors for the Confessing Church. But this was stopped by the police in the spring of 1940. By September, he had been forbidden to speak any more in public, and was required to report regularly to the police. And again, the threat of military call-up loomed large. During that summer, Bonhoeffer talked at length with his brother-in-law Hans von Dohnanyi who was now on the staff of the *Abwehr* (Military Intelligence), and with Colonel Oster, Head of the Central Department of the *Abwehr*. Before the Nazi period, Dohnanyi had been personal secretary to successive ministers of justice, and despite being resolutely non-Nazi had remarkably managed to retain his post even after the Nazi ac-cession. A 'mole' within the Nazi establishment, he compiled a 'chronicle of shame' of misdeeds unknown to the general public so that in the event of a *putsch* the moral grounds for such action could be made clear.

The *Abwehr* was in fact the centre and the cover for the resistance. The Bonhoeffer family circle was thus connected to the very heart of the conspiracy, and in fact it was in Dohnanyi's office that most of the coordination between the military and political wings of the con-spiracy was effected. To fulfil its official responsibilities of gathering information relevant to the war effort, the *Abwehr* had to make use of people from a wide variety of occupations, social backgrounds and political outlooks. Such a requirement also provided a convenient cover for recruiting agents for the conspiracy. So from October 1940, Dietrich Bonhoeffer was taken into the recognized but unpaid service of the *Abwehr* and was attached to its Munich office. The official justification for his appointment was that with his ecumenical and personal contacts abroad he could have access to useful information concerning enemy countries. Though unpaid, Bonhoeffer's service with the *Abwehr* secured him exemption from conscription (a protection afforded some other Confessing pastors also). Others in the family were involved in the conspiracy though not in the *Abwehr*: Klaus Bonhoeffer, Rüdiger Schleicher, and General Paul von Hase, military commandant of Berlin. All were to lose their lives in the final revenge.

Meanwhile, Bonhoeffer continued as a pastor of the Confessing Church, without parochial duties but seconded for theological work. He spent much of the time from late 1940 till his arrest in April 1943 working on his *Ethics*, living either at the Benedictine monastery at Ettal near Munich, or on the estate of his friends the von Kleist-Retzov family at Klein-Krössin in Pomerania, or at his parents' home in Berlin. The Klein-Krössin connexion became specially significant when he became engaged to Maria von Wedemeyer, grand-daughter of Frau von Kleist-Retsov. Few in the Confessing Church knew of his *Abwehr* work, and most would have been shocked had they known what he was actually involved in.

Bonhoeffer's specifically conspiratorial activities comprised five journeys sponsored by the *Abwehr*, ostensibly to glean information about British and allied war aims and policies from contacts abroad. Their actual purpose was to impart information about the conspiracy to those allies, and to seek support for that conspiracy from Germany's enemies. Three of these journeys were to Switzerland, where he visited staff of the World Council of Churches in Geneva, and contacts such as Karl Barth; one was to Norway; and finally the most important visit was to Sweden in May 1942. On this last occasion he met George Bell and gave him detailed information to take to the British government, in the hope that, should the overthrow of Hitler succeed, the allies might negotiate a peace with a non-Nazi government committed to de-Nazifying Germany. As the world now knows, Bell was unable to elicit any such assurances from the British government, and the conspirators had to proceed alone. In addition, Bonhoeffer was involved in another *Abwehr* operation not directly related to the conspiracy but which was to prove compromising during his interrogations later. In October 1941 the first deportations of Jews from Berlin took place. The *Abwehr* was able to save a small number of Jews by ostensibly taking them into its service as under-cover agents to work in Switzerland. Bonhoeffer was partly responsible for recruiting this group, and also for arranging their reception by the Swiss churches. This 'Operation 7' involved a substantial amount of money disappearing into Switzerland as well, and this alone made the Gestapo deeply suspicious about the whole affair.

Bonhoeffer, then, cannot be said to be *central* to the plot which culminated in the attempt of 20th July 1944. He was one of many who accepted complicity in a particular way. If we must not over-dramatize or exaggerate his role, neither must we flinch from recognizing the ethical cost of his total commitment to it. The over-throw of a regime such as Hitler's could only be accomplished if those involved camouflaged their activities under the guise of loyalty. For the sake of infiltrating the system which had to be destroyed, it meant rejecting all scruples about practising deceit. It involved, as Bonhoeffer put it, taking part in the 'great masquerade of evil', from the comparatively trivial level of giving the Nazi salute to working for the country's military intelligence machine. And if the arts of pretence were necessary while engaged in conspiracy, they were absolutely essential for survival under interrogation after arrest.

When Bonhoeffer, with Hans von Dohnanyi, was arrested in April 1943, he was suspected of 'treasonable' activities. As yet the Gestapo had no serious suspicion of a plot against Hitler. They were, however, concerned about the *Abwehr*, and Bonhoeffer himself was accused of repeatedly seeking to evade military service under *Abwehr* cover. In fact he cleverly managed to use this issue – in his eyes a relatively trivial one – as a decoy to divert interest from his journeys abroad. Even the truth about 'Operation 7' was obscured by a well-prepared set of stories. Bonhoeffer was never brought to trial on any of these matters, and not until the fateful day of 20th July 1944 was he ever in real danger again. Even so, it was not until the autumn of 1944 when incriminating files concerning him, Admiral Canaris, Oster and Dohnanyi were discovered, that renewed attention was paid to him. There followed intensive interrogations, though without torture, at Gestapo Headquarters in Berlin. He was transferred to Buchenwald concentration camp in February 1945, and from thence to his final court-martial and execution at Flossenbürg on 9th April.

If a rationale is sought for Bonhoeffer's involvement in the con-spiracy, it has to be admitted that it does not leap from the pages of the theology he had previously written. In 1933 he had raised the question, in discussion with other pastors, as to the possibility of the church making a political intervention to avert injustice and oppres-sion. And as we have seen, the *Cost of Discipleship* keeps the door open for suffering in a righteous cause, although it must equally be said that the whole tenor of the book is pacifist in tone. The rationale for Bonhoeffer's involvement in conspiracy lies not so much in an explicitly prepared theological position worked out beforehand, but rather in that Christian instinct which he repeatedly displayed, the instinct for *solidarity*. When it came to the point, for him it was not so much a matter of whether he should become involved, but of what possible grounds there were for *not* becoming involved with his close relatives, friends and others who seemed to represent the last possibility of retrieving Germany's name from total ruin when other groups, not least the church, had either failed or opted out. The figure that is sometimes painted, especially in muscular Christian circles, of Dietrich Bonhoeffer as a lone crusader, needs to be corrected. He himself would be amazed and disturbed that so much attention would be focussed on him alone. He simply wished to share responsibility with those who, to speak theologically, were doing what they could towards atonement for the nation's guilt. Bonhoeffer's real significance as a conspirator is not simply in what he did for the resistance, but in the way in which, as a believer and theologian, he was able to articulate the moral and spiritual demands that were involved, and out of the darkness to kindle a vision of a 'patriotism' very different from that which hanged him – and very different from most of the notions that are still abroad amongst us today.

This, then, is the man with whom we shall discuss more fully what is meant by loving our country. This chapter has, one hopes, brought out his qualifications as interlocutor, in the rich combination of different elements in his 'patriotism' which a Christian faith was able to hold together in a creative whole. He was a grateful heir of his country's cultural wealth; a man who had travelled abroad sufficiently to enable him to view his country objectively in the world of nations; a Christian theologian who both in his passion for the universal church of ecumenism and for the true church of Germany, never lost sight of his country's proper needs and aspirations; a man who rejected safety in order to be with his country in the hour of its greatest danger and shame; a man who finally identified with those who risked all in an attempt to save their country from utter destruction and unrelieved guilt. Because he was all of these in one, there is an incandescence about Bonhoeffer's life and thought which shines well beyond his own context into ours.

3
How Important is Country?

Patriotism is an ancient sentiment, as shown by the wealth of classical aphorisms on the subject. *Dulce et decorum est pro patria mori*: twenty-one centuries later, Horace's words on the beauty and seemliness of dying for one's country still solemnize many a war memorial and 'In Memoriam' announcement in the press. What is striking, however, is that while 'love of country' is so recurrent down the ages, the notion of *country* itself has changed vastly. Today, most of us assume 'country' to mean the sovereign nation-state such as we live in. Because it is what our parents and grandparents were born into, and what *their* grandparents knew, and because it is what we assume our children's children will grow up in, it has a monumental air of permanence about it. But the political historian points out that such a view of country really dates from no earlier than the end of the eighteenth century. Further, what constitutes a 'nation' or a sense of being 'a nation' seems very elusive. A modern historian admits resignedly: 'Nations may be defined by a supposed common ethnic origin, by use of a particular language, by a shared literary inheritance, by reference to a well-defined geographical region – and so on – but few nations have all of these characteristics and some have none. Indeed, prolonged immersion in the literature written by nationalists and in the writings of scholars primarily concerned with nationalism speedily leads to the conclusion that the nation is a very subjective concept.'[1]

Very subjective it may be, but it is not for that reason historically insignificant. For the present, it is enough to note that the modern nation, as well as incorporating the obvious element of territory, relies for its coherence upon both the feeling of being a people or closely related group of peoples, and upon the legislative and administrative authority of the state. Hence 'nation' and 'state' are almost but not quite synonymous today. Without some sense of community – which is not a matter of feelings alone but is nurtured by and expressed in language, culture and remembered history – no state machinery could function affectively. Equally, without some degree of political institutionalization, no 'people', however intense their self-conscious identity, could become a sovereign entity. Our concern in this book is that we should not be embarrassed by the 'subjectivity' of national identity and loyalty, but should seek to understand it more fully as a proper ingredient in human responsibility. In seeking such an understanding, a fundamental question that must be faced right away is that of the actual value that we place on nationhood. Just *how* highly should loyalty to one's country be rated, relative to other values? Or, put slightly differently, where do we place 'nation' in the total scheme of things which form our world?

All earthly things above?

Since we are dealing with an area where poetry and symbolism so often hold sway, and where it is the popular imagination rather than abstruse concepts which matter, no apology is made for beginning with a look at a hymn which for many British people expresses patriotism at its most sublime:

> I vow to thee, my country – all earthly things above –
> Entire and whole and perfect, the service of my love,
> The love that asks no question: the love that stands the test,
> That lays upon the altar the dearest and the best:
> The love that never falters, the love that pays the price,
> The love that makes undaunted the final sacrifice.

These lines are so ardent in their idealism that it seems sacrilege even to think of questioning them. Especially when sung to Gustav Holst's 'Jupiter' theme the words take on an almost ethereal quality of devotion, and the popularity of the hymn was recently boosted by its inclusion in the grand pageantry of the royal wedding in St Paul's Cathedral, in 1981. And it must be said at once that as poetry the verse has a moving and noble simplicity. Furthermore, expressing as it does the theme of self-sacrifice to a cause greater than one's own life, there is no place here for casual or flippant criticism. The author was Cecil Spring-Rice (1859–1918), a diplomat who was British Ambassador in Washington during the First World War. Immediately on the entry of the United States into the war in late 1917, he was relieved of his post and replaced by a direct representative of the war cabinet. Some days later, just before leaving Washington for Canada, he composed this verse. Awareness of the sense of injury which Spring-Rice bore as a result of his peremptory dismissal certainly adds depth to his lines, for now they are seen to be the expression of devotion offered in spite of seeming ingratitude. By a love which is prepared to sacrifice all, Spring-Rice privately made clear that he meant a love which shared something of the same quality as that sacrifice shown on the cross. Spring-Rice in fact died suddenly just a few weeks after writing the verse, and one can only speculate whether the blow he had suffered, and the effort to transform it into a creative sacrifice of love, had not indeed cost him his life.[2]

It is therefore only with a sense of deep respect that we may question what this verse has to say – and question it we must, especially regarding its use in a Christian context. 'All earthly things above' – on what basis is it assumed that nation is the highest 'earthly' reality claiming our loyalty? On the more immediate level, what of our duty to parents and children? And on the wider level, can we ignore the claim of the total human community on this one earth? Further, while the spirit of self-sacrifice is certainly one that stirs the soul to deepest respect, a 'love that asks no question' is – ironically – a very questionable kind of love. For if the claim of one's country is so absolute, it means that there is no moral frame of reference outside the nation itself. This makes for a distorted form of 'love'. The meaning of 'loving' someone is never as simple as it seems, but generally it will include our willing of what is best for that person. In loving my children I will what I consider is best for them, which includes their health, their protection from danger, their education, and the fulfilment of their potential as human beings. But if my love for them is not to slide into sheer infatuation or dotage, it must also mean seeing them in the light of my beliefs in goodness, honesty, truthfulness and justice. To believe 'he can do no wrong' does the loved one no real service at all. In other words, true love of a human person cannot simply be a wondering adoration and submission, which identifies the beloved with goodness itself. It requires seeing the beloved in the light of a standard of goodness which transcends him or her. There is One, and One alone who is truly good, and who can be worshipped as goodness itself.

Now Spring-Rice does not explicitly divinize his country – he at least keeps it in view as an earthly thing, even if 'all earthly things above'. But the expressions of absolute love and sacrifice which follow – and note the frank reference to the *altar* of sacrifice – are more redolent of that which is due to God rather than to Caesar, and verge on idolatry. Self-sacrifice as an end in itself cannot be the ultimate aspiration, for could not this verse be sung by any patriot, of any country fighting for any cause whatever? On this view, would not the noblest people of modern times be the Japanese Kamikaze pilots who flung themselves to death with their planes against allied warships in the Pacific? It is not enough to admire the love that makes undaunted the final sacrifice. We do have to ask questions about the morality of the national cause for which the sacrifice is made, otherwise devotion becomes indistinguishable from fanaticism. As Reinhold Niebuhr says:

The paradox is that patriotism transmutes individual unselfishness into national egoism. Loyalty to the nation is a high form of altruism when compard with lesser loyalties and more parochial interests. It therefore becomes the vehicle of all the altruistic impulses and expresses itself, on occasion, with such fervor that the critical attitude of the individual toward the nation and its enterprises are almost completely destroyed. The unqualified character of this devotion is the very basis of the nation's power and of the freedom to use the power without moral restraint. Thus the unselfishness of the individual makes for the selfishness of nations.[3]

Some years before 1918, Spring-Rice had written another verse in the same metre, and this he now placed as the second verse of the hymn as we know it today:

> And there's another country, I've heard of long ago –
> Most dear to them that love her, most great to them that know –
> We may not count her armies: we may not see her King –
> Her fortress is a faithful heart, her pride is suffering –
> And soul by soul and silently her shining bounds increase,
> And her ways are ways of pleasantness, and all her paths are peace.

Here, it may be felt, is the restoration of the balance. Here is the recognition of an ultimate realm, transcending that of earthly country and its claims. But is it? The 'other country' depicted here seems remote and mysterious, like a far-off fairy-land of childhood tales ('I've heard of long ago') having no connexion with present, visible realities of the world. Superficially, it is an evocative picture of the 'kingdom of God'. But the verse completely misses what is crucial in the biblical understanding of the kingdom of God, which is that not only is that kingdom *different from* the order of this present world, *but actually and actively impinges upon it*. The kingdom is not to be described solely in terms of its otherness and 'beyondness', but in its present bearing upon all life in challenge for decision and commitment. 'The kingdom of God is *at hand*; repent and believe in the gospel' (Mark 1.15). We do not therefore have simply two quite separate realms existing side by side. If that were so, God's kingdom would have as much bearing on the life of nationhood as Tolkien's Hobbit-land. We have, in the biblical witness, a kingdom of this world subjected to the kingdom of God in judgment and grace, and therefore always to be assessed in terms of that frame of reference.

The two cities

It is significant that the original poem from which Spring-Rice took the second verse quoted above, he called *Urbs Dei*, 'City of God'. Ultimately, behind his two-fold view of 'my country' and 'another country' lies St Augustine's grand cosmic vision of the course of history as a tale of two cities: the temporal or 'terrene' city which is built on human self-love, and the 'city of God', 'that most glorious society and celestial city of God's faithful' which is founded on righteousness and is being built up by God for eternity. Augustine wrote his *City of God* in response to the sack of Rome by

Alaric and the Goths in 410, an event which made pagan and Christian alike tremble, for it seemed as though the very foundations of civilization were being shaken, and that barbarism was about to engulf the whole world. Augustine set out to confute the pagan and comfort the Christian. What he wrote was a remarkable fusion of certain elements in the New Testament, especially Paul's concept of the triumph of God's kingdom, with the Greek, Platonic view of ultimate reality as the invisible, immaterial and timeless realm of spirit which transcends this world. Kingdoms and empires of this world will rise and fall, disasters may befall them. But all the time, invisible and unshakable, grows the city of God whose members are God's elect and whose triumph will be manifest at the great consummation of history. But while this vision indeed lies behind Spring-Rice's imagery, much has happened to transform it in the course of the centuries. By the time we come to Spring-Rice, the terrene city has been reduced and localized, from the *total* structure of the human world in history to 'my country' in the national sense. Instead of a total human solidarity in sin, we now have a nationally circumscribed solidarity with 'my country'.

In its original context, Augustine's simple yet brilliant conception, worked out in the full knowledge that the invading hordes were even then driving through his North African homeland, was much more than a counsel of despair. Not only did it provide a bulwark against panic at the threat from barbarism, but it also came to provide the basis for the grand synthesis of mediaeval thought which was to carry the western world through a thousand years of Christian civilization. Out of the ruins of old imperial Rome arose the new Christendom, designed on the grand scale like the cathedrals which are its most enduring visible monuments. The mediaeval mind sought to grasp heaven and earth, God and man, in a single interlocking system of thought. The heavenly city in the shape of the church ruled the earthly realm. The Catholic Church was the unifying force of the west, and it was as members of Christendom rather than of 'nationalities' in our modern sense that people identified themselves when thinking in terms of anything wider than their immediate local or regional area. Nor was the spiritual sphere simply set apart from this world as 'another country', leaving the kingdom of this world the right to one's love 'entire and whole and perfect'. Secular citizenship was here and now qualified by the claims of heavenly citizenship. 'Man does not belong to the political community with the whole of his being nor with all that he is', stated the greatest mediaeval schoolman, St Thomas Aquinas.

The mediaeval edifice did not last. The framework which sought to keep earthly activity directly subject to the heavenly – which politically and culturally meant the sovereignty of the church on earth – could not contain the pressures of resurgent humanism, which sought fulfilment in this-worldly achievements in their own right. The political and ecclesiastical structure fragmented along with much else. Rome no longer remained the hub of Europe, as the Reformation spread from Germany, and the peoples of the north declared their spiritual and political independence. The movement towards the sovereign nation-state was under way. In England, Henry VIII's defiance of the Pope, in order to secure a male succession to the House of Tudor, was quickly seen to have a significance far transcending dynastic ambition. Once the king declared himself head of an autonomous English Church, the way was open for the development of a much more distinctive English self-consciousness. While Henry himself was theologically and liturgically a conservative Catholic, it was soon apparent that a church refusing to recognize the jurisdiction of Rome could not, in the face of the Reformation thinking arriving from the continent, remain catholic in the old way. And what the English Church should be like, became a people's question, a matter of intense debate in parlours and taverns as well as in Parliament. Through the long and bloody story of the sixteenth century, England (as Scotland) was working out her own destiny, her own peculiar combination of the two threads of religion and politics, shaped by the need to find a measure of internal unity against the threat of Spain from without. Under Elizabeth, a measure of stability was reached, a sense of identity realized, providing the climate for a Shakespeare to extol

> This blessed plot, this earth, this realm, this England.[4]

So 'this England' arrived on the scene as a new object of men's devotion. In the sixteenth century the devotion took various forms. For some, it was already a highly secularized devotion surrounding the court of Elizabeth and the cult of Gloriana. For others, loyalty to England was closely allied to loyalty to Protestantism. More extreme was the view, which has periodically reasserted itself as one of the most potent forms of patriotism, of the country as a specially chosen people, selected by God to fulfil a particular messianic mission to the rest of the world.

Ever since, the relationship of the national city of men to the city of God has been problematic. Not many have taken Søren Kierkegaard's lonely path of rejecting corporate national existence as indifferent and hostile to man's eternal destiny:

as Hegal taught, that from a Christian standpoint . . . the state has a moral significance, that true virtue should be manifested only in the state . . . that the aim of the state is to ennoble man, and so on, of course is all nonsense. The state is rather an evil than a good, rather a necessary and in a sense a useful and expedient evil than a good. The state is human egoism in its great proportions . . .[5]

But if this stark extreme is rejected, and the claims of national loyalty are allowed to some degree, how are those rampant claims to be reconciled with the ultimate claim, whether it be called the city of God, or a transcendent moral order, or whatever? By identifying the nation with the city of God, as essentially happens with the 'chosen nation' concept? By frankly allowing the claim of the nation to pursue its own ends, either relegating the city of God to a remote realm beyond, or dismissing it altogether in atheistic fashion? Or by regarding the claim of the nation and the authority of the state as the channels of divine authority? The fact is that the nation-state is here, and in the twentieth century it has acquired an almost unquestioned status. To quote Reinhold Niebuhr again:

the modern nation is the human group of strongest social cohesion, of most undisputed social authority and of most clearly defined membership. The church may have challenged its pre-eminence in the Middle Ages, and the economic class may compete with it for the loyalty of man in our own day; yet it remains, as it has been since the seventeenth century, the most absolute of all human associations.[6]

In the twentieth century, one factor especially has contributed towards the apotheosis of patriotism to a virtually sacred status: war. The relationship between patriotism and war is not simply, as is commonly assumed, one of cause and effect respectively. War *unleashes* patriotic feelings and eventually *consolidates* them. It can generate a sense of national unity and identity in face of a threat from without – 'backs to the wall', 'their finest hour' – and provoking even the blandest citizens to discover just what their country means to them. This was most marked in the outbreak of the First World War. It was the atheistic Rupert Brooke who discovered that the summons to king and country came with the liberating clarity of an all-or-nothing issue, which required nothing less than a *religious* phraseology to express:

> Now, God be thanked Who has matched us with His hour,
> And caught our youth, and wakened us from sleeping

There was release in at last finding something worth dying for, in a world 'grown old and cold and weary'. On the political stage, David Lloyd George preached the same message in September 1914: 'The stern hand of fate has scourged us to an elevation where we can see the great everlasting things that matter for a nation: the great peaks of honour we had forgotten – duty and patriotism clad in glittering white; the great pinnacle of sacrifice pointing like a rugged finger to heaven.'[7] Sixty-eight years later, in the midst of the Falklands campaign, Mrs Thatcher again voiced a mood of national self-congratulation: 'The world wondered, would the good and true respond? And the good and true did.'[8] Further, the aftermath of war is a solidification of national sentiment, especially in view of the sacrifice of those who died. When blood has been shed for the country, the rightful claim of the country to that blood must be asserted, or else the unbearable, unmentionable and horrific thought might emerge: those lives were wasted. No, the sacrifice *had* to be made, they did not 'die in vain'. The sacrifices which have been made even take on a justifying power of their own. 'If they're worth dying for, they're worth keeping', was a widely-quoted remark of a colour sergeant returning from the Falklands. A soldier who has been involved in the peril cannot be blamed for feeling that way. Whether a whole nation can base its policies on such a feeling is another matter.

Nations then, constitute an extremely important fact of life today, whether we like it or not. Their existence and nature must be recognized. But we need a way of looking at nations, and our own in particular, which relates them to what *is* absolute – in Christian terms, the will and purpose of God. How can the nation be valued yet kept in its place? It is at this point that we turn to Dietrich Bonhoeffer for guidance as to what theological insights the Christian tradition may provide, for the relationship between the structures of human life on earth and the kingdom of God was a central theme in his thought, both during his early career and in his last years.

Germany: the absolutization of nation

When Bonhoeffer returned to Germany from the United States in 1931, the Weimar Republic had less than two years to live. For many of his countrymen, its doom was a matter for rejoicing if it meant the reversal of all the humiliation that had attended the end of the war. The armistice of 1918 had effectively meant defeat for Germany on the western front, but many Germans could not accept this interpretation. The military had not been defeated in battle. Rather, there had been the infamous 'stab in the back' by weak-minded politicians at home, who prevented the army from defending the fatherland any further. Germany had not been defeated, only betrayed, such was the German aftermyth of war. This at least allowed the colossal loss of life to be defended against the charge of futility. All would have been well, but for the treason of those who sued for peace. Many were therefore looking for a re-affirmation of national dignity which, it was held, had been so ignominiously discarded in 1918, and which the terms of the Versailles Treaty seemed determined to deny to Germany.

It was this atmosphere of hurt national pride and deep resentment that was being exploited by resurgent German nationalism – above all by the Nazi party of Adolf Hitler. In *Mein Kampf* Hitler had hardly shown himself a master of coherent argument, venting forth his crude flood of ideas on blood, race and soil. But the absolutist tone of his nationalism was clear enough:

Only an adequate large space on this earth assures a nation of freedom of existence . . . Without consideration of 'traditions' and prejudices [the National Socialist movement] must find the courage to gather our people and their strength for an advance along the road that will lead this people from its present restricted living space to new land and soil.[9]

And for Hitler the unique claims of the nation enabled him to give his own definition of a 'socialist':

Whoever is prepared to make the national cause his own to such an extent that he knows no higher ideal than the welfare of his nation; whoever has understood our great national anthem, 'Deutschland über Alles', to mean that nothing in this wide world surpasses in his eyes this Germany, people and land – that man is a Socialist.[10]

'No higher ideal than the welfare of his nation', 'nothing in this world surpasses . . . this Germany' – such slogans were on the lips not just of Hitler and his party propagandists, but of many academics in Germany, and not least certain Protestant theologians, during the late 1920s and early 1930s. Indeed, there can be traced a German intellectual preoccupation with the concept of *das Volk*, the people or nation, as far back as some of the Romantic thinkers in the early nineteenth century who saw 'the people' as a kind of mystical entity with its own personality and genius.

After the First World War, an explicit metaphysical basis for nationhood was sought. For nationalistically-minded Protestant theologians this involved the concept of *orders of creation*, that is, the doctrine that certain structures of human life are not just biological or historical phenomena, but are deliberately ordained of God as essential and immutable conditions of man's existence and without which he is not man as created by God. The concept of an order of creation was not in itself particularly sinister. Karl Barth, who was to lead the theological onslaught on nationalist religion in the German Church Struggle, was himself employing the term in his lectures on ethics at Münster and Bonn in the late 1920s.[11] And a Christian doctrine of man, in both Protestant and Catholic traditions, has generally maintained that certain features of human existence are specially significant for the way in which the 'image of God' is reflected in man. But the nationalist theologians made a much freer and quite arbitrary use of the idea of orders of creation, and above all claimed that *the* supreme order of creation is the people, race or nation to which one belongs and owes loyalty.

So, for example, a particular meaning is now to be attached to the credal confessional 'I believe in God, the Father Almighty, Maker of heaven and earth . . .' This becomes a confession that God has created me with my particular nationality and its special characteristics. He has therewith bound me to submit myself to the forces working out the destiny of my nation, and to co-operate with its spirit. Indeed in the flowering of a nation's life we see what creation really is. So, while not actually elevating the nation to godlike status, such a view claims for the nation a special, original and fundamental status in man's world. The nation has its own particular laws of development and it is incumbent on all concerned, not least the church, to recognize these. As part of their reverence to the Creator, Christians must play their part in affirming the distinctive nature of their nation as God's creation – which means safeguarding its racial purity and preserving it from alien cultural elements. The so-called Faith Movement of German Christians, the Protestant equivalent of the Brownshirts, made all this a main plank in their campaigns for control of the Evangelical Church. Their manifesto of 1932 stated:

In race, nation and cultural heritage we see the orders of existence which God has given us in trust; it is the law of God that we should be concerned to preserve them. Therefore racial admixture is to be opposed . . . faith in Christ does not destroy the race, it deepens and sanctifies it.[12]

It was in this atmosphere that Dietrich Bonhoeffer took up his duties as a lecturer in the University of Berlin in the late summer of 1931.

Order of creation or order of preservation?

Everywhere, it seemed, churchmen were calling for a new 'theology of creation' with special regard to the place of nation and race. Bonhoeffer knew from the start where he stood amidst all this theological clamour, but he chose the point of his opposition carefully. His lectures during 1931–33 in the university breathed scarcely a word on the issue – and in the context it was an eloquent silence. For during the winter of 1932–33 he gave a series of lectures on 'Creation', expounding the first two chapters of Genesis, and mentioning neither orders of creation, nor 'people' or 'nation' at all. Bonhoeffer's refusal even to mention the issue was probably a sign of his contempt for the nationalist theology, which he perceived to have made a fundamental error: that of claiming to be able to discern the will and purpose of the Creator by an observation of 'creation' as it now is. What *is*, the nationalists had argued, evidently *must* be, and is therefore ordained of God. To Bonhoeffer, more faithful to the Reformation heritage, what *is* exists as part of a fallen, sinful world – the people and nation no less than any other aspect of the world. It is *Jesus Christ*, the Word of God, who reveals to us the will and purpose of the Creator, and the true shape of human existence. Bonhoeffer's interpretation of Genesis was thus a 'theological' one, in the sense of relating it to the specifically Christian perspective given by the incarnation, death and resurrection of Christ. 'Therefore the Church only sees the beginning in the end; from the end. It sees the creation *sub specie Christi*; better still, in the fallen, old world it believes in the new creation world of the beginning and of the end, because it believes in Christ and in nothing else.'[13] Bonhoeffer's theology was clearly in line with that of Karl Barth and the affirmation to be made at Barmen in 1934.

If Bonhoeffer's attack on the nationalist theology was implicit in this exposition of the creation narrative, then it became quite explicit when he entered the pulpit and conference room. Bonhoeffer found himself pitched into the battle on the ecclesiastical front as a result of his appointment as German Youth Secretary of the World Alliance. Part of his work involved arranging ecumenical conferences and it was obvious that to German participants the relationship of the church to the nation, and of the ecumenical movement to the world of nations, was a highly sensitive issue. The first such conference took place in Berlin in April 1932. Following a paper by Professor W. Stählin of Münster, which made heavy use of 'orders of creation', Bonhoeffer launched into a forthright assault on the concept, particularly as applied to the nation. Our only record of what was said comes from Bonhoeffer himself who wrote up the minutes as secretary, but we may at least presume that he reported what he said or wished to say, accurately enough:

It was impossible to single out some features of the world above others as orders of creation and base a course of Christian moral action upon them. This was only possible if the revelation in Christ was the starting point for thought, and that was not the case here . . . It was just this presupposition, i.e. the orders of creation, which provided a justification of war between the nations.[14]

In place of 'orders of creation', Bonhoeffer proposed the concept of *orders of preservation*:

The difference was that in the light of the concept of orders of creation, certain ordinances and features of the world were regarded as valuable, original, 'very good' in themselves, whereas the concept of orders of preservation meant that each feature was only a feature preserved by God, in grace and anger, in view of the revelation in Christ. Any order under the preservation of God should be carried out by Christ and only preserved for his sake. An order is only to be regarded as an order of preservation so long as it is still open for the proclamation of the Gospel. Where an order is basically closed to this proclamation, be it apparently the most original, marriage, nation, etc, it must be surrendered.[15]

Bonhoeffer is spelling out the implications of what Christians usually claim to believe, namely the supreme lordship of Jesus Christ. This means the relativizing of all claims to one's loyalty apart from him. If we recognize the importance of our nation and of being a member of it, then we can do so only for the sake of Christ. The nation is not an absolute good in itself, it does not have an intrinsic right to existence.

Later in 1932, Bonhoeffer gave a paper at the Youth Peace Conference of the World Alliance in Czechoslovakia. He dealt again with 'orders of creation' and 'orders of preservation', and was even more forthright in the need for radical questioning of accepted structures of human life:

Orders of preservation are forms of working against sin in the direction of the gospel. *Any order* – however ancient and sacred it may be – *can be dissolved*, and must be dissolved when it closes up in itself, grows rigid and no longer permits the proclamation of revelation. From this standpoint the Church of Christ has to pass its verdict on the orders of the world. In the historical change of the orders of the world it has to keep in mind only one thing: Which orders can best restrain this radical falling of the world into death and sin and hold the way open for the Gospel? The Church hears the commandment only from Christ, not from any fixed law or from any eternal order, and it hears it in the orders of preservation . . . It can demand the most radical destruction simply for the sake of the one who builds up.[16]

On this view, national life is, theologically, a holding operation for the coming of that which alone is absolutely valuable, the salvation offered by Christ. It draws people together in communities which sustain and enhance life, and enables a certain stability to be achieved. Not in itself of absolute value, it can provide a matrix for the reception of the absolute, that is, the gospel of Christ. But if the nation begins to make absolute claims for itself, it thereby shuts itself up against the one true absolute, and forfeits its right to existence. Or if it should become apparent that nationhood is no longer acting as a preservative force in human life, but rather threatening to bring chaos and destruction, then likewise it is open to dissolution for the sake of a more adequate order.

The nation in biblical perspective

At this point, if it is felt that Bonhoeffer is being unwontedly subversive of the traditional link between godliness and national loyalty, it is worth glancing at the Bible itself. Surprising though it may seem to those who automatically link Christianity and patriotism, the Bible is a very poor source of 'patriotic' texts as compared with Horace, Cicero, Homer, Shakespeare and Wordsworth.

In both Old and New Testaments the existence of man in nations and peoples is noted – and at certain points very realistically indeed. Egypt and Syria, Assyria and Babylon, Phoenicia and Persia, Greece and Rome, all take their turn on the stage with more peripheral

actors and the central figure, Israel. But the fact of nationhood is ultimately incidental to the great drama which moves from creation and
fall through to the great final triumph of God's purpose in a new
heaven and a new earth. In the actual creation narratives (Genesis 1
and 2) there is no mention of peoples or nations, yet it is emphasized
that the decisively human marks depicted there indicate the divine
likeness in man (Genesis 1.27). Man as God's viceroy on earth,
having dominion over other creatures, and man as man-in-
relationship (male and female) – of *this* existence it is said that it is in
the divine image. Whatever other structures of life ensue, may be
good, useful and productive for mankind, but are not the *sine qua non*
of being human. Races, peoples and nationalities do not appear in the
ancient saga until after the flood and the preservation of Noah's sons
(Genesis 6–9) from whom are descended the peoples 'each with his
own language, by their families, in their nations' (Genesis 10.6, 20,
31). 'And from these the nations spread abroad upon the earth after
the flood' (10.32). Here the differentiation and extension of the
peoples is certainly to be seen as a fulfilment of the divine blessing
pronounced upon Noah and his family: 'Be fruitful, and multiply,
and fill the earth' (Genesis 9.1).

However, the Bible presents another aspect to the rise of nationhood, in the mysterious story of the Tower of Babel (Genesis 11).
Here, men who as yet 'had one language and few words' attempt to
build a tower up to heaven to 'make a name' for themselves and to
prevent their dispersal over the whole earth. God comes down and
scatters them, confusing their language 'that they may not understand one another's speech'. Here again, therefore, existence as
distinct peoples is seen as a divine ordering – but this time in
judgment and, in view of man's persistent tendency to overreach
himself, as a preservative against complete self-destruction. On this
view, to be a nation is not a pretext for self-glorification, but a sign of
one's limitedness and dependence.

From this point on, the Old Testament focusses on the story of
Israel, the one people called from the world of peoples to be God's
people. The call affirms the reality of nationhood – but in a peculiar
way. Israel is called from among the nations, *for* the nations; for
service, not for privilege. Abraham, the rock from which this nation
is hewn, is told: 'And by you all the families of the earth shall bless
themselves' (Genesis 12.3). Israel exists not for her own sake, but for
all mankind. God's mighty acts on her behalf are *not* simply on her
behalf, but so that all peoples may rejoice at the saving power of
Israel's God (Psalm 67.1f). Jerusalem will one day be lifted up above
all the mountains of the earth, signifying not Israel's national
eminence over the rest of the world, but the recognition by all

nations and peoples of the authority of the God of Jacob (Isaiah 2.3f). And why has *this* people been chosen by God to be his own, and the means of revealing his glory to the world? The answer is at first sight rather brusque, disregarding any cause of Israel's pride in herself, and giving more credit to God himself:

> It was not because you were more in number that the Lord set his love upon you and chose you, for you were the fewest of all peoples; but it is because the Lord loves you, and is keeping the oath which he swore to your fathers, that the Lord has brought you out with a mighty hand . . .

> (Deuteronomy 8.7f)

The inner meaning of Israel's history therefore lies not in her innate 'genius', religious or otherwise, or in any of the standard national interests of power and possessions that she shares with peoples generally (and just how real these could be is clear from a reading of the books of Samuel, Kings and Chronicles), but in the purpose of the God who calls her. This was so much the case that the prophets who again and again reminded the people of the supreme claims of their God, risked the accusation of betraying their country's interests. Above all it was Jeremiah who was branded as traitor, because he saw the only real and lasting hope for his people as lying in defeat and submission to the conqueror.

Israel's true life is therefore one of total reliance upon the holy and gracious God, for the sake of all peoples – 'a light to lighten the gentiles'. The New Testament sees this meaning fulfilled in Jesus, who consummates Israel's calling by his life of obedient faith, crowned in the self-offering of himself on the cross. Raised by the power of God, he is the head of the new humanity created by the Holy Spirit. At Pentecost the confusion of Babel begins to be reversed. A new community arises through faith in Christ, in which 'there is neither Jew nor Greek, there is neither slave nor free, there is neither male nor female: for you are all one in Christ Jesus' (Galatians 3.28). The universal community of the church signals the end of previous enmities, even what was formerly supposed to be the absolute divide between Jew and gentile: 'For he is our peace, who has made us both one and has broken down the dividing wall of hostility' (Ephesians 2.14–16).

At the end, the kingdoms of this world become the kingdoms of our God, and of his Christ, king of kings and lord of lords. That is the only ultimate sovereignty. The great vision of God's completed purpose is of 'a great multitude which no man could number, from every nation, from all tribes and peoples and tongues' before that unsurpassable throne (Revelation 7.9). The nations walk by the light of the new Jerusalem – and offer to it their glory and honour (Revelation 21.24–26).

In the biblical perspective, then, national existence as we know it is neither an original or final state of humanity. It is provisional. As such it is recognized but also transcended in the kingdom of God. There is a glory and honour of the nations, but these are to be submitted to the one God who alone reigns for ever.

A love of the provisional

Much of the atmosphere and arguments of German academics during 1931–33 will seem exotic to us in Britain today – and so may Bonhoeffer's contribution to that debate. Hardly anyone, it may be felt, is going to lose any sleep trying to decide whether the nation is an order of creation or an order of preservation. But the real issue lies deeper than the phrases and terms used. It is the issue of whether we are to regard the sovereign nation-state as we know it, as the only valid and absolutely necessary form of larger social grouping. As a matter of fact, as far as the phraseology is concerned, it is not at all obvious that a clear line *can* be drawn between the underlying assumptions of 'I vow to thee, my country' on the one hand, and the mystical absolutization of the country by the German nationalist theologians on the other. The Nazis have not been the only ones to elevate nationhood to such a degree. 'The idea of the "nation", indeed, has the most far-reaching biblical endorsement', claims a British Conservative MP, who also seems to think that Paul's words about God fixing 'the bounds of the peoples' (Acts 17.26) are to be found 'Right at the beginning (*sic*) of the Bible'![17] The theology of orders of creation is not yet dead. Equally, Bonhoeffer's critique extends its cutting edge to much more than the obvious theological lunacies of his own immediate context. It challenges all such assumptions and sentiments about the nation being *the* highest object of our love, *the* larger grouping of absolute significance, with its present form as eternally ordained (by God, fate, history or whatever).

Reinhold Niebuhr was quoted earlier to the effect that the nation has outstripped all its rivals among larger social groupings in its bid for loyalty and devotion. As a fact of history, that is so. Yet today we are faced with the situation that a sense of human solidarity wider than the nation, and embracing the whole earth, is quite literally a matter of life and death, of survival or extinction for mankind as a whole. In a world in which the issues of population, poverty, ecology and nuclear weaponry are inescapably everyone's issues, it has to be asked if, in Bonhoeffer's terms, the sovereign nation-state left to itself can even be an 'order of preservation'. Unless it is significantly qualified by a realistic world-consciousness, national identity seems destined to become an order of destruction rather than an order of preservation. This is a spiritual as much as a political issue, for it is a matter of determining where our higher loyalties really do lie, and also of finding the imagery, language and symbolism which can express them with the appropriate passion.

A Christian perspective, then, will strongly qualify the ideal of national loyalty today. But to qualify is not to abolish. Because the nation is regarded as a provisional structure, it is not thereby discarded. There is a loyalty and love proper to it, precisely in its provisionality. Not created directly by God for eternity, it nevertheless does have a role in his total purpose. So long as it is acting as a preservative in human life, it merits gratitude, respect and solidarity. Human powers and structures may not be identified with the kingdom of God, yet the kingdom of God seeks to be present on the earth. This was the theme of a remarkable sermon preached by Bonhoeffer in late 1932, 'Thy Kingdom Come on Earth'. The church's ancient prayer, says Bonhoeffer, tends to be prayed either in other-worldly fashion (seeking God by leaving the world behind), or in secularist fashion (despising God to find the world). Neither way is successful:

The man who loves God, loves him as the lord of the earth, as it is; the man who loves the earth, loves her as God's earth. The man who loves the kingdom of God, loves it precisely because it is *God's* kingdom, and he loves it as God's kingdom *on earth*. The reason is simple – the king of that kingdom is the creator and sustainer of the earth.[18]

The sinful earth now bears the curse, but Christ has come in human flesh and borne that curse on the cross. That, Bonhoeffer continues, has profound implications for our own attitude to our contemporary world:

When we pray for the coming of the kingdom, we can only pray for its coming on earth, this earth, not some earth that we have transfigured. We cannot pray for the coming of the kingdom on earth if we try to flee from the cares and responsibilities of earth, this earth. Our prayer forces us into the company of the children of this world, it commits us to accept the facts of this earth, its care, its hunger, its death. It places us in complete solidarity with our fellow-men in their evil and their guilt. When we pray for the coming of the kingdom of God we stand together with the world. We grind our teeth with them and with them clench our fists. This is no time for lonely piety.[19]

Bonhoeffer does not specifically refer to the nation in this sermon, but it is clearly implicit in his understanding of the 'earth'. We cannot opt out of our earthliness, which includes our national existence as long as nations exist, and it is in this involvement that we seek the kingdom of God. Bonhoeffer, we may see, points towards a true love of country in the light of belief in God's grace. What often goes by the name of patriotism is an attempt to elevate the country to a position of great reverence, if not divinity. Eventually, that becomes a burden of pretentiousness and hypocrisy, as the idol's feet of clay crumble. But when seen quite simply as part of the earth which God loves, the nation itself is freed from the need to justify itself by grandeur and dazzling achievement, and we are freed from the burden to pretend that it is greater than it actually is. We can love it and appreciate it as it is – the nearest circle of humanity that we know on this earth which God loved to the cross. No more, and no less, than that.

It will therefore be seen that Bonhoeffer's view of people and nation as orders of preservation not only prevents a falsely exalted view of country and a pathological form of patriotism, but equally affirms the reality of nationhood, however provisional in the ultimate scheme, in the face of attempts to belittle it or trivialize it. This is an intellectualistic temptation once we embark on a thoroughgoing sociological critique of institutions generally. All forms of social institution, however venerable, are in origin human creations – so the post-Marx analysis runs – from the simplest family habits and customs to the most complex national and international structures. But we very rarely observe the creation of the institutions or structures for ourselves. They precede our arrival in this world. We are born into them and we grow up having to adapt to them ('socialization'). They are there in all their seeming objectivity, over against us. They therefore seem to have an unquestioned authority simply by existing, especially when hallowed by long tradition. *Reification* is how the sociologist describes this apprehension of human artefacts as seemingly extra-human or even supernatural in origin.

Nationality may certainly be considered such an artefact. But to see the historical relativity of the nation does not license the view that it is of no account, or should be of no account in a properly enlightened world. As Daniel Jenkins points out,[20] many of the things most admired by those (especially academics) who are contemptuous of nationhood, only become possible through the strong sense of identity and mutual responsibility which are created by national feelings. Social service networks and public education are but two examples, together with the sense of shared tradition which enables knowledge and skills to be transmitted from generation to generation.

Bonhoeffer sought to maintain the theological perspective on the nation throughout his life. No-one saw more clearly, more quickly, the falsity of the claims being made for the nation during 1931–33. No-one rejected more decisively the basis of the state symbolized by the swastika and the absolute claims of the *Führer*. No-one realized more painfully the vast gulf between the glories proclaimed by the Third Reich and the brutalities committed in its name. Yet, no-one stood by his people more faithfully in their darkest hour and, from the moment of his decision to return from the United States in 1939, no-one cherished the name of Germany more than he. In rejecting the false love for his country, he was freed for its true love.

To love the earth, including our country, according to Bonhoeffer, we must love it *as it is*. To explore that thought further is the theme of our next chapter.

4
Loving the Real

Following the skirmishes of 1932–33, Dietrich Bonhoeffer appears to have lost interest in a theology of nationhood, or indeed any re-worked understanding of the doctrines of creation and preservation at all. The need now was to concentrate on the true confession of faith as enunciated at the Barmen Synod, and on the struggle of the Confessing Church to remain loyal to that confession in word and deed. Jesus Christ as the one Word of God to be obeyed in life and death now became the key issue, and with it, the marks of the true church of Christ. After the summer semester of 1933, Bonhoeffer effectively left the university lecture-room for the pulpit and the seminary. From the autumn of 1933 until 1935 he was in charge of the German congregation in London, and then returned to Germany as director of the Confessing Church's seminary at Finkenwalde. The Findenwalde period was the time of the writing of *Cost of Discipleship* and *Life Together*. The exclusive, absolute nature of the call of Jesus and the 'special' nature of the Christian life and community now took precedence. All else was in the background – though it should be noted that the background was still there! The world as a whole is not completely lost to view, nor are the 'natural' human instincts and loyalties simply deprecated or ignored as in some forms of pietism, even though they take second place to the demands of Christ. 'When we love those who love us, our brethren, our nation, our friends, yes, and even our own congregation, we are no better than the heathen and the publicans. Such love is ordinary and natural, and not distinctively Christian.'[1]

Ethics

Such love is ordinary and natural. As time went on, Bonhoeffer felt that the 'ordinary and natural' deserved reassessment by theology, especially German Protestant theology which had tended to emphasize 'grace' at the expense of 'nature'. As we have seen, from the autumn of 1940 until his arrest in April 1943 Bonhoeffer was occupied in writing his *Ethics*, while also engaged in the conspiracy. Here, in this boundary situation between ecclesiastical service and political resistance, the claims of the world came high on the theological agenda. While for obvious reasons of security there is no overt reference to the resistance (and indeed hardly any to Nazism itself) much of *Ethics* reflects the ambiguities and tensions of that situation and Bonhoeffer's efforts to resolve them theologically. So we find trenchant criticism of that whole caste of mind induced by a debased Lutheranism, which Bonhoeffer calls 'thinking in two spheres', spiritual and secular, sacred and profane. In contrast, says Bonhoeffer, 'There are not two realities, but only one reality, and that is the reality of God, which has become manifest in Christ in the reality of the world. Sharing in Christ we stand at once in both the reality of God and the reality of the world.'[2] The world – even the disordered world – has been reconciled to God by Christ. 'The world belongs to Christ, and it is only in Christ that the world is what it is.'[3] Bonhoeffer's earlier immense stress on the centrality of Christ – owing so much to Karl Barth's influence – therefore did not prove to be the blind alley which it might have been if his interest had simply centred on the relationship between Christ and the Christian. Even in *Cost of Discipleship*, we have seen, it is a Christ who is Lord of the world rather than the possession of the church, who is ultimately in view. Via the narrow christocentric defile, Bonhoeffer attains to a new panorama of the world as the place which God has made and re-conciled to himself through the incarnation, cross and resurrection of Jesus Christ. In *this* light, therefore, Bonhoeffer can look seriously again at the world and its structures, as the place where man meets God in responsibility.

  Ethics is not easy reading. Students hastening to become Bonhoeffer addicts are slowed down to walking pace on meeting what at first appears to be an odd combination of rather pietistic language and abstract terminology, not to mention statements made as confidently as they are paradoxical: 'The knowledge of good and evil seems to be the aim of all ethical reflection. The first task of Christian ethics is to invalidate this knowledge.'[4] Moreover, in his treatment of some concrete ethical issues, liberal-progressive readers of today must be prepared for some disappointments – his views on abortion for example. Most surprising of all, only *very* reservedly does he suggest certain qualifications to the traditional Lutheran attitude towards the authority of the state. But the best way to penetrate the *Ethics* – on first reading at any rate – is to ask repeatedly: What light does Bonhoeffer's involvement in the conspiracy throw on this passage – and *vice versa*? It would be too much to say that the *Ethics* is a theological justification for the conspiracy, since Bonhoeffer writes with a deliberate consciousness of the destiny of the whole western world. Nazi Germany and its hoped-for over-throw are but one part of a very large canvas. But there is no mis-taking the deeply existential tone of the sections dealing with responsibility in the face of massive evil, with conscience, freedom and above all the acceptance of guilt in responsibility. Only the believing theologian who had dared to put himself where his integrity was tested by the 'great masquerade of evil' could have written such passages.

All this is by way of introduction to an unfinished book on which we shall draw heavily in this and succeeding chapters. For the present we shall look at two themes from *Ethics* which offer further insights into the matter raised in the previous chapter, namely taking one's country seriously, but not *too* seriously. These themes are what Bonhoeffer calls the relationship between the 'ultimate' and the 'penultimate', and his concern with 'the real'.

Ultimate and Penultimate

'The Last Things and the Things Before the Last' is the title of the relevant chapter.[5] According to Reformation doctrine, the Christian gospel of God's mercy and forgiveness, whereby man is 'justified' by God's grace alone, is unequivocally the 'last thing' which man can encounter. Here is the final, absolute and eternal word from God to man. Beyond this and behind this man cannot hope to go in his dealings with God or his understanding of God. Moreover, man himself, by his own understanding, or actions, or piety, cannot reach this 'last thing'. It comes to man by God's own initiative, cutting across and disregarding all that man may have hitherto understood about his life and its possibilities. Man cannot conjure up this word for himself, still less speak it to himself as though he could forgive his own sins. He can only accept it as it comes, in a faith which issues in hope and love.

So Bonhoeffer expounds the old faith of his own Lutheran tradition – and in doing so he can sound every bit as evangelical as the Wesley hymns. The *finality* of the word of justification of the sinner has to be asserted without compromise. Now this finality, says Bonhoeffer, has two aspects. It is final 'in a qualitative sense, by the nature of its contents. There is no word of God that goes beyond his mercy. There is nothing that goes beyond a life which is justified before God.' This is completely discontinuous with everything that precedes it, 'of everything that is before the last'. But – and here is where Bonhoeffer becomes particularly interesting – it is final also in the literal sense of *time*:

> It is always preceded by something penultimate, some action, suffering, movement, volition, defeat, uprising, entreaty or hope, that is to say, in a quite genuine sense by a span of time, at the end of which it stands. Only he can be justified who has already become the object of an accusation in time. Justification presupposes that the creature has incurred guilt . . . There is a time when God permits, awaits and prepares, and there is a final time which cuts short and passes sentence upon the penultimate.[6]

So, while the ultimate word of mercy in one sense annuls and invalidates the penultimate state, the penultimate does have to be recognized. It does not last for ever, but while it *does* last it must be respected.

Bonhoeffer asks whether Christians do not piously deceive themselves in claiming that they live *only* by the ultimate in every moment. Is there not a sense in which each day we are traversing the length of the penultimate for the sake of the ultimate? With superb insight Bonhoeffer draws on a common instance of pastoral experience:

> . . . precisely in thoroughly grave situations, for instance when I am with someone who has suffered a bereavement, I often decide to adopt a 'penultimate' attitude, particularly when I am dealing with Christians, remaining silent as a sign that I share in the bereaved man's helplessness in the face of such a grievous event, and not speaking the biblical words of comfort which are, in fact, known to me and available to me. Why am I often unable to open my mouth, when I ought to give expression to the ultimate? And why, instead, do I decide on an expression of thoroughly penultimate human solidarity?[7]

Bonhoeffer argues that this is not because of any distrust of the power of the ultimate word, but a true respect for it. By deliberately remaining in the penultimate, one might in fact be pointing all the more genuinely to the ultimate 'which God will speak in his own time (though indeed even then only through a human mouth)'.

This approach, Bonhoeffer makes clear, covers the whole range of Christian social responsibility. Again, it is not difficult to detect the bearing of this upon his own strange form of responsibility at the time of writing. Instead of an out-and-out rejection of his country in the name of Christianity, he had indeed chosen a 'thoroughly penultimate human solidarity' in its fate, sufferings and guilt, identifying with it not in order to condone what was happening, but so that a responsible act might be undertaken which could preserve the country for the time when the final word of mercy could again be preached to it. This human community, in all its 'penultimacy' shared with all other human structures, was not yet to be written off in face of the ultimate. In general terms, Bonhoeffer writes:

> For the sake of the ultimate the penultimate must be preserved. Any arbitrary destruction of the penultimate will do serious injury to the ultimate. If, for example, a human life is deprived of the conditions which are proper to it, then the justification for such a life by grace and faith, if it is not rendered impossible, is at least seriously impeded.[8]

In other words, if divine grace is to be preached to man, humanity must at least be preserved in all its aspects – physical, mental, social and cultural – for the reception of that word. There is thus a rightful place for the 'natural', in which the way is prepared for the coming of the Lord. Bonhoeffer has moved on to a more positive stage from his earlier distinction between 'orders of preservation' and 'orders of creation'.[9] The world is now more definitely asserted to be a realm of God-given responsibility, and on this basis later in *Ethics* Bonhoeffer discusses the rights to bodily life, the freedom of bodily life, and the concept of the four 'mandates' given by God to man for responsibility in the world: labour, marriage, government and church.

On this basis, too, we may plot further the basic shape of a patriotism qualified by Christian faith. The nation is not the ultimate. It merits neither worship nor absolute and unquestioning allegiance. It cannot, any more than any other human structure, provide out of itself an ultimate scale of values. It cannot claim the finality which much of the usual language and symbolism of patriotism – especially in time of war – suggest. But, not being the ultimate does not mean it is nothing. Precisely in its very human nature, it has a rightful claim on our solidarity. However repugnant he may find some features of its behaviour, however embarrassed he may be by displays of 'My country, right or wrong' attitudes, the true patriot will not try to shrug off his national identity in a fit of superior moral wisdom. In the light of the ultimate, criticism and even severest condemnation may at times have to be brought upon the country, if it is believed that basic laws of justice and humanity are being denied. But then, and especially then, the true patriot stays with the country and does what can be done for the preserving of the country in a way that keeps it open to the awareness of those laws.

The real

Right from the start of his theological career in the writing of *Sanctorum Communio* to the last of his prison letters, two interlocking themes run through Bonhoeffer's thought: encounter with the real, concrete human person as distinct from abstractions about humanity; and Jesus Christ as the very incarnation of God, the revelation of true God and true man. No better illustration of the former point can be found than in the little book *Life Together*, written out of the communal experience of the seminary and community house at Finkenwalde. Sometimes apt to be dismissed as lacking the sophistication of his other works, *Life Together* in fact drives home the message which the sophisticated have to learn repeatedly and often painfully, namely, that if we would seek community with others we must drop our lofty conceptions and romantic illusions as to what that community experience should be like. True community involves an acceptance of the brother *as he is*, in all his human akwardness and indeed sinfulness.

By sheer grace, God will not permit us to live even for a brief period in a dream world. He does not abandon us to those rapturous experiences and lofty moods that come over us like a dream. God is not a God of the emotions but the God of truth. Only that fellowship which faces such disillusionment, with all its unhappy and ugly aspects, begins to be what it should be in God's sight, begins to grasp in faith the promise that is given to it. The sooner this shock of disillusionment comes to an individual and to a community the better for both.[10]

Visionary dreaming breeds pride and pretentiousness, and is destructive, for the visionary person demands that the community should conform, willy-nilly, to *his* ideal, which is doomed to failure. Christian community, on the other hand, is based on the forgiveness of sins through Christ, and the forgiveness of sins involves the mutual recognition of the frailness of each other's humanity no less than each other's individuality. 'To bear the burden of the other person means involvement with the created reality of the other, to accept and affirm it, and, in bearing with it, to break through to the point where we take joy in it.'[11]

In *Ethics* of course the perspective has been widened from the Christian fellowship to that of the world as a whole. But the stress on the real person is at least as strong:

God loves man. God loves the world. It is not an ideal man that he loves, but man as he is; not an ideal world, but the real world. What we find abominable in man's opposition to God, what we shrink back from with pain and hostility, the real man, the real world, this is for God the ground for unfathomable love, and it is with this that he unites himself utterly.[12]

Still more pertinently, Bonhoeffer puts his finger on the almost inescapable peril of all philosophical, theological and ideological discussion of what is 'good', taken in isolation from what is actually happening to real men and women:

Christ teaches no abstract ethics such as must at all costs be put into practice. Christ was not essentially a teacher and legislator, but a man, a real man like ourselves. And it is not therefore his will that we should in our time be the adherents, exponents and advocates of a definite doctrine, but that we should be men, real men, before God. Christ did not, like a moralist, love a theory of good, but he loved the real man . . .[13]

We do well to note that Bonhoeffer is underlining a biblical and Christian view of love, and one feature in particular which is apt to be overlooked because it is so elemental. In modern theology, a popular approach to the nature of love is to distinguish between various types of love, notably erotic love (*eros*), affectionate love or friendship (*philia*) and specifically 'Christian' love, *agape*.[14] Theologians characteristically set *agape* apart from the others and exalt it for its distinct quality of self-giving, that is, willing the good of the loved one regardless of the cost or rewards to oneself. This need not be disputed, though whether the distinction between the various loves implies that in actual life they can exist apart from each other, is another matter. But such discussion has focussed on the psychology

of loving, the inward motivation of the lover. In the Bible, it has to
be recognized, at least as much emphasis is put on the fact that it is the
real and actual person or thing that is beloved of God, as distinct
from idealizations or abstractions. 'And God saws that it was good':
it is the actual, created world of space and time, dry land and sea,
plants and animals, man and woman, whose existence God joyfully
affirms (Genesis 1.12, 18, 25, 31). This is the real world in distinction
from God himself, and not merely his eternal dream of such a world,
which is affirmed. It is not a primitive and naive view of divine-
human relations which in the early chapters of the Bible tells of God
dealing with individualized figures such as Adam and Eve, Cain and
Abel, Noah and his sons, rather than with 'man' at large (an abstraction alien to the Bible). For by this means God is seen as travailing
with the awkward reality of persons in all their particularity – which
is the only way in which 'man' exists. It is above all in the tangled
story of Isreal that God's love for the real emerges so clearly. 'For the
mountains may depart, and the hills be removed, but my steadfast
love shall not depart from you, and my covenant of peace shall not be
removed, says the Lord, who has compassion on you' (Isaiah 54.10).
Yet Israel, the recipient of such undying love, is never idealized into
the perfect nation, never romanticized into a beauty beyond
compare. Her pride is continually pricked. The prophets repeatedly
strip the illusions from her eyes, tearing the conceit from her, and
call her to account in no uncertain terms: 'Rejoice not, O Israel! Exult
not like the peoples; for you have played the harlot, forsaking your
God' (Hosea 9.1). None felt more sharply than Hosea the pain of
loving a people in their waywardness, evidently paralleled by the
prophet's knowledge of his own wife's unfaithfulness. Yet not to an
ideal Israel, but to the actual Israel, does the divine love return
(Hosea 11.8f). *This people* is the blunt term by which Israel is so often
referred to, in receiving condemnation and pardon. The prophets
knew well enough that 'this people' in their actual behavior were an
embarrassment. Yet it was as the God of just 'this people' that God
wished to be known. So too Jesus himself weeps when he is in actual
sight of Jerusalem, because of the city's ignorance of the things that
make for her peace (Luke 19.41–44). 'Let love be genuine' (Romans
12.9) – the genuineness of love must include acceptance of what is
genuinely there, as contrasted with what we simply imagine or wish
to be there.

Loving the real country

If there is to be love of one's country, it must be a clear-eyed
recognition of the reality of the country, and not a wishful, indulgent
admiration of what once might have been but no longer exists, or of

what one would like to be there but quite simply is not there and can never be. It is the real country we must love. Now of course this simply invites the question of what and where the 'real' country is. It is true that we never attain to the reality of anything in itself, apart from our perceptions and mental constructions concerning it. We are never free from our imaginative spectacles. This is the philosophical problem with which western thought has teased itself ever since Hume and Kant. But to say that we can never opt out of our subjective perspectives does not mean that we should give up the search for truer understanding. And to say that we may never wholly attain to 'the truth' is no excuse for not being prepared to be disabused of illusions. Indeed, as John Macmurray tersely put it, the desire to know the truth *is* the desire to be disillusioned. In knowing a person, for instance, I do at least know when some assumption about him or her proves to owe more to my imagination and prejudices than to his or her actual self – I am brought up short by a sense of reproof, of suddenly being found ignorant. We are on the way to truth whenever we give the world a chance to revise our theories and dreams about it, and allow there to be more to know than we previously imagined. That means allowing other people their say, and even more to the point, allowing them to question us too.

Something of the sort must also apply to a genuine love of country. A genuine love of country will not be a sentimentality which cherishes only part of the picture and mistakes it for the whole. And the alternative to this is not a cynical dismissal of the whole, because it does not register with one's lofty expectations.

When we come to consider characteristic British attitudes to Britain, much of Bonhoeffer's emphasis on 'the real' may at first sight seem unnecessary. After all, compared with grandiose Teutonic theorizing about the nation and *Kultur*, and fatefully romantic dreams of the role of the state, do not the British take delight in being more down to earth, pragmatic, commensensical – even prepared to laugh at themselves for the way they seem to 'muddle through'?

> Before the Roman came to Rye or out to Severn strode,
> The rolling English drunkard made the rolling English road.
> A reeling road, a rolling road, that rambles round the shire,
> And after him the parson ran, the sexton and the squire;
> A merry road, a mazy road, and such as we did tread
> The night we went to Birmingham by way of Beachy Head.[15]

Certainly, the British often derive amusement from what they see as a German passion for imposing *Ordnung* on the untidiness of life, and contrast this with their own tolerance of eccentricity and individuality. But it is an exercise in self-deception to play down too much

the role of ideology in British life. The very fact of the Mother of
Parliaments is a sign of the recognized need for debate at the centre of
national affairs. It is possible to be cynical about the degree of difference of course (the word 'consensus' is now almost obscene in some
quarters), and from a theological perspective they are boung to be
relativized. A certain Baptist minister is reputed to have had a large
poster pasted up outside his church after a general election: 'One lot
of sinners out – another lot of sinners in.' That was highly salutary –
even more so had it been put up at Westminster itself. But within
their penultimate context, the distinctiveness of the ideological
approaches must be respected.

It has often been pointed out that the long-term stability and
continuity of British life incorporates a balance between broadly
conservative and progressive forces. To a large extent but by no
means completely, these are reflected in the dominant two-party
structure of today. The exact political expression of these tendencies
has in fact varied considerably from age to age. Daniel Jenkins
characterizes the two tendencies as 'Cavalier' and 'Roundhead'.[16] I
myself would prefer to go further in personalizing these two main
approaches to political and social life, and to see them embodied in
two figures who were contemporaneous with each other in the late
eighteenth century: Edmund Burke and Tom Paine. Both have left
their mark on the way their countrymen view their country. Both
claimed to be patriotic. And the approaches of both, while demon-
strating characteristic ways of engaging with the issues of society,
also illustrate how they can hinder their adherents' perception of
what is really going on around them.

Edmund Burke: idealizing conservatism

Burke was member of Parliament for Bristol in the late eighteenth
century. He stands as the most eloquent spokesman of conservatism,
in the broadest sense, in British political life. A Whig who supported
Wilberforce's anti-slavery campaign and the rights of the American
colonists, like so many others he recoiled in horror at the French
Revolution, and the caste of mind it revealed:

I cannot conceive how any man can have brought himself to that pitch of presump-
tion, to consider his country as nothing but *carte blanche*, upon which he may scribble
as he pleases. A man full of warm, speculative benevolence may wish his society
otherwise constituted than he finds it; but a good patriot, and a true politician, always
considers how he shall make the most of the existing materials of his country. A disposition to preserve, and an ability to improve, taken together, would be my standard
of a statesman. Everything else is vulgar in the conception, perilous in the
execution.[17]

In Burke's view, a country is an organic whole, with its peculiar, innate features extending through time. As with any living organism there must be some capacity to change and adapt, but the changes must accord with the given character of the organism. The terrors of the French Revolution were ample testimony to the mistake of trying to impose an alien and wholly artificial system in place of the inherited institutions. Balance, tradition, continuity form the foundation of national life: 'our old settled maxim, never entirely nor at once to depart from antiquity'; 'Good order is the foundation of all good things.' Burke held to an almost mystical conception of the nation as the total community of citizens, past as well as present, sharing in the inheritance of the nation. Indeed, the linchpin of Burke's conservatism is the notion of an entailed inheritance, an *obligation* to maintain the constitution bequeathed by the past, irrespective of present wishes. For example, those who in past ages had placed themselves under the authority of the monarch, bound their descendants to do likewise.

It hardly needs saying that time has dealt its own answer to Burke. He seems to speak from a different universe to ours. Yet he has left to British social and political thought a highly influential attitude. His sense of continuity and organic wholeness has outlasted his peculiar theory of inheritance, and has probably even entered into some socialist conceptions of the corporate nature of society. His splendid prose abounds in aphorisms cherished by politicians of all hues. He is, above all, the most articulate spokesman of reverence for tradition. However, he also exemplifies the dangers wrought by such an approach for our perception of what is actually happening in the nation. 'There ought', he says, 'to be a system of manners in every nation, which a well-formed mind would be disposed to relish. To make us love our country, our country ought to be lovely.'[18] Burke is in no doubt that Britain has been endowed by tradition with an abundance of such appealing 'manners', and exhibits a unique loveliness. But if the country is so 'lovely', why is there such discontent within it? Is it really Britain *as it is* that Burke loves, or is it his ideal of ordered wholeness and continuity which captivates his mind? Is British life really the expression of that ideal in every respect, or is it an image which he imposes on the more complex and untidy reality?

Such questions must always be asked of those who would view the nation in terms of some great, everlasting ideal which they believe it embodies. Mr Enoch Powell is an avowed Burke enthusiast. His celebrated House of Commons speech in 1953, opposing the Royal Titles Bill, seemed to argue that the slightest modification of the status of the monarch in relation to former British territories amounted to sacrilege. Moreover, he admits to a fascination with the essence of 'Englishness' emanating from the mists of antiquity:

Tell us what it is that binds us together; show us the clue that leads us through a
thousand years; whisper to us the secret of this charmed life of England, that we in our
time may know how to hold it fast . . .[19]

It is clear that from the start of this quest, it has already been decided
that the answer must be super-normal, magical or mystical; there
must be some Holy Grail which vouchsafes the meaning of being
British (or at least English). But if the answer has to be so idealized,
there are problems in store. Supposing that instead of a mystical
silver chalice, all that the quest reveals is a very earthen vessel? Either
the ideal is clung to at the expense of any real engagement with
reality; or total disillusion sets in. This problem, if Mr Powell's
admissions no less than the comments of some of his biographers are
to be accepted, has indeed arisen for him. One commentator states:
'There has always appeared to be inside Powell, what can be described as a moral and intellectual necessity in his life, namely pride in
a nation or institution. In the course of his life Powell has felt pride
and intense love for the Army, Germany (his spiritual home), India,
the British Empire, the Monarchy, the House of Lords, the House of
Commons, and now, as he explains, the English nature of the
Anglican Church.'[20] In the context of this study, Powell's early love
for Germany and his sudden disillusionment is worth further comment. It was while an undergraduate and don at Cambridge that he
embraced German thought and culture, Nietzsche became his hero
and mentor, and he published academic papers in German. Then in
the summer of 1934 came Hitler's murder of Röhm and his brownshirts. In Powell's own words:

I still remember clearly how I sat for hours in a state of shock, shock which you experience when, around you, you see the debris of a beautiful building in which you have
lived for a long time. So it had all been illusion, all fantasy, all a self-created myth.
Music, philosophy, poetry, science and the language itself – everything was
demolished, broken to bits on the cliffs of monstrous reality.[21]

When what was completely idealized now proves not to be ideal, it
has to be totally rejected.

Something of the sort also appears to have occurred in Powell's
relationship with his own country and certain of its institutions.
Captivated by the imperial vision, he dreamed of becoming Viceroy.
But then even India was 'lost' to the empire. Had the empire itself
been real? Powell came to decide that it, too, had largely been
illusion. Perhaps most revealing of all is what Powell said in 1977
about the House of Commons, which since the war he has regarded
as his 'home':

. . . I have grown simultaneously more convinced of its indispensable centrality to the
life of the nation and more dubious or even critical of its actual condition and spirit and

motivation and self-respect of its membership . . . The more vital the institution, the
greater the temptation to idealise, and the harder it becomes to match the ideal with
the reality.[22]

Actual flesh-and-blood community, as distinct from abstract conceptions of it, appears to present a person like Powell with an in-
soluble dilemma. It is the problem of idealization, which clouds our
perception of what is actually there, either by investing it with
grandeur – something to 'take pride in' or, when it falls below the
'ideal', totally discounting it and refusing to see any good in it at all.
It is a love of the ideal, rather than the real object. A patriotism of this
type either complacently (or romantically) imagines that the country
is as perfect as can be, or is desperately anxious that it should offer
grounds for 'pride'. Either way, there is little identification with
what actually exists.

Tom Paine: idealizing radicalism

Burke's statue stands in Bristol's city centre, with the traffic
swirling round. Very close to that spot, on an October night in 1831,
rioters wreaked havoc over much of Bristol, burning and looting,
and destroying among other buildings the bishop's palace. The riot
was prompted by the visit of Sir Charles Wetherall, Recorder of
Bristol, who had been among those who just recently had voted
down the Reform Bill in the House of Commons. Burke, had he still
been alive, might well have thought that the fracas only too
tragically confirmed his view that to agitate for departure from
tradition could only lead to dire consequences. It is doubtful whether
many of those who set Bristol ablaze did so with any articulated political purpose in view, incensed though they were by the presence of
such a prominent opponent of reform. But if they had been asked to
name someone who might count as the fountainhead of their aspirations, as likely as not they would have mentioned Tom Paine,
Burke's radical counterpart at the end of the eighteenth century, and
associated ever since with the notion of 'the rights of man'.

It was in answer to Burke's *Thoughts on the French Revolution* that
Paine wrote his *Rights of Man* in 1791. In this seminal work, written
out of Paine's involvement in the revolutions of both America and
France, the radical Enlightenment meets English traditionalism.
Paine, no less than Burke, was concerned for the well-being of the
nation, and could argue his claim to be a good patriot as strongly as
Burke. But the well-being of the nation is seen in very different
terms. Whereas Burke deduces what is good for the nation from its
traditional, established order, Paine insists that the order of government must derive from the moralized will of the nation in the
present.

What is government more than the management of the affairs of a Nation? . . . Sovereignty, as a matter of right, appertains to the Nation only, and not to any individual; and a Nation has at all times an inherent indefeasible right to abolish any form of government it finds inconvenient, and establish such as accords with its interest, disposition, and happiness.[23]

According to Paine, every citizen, by virtue of his being a citizen, is a member of the sovereignty – an assumption now built into our concept of democracy. Behind this there lies an insistence on the immediate application in the social and political sphere of a belief in the original and essential equality of all human beings, a belief which Paine argued both from a philosophical standpoint, and from the biblical view of the creation of man. All talk of the rights and duties of man, if they cannot be grounded on this fundamental unity and equality, is futile. Hence the notion of the absolute rights of monarchs and the duties to them of their subjects, are undercut by this primal understanding. Likewise, Burke's notion of an inherited obligation to maintain a given social order or system of government, is dismissed. It is the present people's will which is sovereign.

Paine, villified by ruling circles in his lifetime, kindled the radical fire which in various forms has burned in Britain ever since. If Burke is the supreme spokesman for tradition and continuity, the pre-eminence of the established order, Paine is the orator on behalf of the radically new beginning. Burke and his lineage view what exists, or is imagined to exist, as the necessary embodiment of a superlative ideal. Paine and the radical tradition fundamentally question what exists, as contradicted by their ideal of what is right, fundamental, essential, but as yet unrealized. For Burke, good is what must be conserved. For Paine, it must be applied. It is the tension between these approaches which has supplied much of the dynamics of British political debate ever since.

Paine encouraged the moral imperative to enter political speech, and those who acknowledge their spiritual debt to him frequently speak not of what is best, or most useful, or most expedient, or in the best interests of the nation, but of what is morally demanded as a political necessity. Note, for example, the frequency of imperative forms of speech in the addresses and writings of Tony Benn (for a quick comparison, I counted the number of times a phrase such as 'must', 'ought', 'should', 'it is essential that' occurs in the middle ten pages of his *Arguments for Socialism*,[24] and did a corresponding examination of Shirley Williams's *Politics is for People*.[25] Benn outscores Williams by a ratio of four to one). Not that Paine preached socialism, important though he is as an ingredient in the development of the politics of the left. But he is the great prototype of that approach to politics which brings to bear a single overriding and clear conception of human nature and its social implications, according to which policy is to be defined. It is the plumb-line approach. In a way it is as idealistic as Burke's conservatism. But whereas the latter tends to idealize what he imagines exists, and thus to accord it absolute value, the radical sees the ideal in what does not (yet) exist, and criticizes the existing order in its light. It is preferable to call the radical approach *ideologization*, an assessment of the human condition in terms of some over-arching world-view regarded as definitive and final, and which has yet to be actualized.

Both idealizing conservatism and ideologizing radicalism offer ways of engaging with one's society. Each also offers a way of detaching oneself from the reality of that society. The idealizing conservative can so easily come to love his ideal of ordered community and continuity, at the expense of the actual community which he professes to admire, including the suffering of those who bear the cost of maintaining the stability he so much enjoys. Paine had no difficulty in showing just how partial and complacently sentimental Burke could be in painting his idealized pictures of both contemporary Britain and pre-revolutionary France. 'Not one glance of compassion, not one commiserating reflection . . . has he bestowed on those who lingered out the most wretched of lives, in the most miserable of prisons. It is painful to behold a man employing his talents to corrupt himself.' The upper classes, Paine suggested, would think very differently if they could descend 'to the cold regions of want, the circle of polar poverty'. Beneath the polished veneer of established society lay a very different reality:

When, in countries that are called civilized, we see age going to the workhouse and youth to the gallows, something must be wrong in the system of government. It would seem, by the exterior appearance of such countries, that all was happiness; but there lies hidden from the eye of common observation, a mass of wretchedness that has scarcely any other chance, than to expire in poverty or infamy. Its entrance into life is marked with the presage of its fate; and until this is remedied, it is in vain to punish.[26]

But Paine himself illustrates the limitation of the ideologizing approach, which may be summarized as an attempt to impose a rational order on life which so often insists on being chaotically irrational. Paine tragically discovered this for himself soon after his arrival in France in 1792 to serve in the National Assembly. By then, the former advocate of the revolution found himself under suspicion as a counter-revolutionary, especially as he went on to vote against the execution of the king in 1793. He was imprisoned, and only narrowly escaped execution. When life moves on, the ideologist has to decide between adjusting his theory to suit reality, or cling to his theory and lose touch with reality.

Loving our country means striving to discover more of what is really there, in order to relate to it responsibly; and whether we be idealizers or ideologizers or whatever, we must beware of the seductive tendencies of our dreams and concepts to become objects of loyalty in themselves, and to divert us from the actual people, communities and needs which can never be wholly apprehended in abstract ideas of good, or of history, or even of 'society'. Our rhetoric can itself come between us and those it claims to speak for. To quote Chesterton again:

> Smile at us, pay us, pass us; but do not quite forget,
> For we are the people of England, that never has spoken yet.[27]

Idealizing and ideologizing today are the monopoly of no one political camp. The polarization into so-called conviction politics, in both its Thatcherite-monetarist and its neo-Marxist manifestations, is symptomatic of the desire to find some single, simple, ideal key to explain and control the complex, messy and often unhappy human condition that we call society.

Dietrich Bonhoeffer: encounter with life

Bonhoeffer could speak trenchantly on the failures of abstract concepts of good to affect life at any depth. The importance of his observation is that it perceives that abstractions are not just the property of intellectual theorizers, but of some of the most enthusiastic people who are 'active for change' as they themselves would put it.

Here again the appropriate form of life may vary, according to the principles adopted, from that of the great political fanatics and ideologists down to that of all the various shades of stupidly importunate reformers of life . . . Theirs is an idealizing failure; it is a failure already in its momentary triumph; it is a failure ultimately because here no true encounter has taken place at all with life, with man; it is rather that something alien, false, factitious, imaginary and at the same time completely tyrannical has been superimposed on man without really and essentially affecting him, changing him and forcing him to a decision. Ideologies vent their fury on man and then leave him as a bad dream leaves the waking dreamer. The memory of them is bitter. They have not made the man stronger or more mature; they have only made him poorer and more mistrustful.[28]

Bonhoeffer's insights into the proper claim of the penultimate sphere of human life, and his insistence on engagement with this human reality as it is, are of the greatest significance for a Christian understanding of loyalty to one's own people and country. For the Christian who believes that in Christ God has decisively made himself one with the creation and reconciled the sinful world to himself, neither the idealizing of the world as it is, nor an ideologizing rejection of the world as it is, are adequate. The world cannot be left as it is. Neither can it be forced into a mould of our choosing. Responsible action is that which, in the actual situation, most fully serves our real neighbour in enabling him or her to live more fully as a human being before God.

We cannot pretend that the ultimate does not exist either by removing it to another realm altogether ('another country') or by viewing the existing order as itself the ideal. Bonhoeffer states of this view: 'The ultimate remains totally on the far side of the everyday; it is thus, in fact, an eternal justification for things as they are; it is the metaphysical purification from the accusation which weighs upon everything that is.'[29] But neither can the ultimate be forced upon the penultimate:

Radicalism always springs from conscious or unconscious hatred of what is established. Christian radicalism, no matter whether it consists in withdrawing from the world or in improving the world, arises from hatred of creation. The radical cannot forgive God his creation. He has fallen out with the created world, the Ivan Karamazov, who at the same time makes the figure of the radical Jesus into the legend of the Grand Inquisitor.[30]

Compromise (keeping things as they are) and radicalism (hating things as they are) are both inadequate in face of Jesus Christ, in whose incarnation is seen God's love for his creation, in whose crucifixion is seen God's judgment on all flesh, and in whose resurrection is seen God's will for a new world. This whole view of Christ is what, according to Bonhoeffer, determines truly responsible action – taking the human reality seriously, refusing to escape from it, 'as that which is before the last'.

A true love of country, then, will view it as part of this world which is God's creation, which has sinned and stands under his judgment, and which God nevertheless wills that it should experience his new creation. Thus, in all its particular human features, it will be loved. As it is, before God, it will be loved. Not as we would like it to be, clouded in mists of illusory grandeur, but as it is – it will be loved. Nor as we imagine it might become once it has conformed to our utopian blueprint, but as it is – it will be loved. Patriotism, so often associated with pride, therefore really begins with gratitude, gratitude for what one has genuinely received from God via one's country. We therefore now need to explore what it means to accept a national 'heritage'.

5
Accepting a Heritage

Patriotism, we have said, means being grateful for the country that is. Loving a country, as with loving a person, presupposes that the one we love has a recognizable identity. And a country, like a person, can only acquire an identity through time. It is as a community with its tried and tested ways of doing things, with its history of achievements and frustrations, victories and defeats, glory and suffering, that in the course of the years a country acquires that image of itself which it would present to its own children in each generation, and to the world at large. The character that emerges has a reality which has to be recognized, even as the provisional, penultimate, human and earthly reality that it is. For whatever else it may be, the story of the country is the story of how people have been sustained in communal life. It is, in Bonhoeffer's phrase, an *order of preservation* at work, and requires no more and no less allegiance than this implies. To love one's country therefore requires that one learns as fully as possible all that the country has acquired in its history, which is of sustaining and enriching value for its citizens. It is a matter of appreciating the good that is in it. The word 'heritage' is commonly used as a summary term for this valuable deposit of history which is available to us in the present.

To speak of a nation's 'heritage' is to indicate, first, that none of us creates our nation *ex nihilo*. We are born into a country which has existed prior to us, whose traditions, institutions, 'way of life' and ethos meet us and claim us with the quality of the 'given'. Indeed, before we are even aware that there is such a thing as a heritage it is already influencing and moulding us through our parental upbringing. Second, it indicates that what has been acquired in the past is of value to us in the present, and to be cherished and enjoyed accordingly. 'Heritage' is of course a metaphor drawn in the first instance from the hereditary transmission of property in the family sphere, and the concept of a national heritage involves the powerful underlying image of the nation as a kind of extended family. 'Fatherland', 'motherland' are terms which make explicit this domestic understanding of the nation, with its sense of gratitude and duty towards either 'our forbears', or the nation personified, or both. The Latin roots of the word patriotism itself also make this connexion clear (*patria*, country; *pater*, father).

Heritage: expert Britain

Britain, more than most other countries, makes much of its heritage. Admittedly, it is sometimes a rather partial view of heritage which is popularly conveyed, as in calendar scenes of castles, cathedrals and country cottages. But there is good reason for the British to be more heritage-conscious than almost any other western nation. The reason lies in the extraordinary continuity of British life for nigh on a thousand years, and with recognizable, living connexions going back still further. The British cannot but be mindful of their heritage – they have so much of it. It has accumulated by compound interest century by century. Since 1066, its capital has been safe from foreign plunder. Much of the internal conflict on British soil, whether religious, political or social, far from depleting the account has frequently bequeathed further legacies to it. We may find Burke's extreme reverence for tradition unreal, but he was accurate in his identification of the principal British maxim as 'never entirely nor at once to depart from tradition'.

It is of course another question as to whether by now we have more heritage weighing us down than is good for us. But for the moment, if we are attempting to be true to the line that genuine love must be a love of what is genuinely there, we need to explore the items which are claimed to be components of the British heritage. To speak of 'components' is a little misleading, however. We are not dealing with something which can be precisely analysed and defined, and in any case as with so much else that is vital in human awareness it is the interconnexions and the wholeness which are as important as the variety of constituents.

Land

Edward Thomas, that most evocative poet of the southern English countryside, enlisted in the army in 1915 despite being over the usual age-limit. Asked by a friend as to what he thought he was fighting for, he bent down, picked up a piece of earth, crumbled it through his fingers and replied, 'Literally, for this.'[1] Where a people have for many generations occupied a piece of land, it would be astonishing if a strong emotional bond did not grow up with it. In the first place, it is 'home'. How can we put into words the difference we feel in seeing the place where we know we 'belong', as distinct from many another place to which we feel attached because of its beauty? I may say that I love the south Brittany coast, or the Rhine valley, or the Tuscan hills. But one cannot actually 'own' them like one's own country. In the second place, the physical features and scenery of the land, having been the setting for so much of the drama of the people's history, provide some of the most important symbols and images of the national identity and character. The white cliffs of Dover are not just geological features; they are the 'walls' of the island home. Moreover, where much of the landscape has over the centuries been shaped by human craft and toil, and yet where nature is still allowed to make a contribution of its own, it is indeed tempting to imagine a specifically British natural history:

> Unkempt about those hedges blows
> An English unofficial rose.

Rupert Brooke was of course speaking about the relaxed and voluntary English style of life as much as the English hedgerow, and contrasted it with the punctiliousness he saw on the Unter den Linden. Indeed a good deal of the British landscape has acquired enhanced significance because of its treatment by particular writers. We speak of 'Hardy country', 'Brontë country', and so on.

This is not the place to indulge in yet another panegyric on the extraordinary variety of scenery, coastal and inland, which Britain exhibits within so small a compass. The heritage is rich indeed. What does need to be said, however, is that for a people who claim to love their land, many British people are in fact woefully ignorant not only of the beauties of their own landscape, but even of the most basic facts of the country's physical and human geography. Northerners have long grown used to the uninformed prejudices of south-easterners who imagine that gentility ends at Watford and who equate the north with industrial grime. At an English polytechnic recently, a class of business-studies degree students produced some remarkable 'facts' in their written work on the regional distribution of unemployment in the United Kingdom. One referred to unemployment being higher in 'the north of England, including Wales'; another wrote of 'less populated areas like the West Midlands'; yet another, having drawn what purported to be a helpfully illustrative map, located Bristol and Gloucester comfortably in the south-east of England. As far as the land itself is concerned, many of the British appear to have little real idea of what they are loving.

Language

If the setting of the drama is the land, then the medium of the drama and its record is language. Language supplies the bond within a community, and separates that community from other groups. Language and nationhood are of course by no means co-terminous. A nation may include more than one linguistic group within it, and the same language may be shared by more than one nation. Indeed the most notable feature of the English language today is that it is the

tongue of so many peoples, and the medium of so much international discourse in politics, art and science. English is so successful
as a language not only because, on a slightly cynical or even realistic
view, it is the language of imperialistically successful peoples (as was
Latin at one time), but because of its great flexibility, its facility for
both concrete and abstract expression, and its ability to convey extremely subtle gradations of meaning and nuance. This itself is but
another witness to the stability of the society within which the
language has operated over the centuries, allowing words acquired
from various sources to find their precise level of meaning. If understatement is an art of the British, it is at least partly because they have
a language which allows them such a wide *liberty* of expression:

> We must be free or die, who speak the tongue
> That Shakespeare spake;

That the British have a rich historical heritage *and* a rich language is
therefore no accident. Each reinforces the other. But the heritage of
the language and the heritage of its greatest literature are not absolutely one and the same thing. To make this identification is the
mistake of those who, for example, see the Book of Common Prayer
or the Authorized Version of the Bible as *the* guarantors of a
common tradition of English usage. Such works have indeed immensely shaped and influenced the English language over the last
three and a half centuries. But it is sometimes forgotten that, equally,
they were the creations *of* the English language. To love the
language, therefore, means something more than elevating certain
great and classical expressions of it into the only permissible ones. It
means being ready to explore what new and surprising forms may
yet spring from this medium. Education in English therefore means
more than inculcating a reverence for Shakespeare. It means exploring for oneself what can be done with and through the language.
Edward Thomas wrote of English words:

> I know you:
> You are light as dreams,
> Tough as oak,
> Precious as gold,
> As poppies and corn,
> Or an old cloak:
> Sweet as our birds
> To the ear,
> As the burnet rose
> In the heat
> Of Midsummer.[2]

That is the kind of intimate and respectful affection which signifies a
true love of the heritage of language. Educationally, it means

keeping alive that natural poetic instinct and experimental delight in words which so many young children display, until the study of their own tongue becomes a formal and boring imposition.

Institutions

The heritage includes the machinery of government and administration. In describing their country as a parliamentary democracy, the British are not describing simply the state of affairs in the present. The phrase to them always carries the overtones of an age-old struggle towards ways of making those in power more accountable to the people as a whole. In Britain, more than most countries, parliamentary democracy is not just an ideal, or a theory – or even a written constitution, since Britain does not have one – but a story. Admittedly, the barons who pressured John to sign Magna Carta at Runymede were moved by their own interests rather than any lofty desires on behalf of the whole populace. But Magna Carta marks the establishment of two fundamental principles which, while relatively narrow in their original application, subsequently proved themselves capable of enormous extension across the whole constitutional and legislative field. The first principle is that of the rule of law, from which even the monarch is not exempt, thus excluding arbitrary wielding of power. The second is the rejection of fiscal demands without representation from those on whom the demands are made, thus excluding absolutist power. Much of what has come to be understood as parliamentary democracy can be seen as implicit in these principles.

The actual origins of Parliament itself are obscure. Advisory gatherings of nobles and bishops around the king had evidently long been standard practice, but that these should include knights representing particular shires, and burgesses representing their own towns, apparently dates from Simon de Montfort's Parliaments of 1264 and 1265, established under the Provisions of Oxford imposed by the feudal aristocracy of Henry III. Thereafter, slowly and in meandering fashion, central to the story of English politics is the issue of where final power lies, between king and parliament. In reaction to Stuart absolutist claims, the seventeenth century established the sovereignty of Parliament. Indeed under the Bill of Rights it made clear that the king reigned solely by consent of Parliament. Since then, essentially, the main question has been that of the representative nature of Parliament. Fitfully and painfully the nineteenth and early twentieth centuries saw the extension of the franchise to include, eventually, all adult citizens. Today, however, questions about the actual sovereignty of Parliament are returning, as for instance in the issue of whether elected governments really do have the capacity to effect policy changes in the face of extra-Parliamentary interests, in the civil service for example. Even the question of the representative nature of Parliament is not yet really settled.

The important element in all this, however, is that in asking such questions in the present, the British can sense a marked affinity with many earlier stages of the story. The heritage of democracy is such that in Britain the most effective and penetrating questions about the political system and the behaviour of governments are framed in terms not of Marxist theory, or any other doctrine of political science, but of the spirit and tendency of the old story. Is power being misused? Are those in high office really accountable? Do the people feel they are really represented? Where such questions are fiercely asked, it does not signify a lack of confidence in the institutions so much as a live concern that they should be true to their heritage.

Monarchy

Monarchy, of all the British institutions, deserves special mention here simply because it is the focus of so much patriotic sentiment. To combine a parliamentary democracy with a hereditary monarchy seems either a contradiction or, as many British people would say, a delightful example of the British skill of balance and compromise. In fact the monarchy has survived into the present largely because its theoretically remaining prerogatives have not been used. The monarch's functions are now formal as far as the business of government goes, and symbolic as far as the role of head of state is concerned.

But while the effective powers of monarchy are now minimal, it is probably the case that the British crown has never enjoyed more popular esteem than now. In fact it is another British paradox that an institution so ancient should have acquired such a fascinating mystique so relatively recently. That aura of reverential admiration, at times slipping into the mawkishly sentimental, which is now assumed to be a royal prerogative, dates only from the latter part of Victoria's reign. Until she acquired the status of national matriarch and imperial godmother, even she suffered a good deal of satire and mockery in the press. Britain's twentieth-century monarchs have largely earned the public esteem and affection through their personal qualities. Edward VII presided over the golden afternoon of empire with an avuncular benevolence. George V exhibited a solid dignity which befitted the misery of the First World War and the years of disillusionment that followed. George VI drew sympathy for the very fact of having the crown thrust upon him by his brother's abdication, and for his determination not to allow his speech impediment to deter him from his public duties – not to mention his continued residence in London during even the most dangerous days of the Second World War. His consort survives as probably the most popular figure in the country at large. In their present Queen the British have an image of unswerving public dutifulness and intense family loyalty.

It may well be that the large-scale popular sentiment towards royalty in a peculiar way owes something to the public's consciousness of the vulnerability of the crown in the modern world. Rationally, hereditary monarchy is an anachronism, but those born to it have little option but to fulfil its obligations. Hence royalist sentiment has a certain element of *sympathy* in it. Scarcely any other public position today depends so heavily on the personal qualities of the holder for its continued existence. The Queen *has* to be seen as a person of transparent devotion, and this evokes the sympathy for the unenviable position in which she is placed, and a deep sense of respect when the demands of her situation are met so unflinchingly. But why continue to place anyone in such a predicament anyway? In a parliamentary democracy, is the continuance of the crown purely an act of self-indulgent sentiment on the part of the people, aided and abetted by the media who are only too eager to make the most of royal weddings, births and anniversaries? Does it perform any service beyond its own maintenance as a kind of entertainment for the populace?

Because the monarchy has undergone great changes in its power and status in the past, to accept the institution as part of the British heritage today should not preclude the asking of some pertinent questions about its role and style. Only if questioned is it likely to reveal its true strength, and the elements which are really worth cherishing to be understood. For it is evident that the monarchy does perform a certain important symbolic function for society – and this should never be dismissed as *merely* symbolic. Philip Howard states what is probably as sensible a justification of the crown as can be found today:

The monarchy is the supreme national and unifying symbol for Great Britain, and it is difficult to think of any substitute that would do the job as well. People need symbols to live by, and to give meaning to their random little lives. The Americans have their Declaration of Independence, their founding father figures, and, at least until recently, their national flag. Russians have dreams of world revolution, or older and hazier dreams of Mother Russia. None of these are as symbolically satisfying as the Crown, personified by a real person; and most of these national unifying symbols of other nations are now looking shabby and unconvincing.[3]

Religion

The idea of a 'Christian nation' is hard to define, but as a fact of history the story of Christianity and the story of the nation as a whole are extremely hard to disentangle from each other. It is not simply that from early mediaeval times ecclesiastical authority and secular powers confirmed and supported each other (and sometimes fought each other as well), nor that the monarch is titular head of the Church of England and the Church of Scotland. The influence has been deeply cultural as well. The English Bible had an enormous influence in creating a commonly accepted form of English from the sixteenth century onwards. For centuries, Christianity has helped to define the accepted norms of personal and public behaviour. Further, while secularization is now far advanced in the sense that the direct influence of the organized churches is now restricted to a relatively small sector of national life, the life of Britain is quite un-thinkable without church and chapel. And no-one needs reminding that it is in the stone and stained glass and music of its cathedrals and churches that, artistically no less than religiously, much of the rich-ness of the British heritage lies. So deeply has the Christian tradition been embedded within the British ethos, that even those who today consciously reject Christian belief frequently acknowledge the power and indeed requirement of Christian symbolism. Such an extraordinary, virtuoso arts-and-science man as Jonathan Miller confesses to the way Christian imagery continually reinforces his sense of 'the tragedy of being human, and the idea of the incarnation is one of the great imaginative inventions of the moral imagination. I would find it very hard to think forcefully and properly without in fact being stocked with such images.'[4] 'Being stocked with such images' is an excellent way of describing what it means to live with the religious element within the British heritage.

Culture

We have of course ventured into this field already, not least in the section immediately above. But it is notoriously difficult to define what culture is. The more precise the definition, the more that is arguably 'cultural' is excluded. But the more general definitions can veer towards the almost uselessly vague. Yet if we are to err, it is better to err on the more inclusive and general side, and there is much to be said for Raymond Williams's definition of culture as 'a whole way of life' shared by a people.[5] The intellectual, imaginative and co-operative work of a society which makes up 'culture' goes much further than the 'refined' understanding of culture which grew up in the last century and which confines it to specialized artistic work and its enjoyment. It certainly does mean the work of poets and drama-tists, musicians and painters, and Britain has produced no shortage of these (excelling especially in the literary fields) – but not only these. Nor does it simply mean the tradition of scholarship, research and teaching established in the universities, ancient and modern, great though this is (as has often been stated, whatever Britain's shortcomings have been since the last war, a shortage of ideas and inventive genius has not been one of them, for the problem has rather been that of exploiting these effectively). Nor does it mean just the folksy arts-and-crafts and song-and-dance industries. It covers all that people consider worth doing to make themselves a world that is both habitable and enjoyable. It is a serious business, but one about which one cannot be pompous. No-one took it more seriously than T. S. Eliot, yet his famous catalogue of the sort of things which make up 'culture' is worth quoting repeatedly to make just that point:

It includes all the characteristic activities and interests of a people: Derby Day, Henley Regatta, Cowes, the twelfth of August, a cup final, the dog races, the pin table, the dart board, Wensleydale cheese, boiled cabbage cut into sections, beetroot in vinegar, nineteenth-century Gothic churches and the music of Elgar. The reader can make his own list.[6]

Making our own list today, nearly four decades later, we would want to add items referring to television soap-operas and personalities, pop music, package-holidays and the like. Culture is that mosaic of human activity which people feel enriches their lives, not least because of the sense of community which results. In Britain, sport is a particularly important example of this. Britain has been a great inventor of team-games which have been taken up by other peoples and 'fair play' is supposed to be a British virtue. Yet while success or failure at the international level is a matter of public concern, it has never become the be-all and end-all of national status as in some countries, especially eastern Europe. The game's the thing. Cricket, the most distinctively English sport of all, is virtually a culture on its own, with not only its own rules, but its own language and folk-lore and scientific theory, its legendary heroes and, above all in the BBC Radio commentary box, its own gurus and interpreters. It is not so much learnt as grown into, like the national identity itself.

Values: freedom and community

The national heritage, then, comprises all the items and accepted practices which history, ancient and modern, has established for the preservation and enrichment of life in these islands. Some parts of the heritage are literally tangible, others less so – Britain after all does not even have a written constitution. Even less tangible than her forms of government are the norms of conduct and aspiration in personal and communal life, yet it is these which so greatly affect the tone of a society. The qualities which the British exemplify (at least in the opinion of their well-disposed neighbours) are those which have both encouraged and been strengthened by a social experience of such long continuity and stability. These include a sense of 'fair play' (the law applies to all without discrimination); a sense of moderation (on an island, as on a boat, people have to learn to live together); a tolerance of diversity as an enriching factor (a German recently told me, 'You have a *National* Portrait Gallery which includes figures of note of all kinds and of all outlooks'); a strong sense of solidarity, especially at the local community level and, in times of great crisis, nationally also; a strong preference for voluntary endeavour as far as possible, and a dislike of 'state interference' (Britain, for instance, has a much greater tradition of voluntary social services than most continental countries).

Underlying all this, is the one word which most British people would, if asked, say is what the country stands for: freedom. There will not be universal agreement as to the extent to which freedom is enjoyed in Britain today, or even as to what freedom consists of. But it is the argument about freedom which is the link in so much of the political, religious, social and cultural story of Britain. As G. Kitson Clark writes:

The freedom of Englishmen was held to be the object of the English law, it was the subject of the constitutional struggles of the seventeenth century. It was enforced, if also menaced, by the Puritan, claiming for himself a freedom which he believed to be endorsed by God. The Established Church believed that it protected freedom when it tried to check the forces of superstition and enthusiasm, and acknowledged the rights of human reason; the Dissenter believed that he vindicated it when he attacked the privileges of the Established Church. The manufacturer and the Liberal claimed it against the State in the nineteenth century, and the social reformer and the trade unionist against the manufacturer.[7]

Yet, with all its emphasis on freedom, Britain has traditionally been a very orderly society. People form queues at counters and bus stops, not because they are told to do so but simply because nearly everyone thinks it is 'the thing to do'. Self-discipline, self-restraint, have been seen to be the corner-stones of 'law and order', rather than the heavy hand of the law. This 'gentleness', as George Orwell described it, witnesses to a strong tradition of communal solidarity at the local level, particularly in rural villages and in urban working-class areas, and also associated with particular centres of interest and activity, ranging from pub to church, bowling green to Rotary, hospital friends to cricket team. It is, perhaps, the island mentality writ small, the consciousness that space is limited. One has a right to elbow room, but no-one is disliked so much as the 'pushy' type. One can see the relation of this to those other British characteristics which anglophiles describe as the relaxed style, the sense that life's pleasures and satisfactions come most readily to those who do not panic about them, and the art of understatement.

The heritage: facing reality

Britain, then, has a rich inheritance in every way, and few need any prompting to wax eloquent on this. 'The British are a nation who have sustained a creative culture of the first magnificence for five hundred years. No other people except the French and Chinese has done this.'[8] But the danger with an inheritance, especially so rich a one, is that it may be lost through complacency and indolence. As Daniel Jenkins warns, 'It is one of the hardest lessons of experience that you cannot continue to enjoy the best of your heritage if all you are content to do is simply to enjoy it.'[9] The danger signals are already apparent in the way in which the British frequently talk of their heritage. It is the ease, the superficiality and partiality in their attitudes to the past and its legacy, which reveal that all too often there is indeed simply a desire for 'enjoying' the heritage. But if, as was maintained with Bonhoeffer in the last chapter, real love is love of what is really there, we must continually ask ourselves whether we are letting illusions and wishfulness cloud the reality of the national tradition. If the heritage is worth loving at all, it is worth taking a good deal more seriously than is allowed by a vague reverence for what is old. Attitudes to the heritage need challenging at three points in particular, if reality is to be faced more squarely.

First, 'heritage' in the singular must be recognized as misleading. There are many heritages in Britain. If we say that there is a British genius for compromise, that in itself is an admission that there has had to be accommodation of different, divergent and at times violently conflicting interests and viewpoints in politics, society and religion. Church *and* dissent, conservative *and* radical, liberal *and* socialist: all claim a part in 'the heritage'. Nor has there been just one culture overall, but a mosaic of cultures, related to class and region. We must therefore beware of reifying 'heritage' into something monolithic, which also means something static, fixed and final, and usually the property of one particular group. The 'stately home' image of heritage certainly needs challenging, as does an Anglican monopolizing of Britain's Christian heritage. Few would be so foolish as to deny the central and crucial role played by the Church of England in the story of the people. But equally, not only was there dissent from the established church, but that dissent came to play a highly significant role in the radical democratic tradition and in the rise of the industrial revolution, as well as in strengthening and extending the hold of organized Christianity in the land.

Second, even a cursory examination of the British 'heritage' shows how relatively little of its origins can be ascribed exclusively to Britain itself. The British have not been as insular as they themselves would often like to pretend. In any area of the nation's history a purely indigenous 'genius' is hard to find, for the history has been one of continual interaction with the outside world. Celt, Roman, Saxon, Dane . . . all went into the making of 'the people'. English feudal society resulted from the imposition of a Norman aristocracy upon Anglo-Saxon society, an amalgam both oppressive and creative. Even the English language itself exhibits the fusion of 'native' and 'foreign'. The tongue that Shakespeare spake owes much of its range and subtlety to the enrichment that Danish, Latin and Norman French brought to the Anglo-Saxon base. Nor would Shakespeare have been Shakespeare without the influence of Italian Renaissance poetry. So too with many other British cultural activities, from music to science: they have lived and grown in an atmosphere transcending British shores. It is still more the case with the Christian story in Britain. While there were strong British undercurrents in the direction of protest against the existing church order from the time of Wycliffe in the fifteenth century, and while Henry's break with Rome was determinedly nationalist in motive, the actual reformation in England required the import of Lutheran and Calvinist ideas from the continent. Nor would Protestantism have survived without the refuge afforded by reformed cities in Holland and Germany to English and Scottish protestants during times of persecution. The British heritage in fact is only understandable, in the end, as part of the wider story of Europe. If there is indeed a British 'genius' at work in the heritage, a chief characteristic of it would seem to be the capacity to work what at first sight seems alien, new and hitherto 'un-British' into new and creative combinations with the old.

Third, there is the strange and unsettling paradox, that *the* distinctively British creation has not been unreservedly welcomed as part of their heritage by the British themselves. The industrial revolution is the one item in their history of which the British can really claim to be originators, and in which for a time they led the world. It is also the item least popularly recognized as an element of 'Britishness'. It seems to contradict the calendar-picture ideal of heritage as sweeping lawns, and sunlight falling on mellow stonework. The dark satanic mills are an intrusion on this green and pleasant land. True, Victorian Britain called itself the 'workshop of the world', and the Great Exhibition of 1851 was a breath-taking display of British manufacturing success on which the nation justly congratulated itself. But there is a strong case for saying that in its public ethos, and especially in the attitudes of its leading citizens, Britain never became fully 'industrialized', and has never fully committed itself to all the implications of a society based on manufacturing. This, some would argue, is the basic root of Britain's long story of industrial decline in the twentieth century.

The most recent and forceful statement of this argument comes from the American economic historian Martin Wiener, who cites the evidence that even while the industrial revolution was growing apace in the nineteenth century, the ruling echelons of English society despised the manufacturer and engineer on principle.[10] The *nouveau riche* manufacturers themselves frequently aspired after 'gentlemanly' ideals, gradually distancing themselves from the activities which had created their wealth, in order to enjoy the fruits of their labours in classic, refined fashion: the house in the country, and for their sons, a public-school education highly prejudiced against science and engineering.

The new society created by the later Victorians rested on a domestication of the wilder traits of earlier British behavior: the riotous populace, the aggressive and acquisitive capitalists, and the hedonistic aristocrats of the Georgian world became endangered, if not extinct, species of Englishmen. Their descendants were more restrained, more civilised, and also more conservative, in that they now had an established and secure place in the social order, or, in the case of the aristocracy, had come to terms with social change and recemented their place in the status quo. By Victoria's death, British society had weathered the storms of change, but at the cost of surrendering a capacity for innovation and assertion that was perhaps the other face of the unruliness and harshness of that earlier Britain.[11]

This process, it can be argued, established a basically contemptuous opinion of industry which continues into the present, and one of the most salient features of which is the identification of real 'Englishness' with rural peace and charm as in the Second World War song:

> There'll always be an England,
> While there's a country lane,
> Wherever there's a cottage small
> Beside a field of grain.

(Ironically, that war for the survival of such an England depended on industry, most particularly on the industrial resources of the United States whose commercial ethos so many British people affect to despise.) All this points towards some uncomfortable implications that a reversal of Britain's economic decline requires a shift in cultural values and indeed some upheaval in social structure which is still dominated by 'gentlemanly' ideals at the top.

Some, while accepting Wiener's picture as an accurate historical analysis, would however wish to insist that the process he describes, far from showing a lack of nerve for continuing innovation and industrial enterprise, is defensible as a genuine choice of values: relaxed enjoyment instead of the relentless pursuit of wealth, and a recognition that industry had an unacceptable face to it in the slums and inhuman working conditions of the factories. The British 'compromise' was in fact a choice for mature and civilized values, the refusal to opt for a one-track culture. Some in fact would argue that today, when the western world is moving into the 'post-industrial' age thanks to the new technology and the growing ecological crisis, Britain is strategically placed to come to terms with the new situation. So Bernard Nossiter, an American observer comments sympathetically: 'Britons . . . appear to be the first citizens of the post-industrial age who are choosing leisure over goods on a large scale . . . Britons have not renounced material things. But many appear to have arrived at a level of income at which they regard the extra effort to obtain extra income as not worthwhile. They prefer the slower pace, the underworked style to a more painful expenditure of energy that pulls some extra income.'[12]

This may be so, but one cannot afford to be too bland in face of the kind of challenge offered by Wiener. Perhaps Wiener himself has offered a clue towards a resolution of the British problem of reconciling industrialism with the British ethos, by referring to 'innovation' as distinct from 'industrialism' *per se*, in the quotation cited above. It was inventiveness which produced the industrial revolution, and maybe it will be inventiveness which will take us beyond it. But that still means that there is an element in their heritage with which the British need to be confronted more truthfully than has been the case hitherto.

It is the real heritage which has to be accepted. Meanwhile, Dietrich Bonhoeffer has been sitting quietly through all this characteristic British chatter. What more has he to say about accepting one's heritage?

Bonhoeffer on heritage

In one respect, Bonhoeffer has little to offer except by way of endorsing, as profoundly as possible, that regard for the long-standing heritage to which the British lay claim. Bonhoeffer himself believed deeply in the importance of cultural tradition, and, as we saw in Chapter Two, owed much to the way in which he was nurtured in the best traditions of his own country. 'Now I stand before you not only as a Christian, but also as a German . . . who confesses gratefully that he received from his people all that he has and is', Bonhoeffer told American audiences during 1930–31.[13] Ten years later, slightly tongue-in-cheek, Bonhoeffer edified the head of the Berlin Gestapo with an impressive catalogue of his forbears and illustrious family connexions, in order to underline his Germanness and unimpeachable national loyalty, in protest against the police order forbidding him to speak in public because of his 'disruptive' activities. He concludes: 'It has been the concern of all these men and their families to serve the German state and its people at all times, and to risk their lives in its service. In deliberate affirmation of this spiritual heritage and this inward attitude of my family, I cannot accept the charge of "disruptive" activity.'[14]

The Gestapo were not impressed by this or any of the other arguments Bonhoeffer used, and the ban stayed. In any case, Bonhoeffer was here indulging in one of the necessary pieces of 'camouflage' on behalf of the resistance. But what he wrote does illustrate a very noticeable feature of Bonhoeffer's war-time thinking – his consciousness of the past, and his responsibility to the tradition which he inherited and represented. Indeed, it seems that the more disrupted and uncertain his own situation became, the more he turned to the past for strength and inspiration – the inspiration which is given by the sense of being part of a long and continuing story. This was for him no idle preoccupation, no sentimental journey of escape, but a deeply felt existential need for sustenance in face of the grim realities from which he could not flee. In the prison writings, we even find him musing on the German landscape, and the particular features of it that he loved:

Are you having a taste of spring yet? Here the winter is just beginning. In my imagination I live a good deal in nature, in the glades near Friedrichsbrunn, or on the slopes from which one can look towards Treseburg to the Brocken. I lie on my back in the grass, watch the clouds sailing in the breeze across the blue sky, and listen to the rustling of the woods. It's remarkable how greatly these memories of childhood affect one's whole outlook; it would seem to me impossible and unnatural for us to have lived up in the mountains or by the sea. It is the hills of central Germany, the Harz, the Thuringian forest, the Weserberge, that to me represent nature. Of course there are a conventional Harz and a hikers' Weserberge . . . So perhaps 'my' central hills are 'bourgeois' in the sense of what is natural, not too high, modest and self-sufficient(?), unphilosophical, satisfied with concrete realities, and above all 'not-given-to-self-advertisement'.[15]

He would, one feels, have approved of the English unofficial rose. But for all his cosmopolitan experience it was to his native German soil that he returned to find a scenic symbol of his own approach to life.

It was the Germany of a long and still incomplete history, in which he placed himself. While on a train journey in 1942, he wrote a birthday greeting to Eberhard Bethge's younger brother:

While I'm going through ancient cities and the summer countryside in the glorious sunshine, I keep thinking of you . . . I live a life which is hardly like yours at all, and which must be strange to you. And yet it is this long journey, looking at the cathedrals of Naumburg, Bamberg, Nuremberg, at the cultivated fields which are sometimes so poor, and the thought that all this has been work and joy for many, many generations, that gives me confidence that here there is still common ground, a common task, a common hope, something which overcomes the gap between the generations. When one thinks of that, one's own short personal life becomes relatively unimportant; one begins to think in terms of greater periods and tasks.[16]

Bonhoeffer was only thirty-six when he wrote this letter, yet he speaks to a younger man with all the acquired wisdom of age. In similar vein to this letter, he wrote from prison a baptismal sermon for Eberhard Bethge's infant son, recalling again the importance of a sense of the past, and of the richness of the heritage of both the boy's parental families: 'To be deeply rooted in the soil of the past makes life harder, but it also makes it richer and more vigorous. There are in human life certain fundamental truths to which men will always return sooner or later.'[17]

In prison, this sense of continuity with the past was both reflected in and reinforced by his plunge into historical literature and the novelists of the last century – 'I really want to become familiar with the nineteenth century in Germany.' He read with mixed feelings the *magnum opus* of his teacher Adolf Harnack, *The History of the Prussian Academy*:

There are so few people now who want to have any intimate spiritual association with the eighteenth and nineteenth centuries: music tries to draw inspiration from the sixteenth and seventeenth centuries, theology from the time of the Reformation, philosophy from St Thomas Aquinas and Aristotle, and the present *Weltanschauung* from bygone Teutonic days. But who bothers at all now about the work and achievements of our grandfathers, and how much of what they knew have we already forgotten? I believe that people will one day be quite amazed by what was achieved in that period, which is now so disregarded and so little known.[18]

Many more citations could be given to illustrate Bonhoeffer's feel for the past. Suffice it to say that if 'patriotism' means an awareness and love for the reality of one's national heritage, then on this count alone Bonhoeffer would earn the title of 'true patriot'. He never complacently presumes upon that heritage, never assumes that he knows all there is to know about it. He is prepared to be continually surprised by it, to look critically at the familiar parts and to search for the currently neglected ones. Encounter with Bonhoeffer can only encourage us to discover (or rediscover) and cherish the best in our own traditions.

There is, however, another and equally characteristic note in Bonhoeffer's view of heritage, which forbids a love of the past becoming an end in itself.

True responsibility: the future

In view of Bonhoeffer's final tribute to his great teacher Harnack, which we have just referred to, it is interesting to note what he said in an address on behalf of his fellow-students at Harnack's memorial service fourteen years earlier: 'Today his legacy comes down to us, and we enter into it with pride, deeply conscious of our responsibility. *At the same time, our eyes are turned towards the future*, towards the permanent significance of Adolf von Harnack for the younger generation of theologians'[19] (emphases mine). This forward gaze coinciding with the backward look is one of Bonhoeffer's most striking characteristics, and this whole attitude is summed up in the simple, magnificent statement of the winter 1942–43: 'The ultimate question for a responsible man to ask is not how he is to extricate himself heroically from the affair, but how the coming generation is to live. It is only from this question, with its responsibility towards history, that fruitful solutions can come, even if for the time being they are very humiliating.'[20]

By a responsibility towards history, Bonhoeffer means neither a worship of the past in its supposed glory, resisting all change as a 'betrayal' of the heritage; nor the vain idea that history can, so to speak, begin anew *ex nihilo* here and now, requiring only the grand vision to be put into effect. Responsibility towards history means the carrying forward of a story, the plot of which has already been part-written, and in which one is now part-author, part-actor. To make sense, one's own writing and acting must have a recognizable continuity with what has gone before. There must be further development of the main themes, a further examination of the values that have emerged thus far. But to be a true story, one's present contribution cannot be a mere repetition of what has gone before. And, since it is not up to any of us to draw the story to a conclusion, the plot has to be carried onward in such a way that leaves the next writer, the succeeding generation, with material to work on creatively. At the very least, this means not handing on a situation of utter and inextricable disaster. It was this sense of responsibility towards the future which provided a light, albeit at times a flickering one, to Bonhoeffer and his fellow-conspirators amidst the uncertainties and perils of the resistance. Whatever else, the coming generation of Germans should not have to identify with a country synonymous with tyranny, falsehood and mass murder. But Bonhoeffer clearly had a wider audience than himself in mind when stating this view of responsibility. Each person, in whatever social context, has to ask himself or herself what the next generation will find when he or she has gone.

Love of country therefore means a gratitude for the good that has been bestowed by the past, combined with an equal concern for the good of those yet to be. 'Thinking and acting for the sake of the coming generation' provides the criterion of whether or not we are really committed to our country's cause, as distinct from seeking to gratify our personal interests in the name of loyalty to some aspect of our 'heritage'. With our country, as with any institution, school, college, society or whatever, it is tempting simply to use what the past has given us as a kind of shelter from hard decision and painful responsibilities; reciting the last page of the story up till now, instead of taking it further into the unknown. It was this total indifference to the future which so alarmed Bonhoeffer in the attitudes of many of his contemporaries. In another letter to Eberhard Bethge's brother he says:

Perhaps one could say: today you are so completely occupied with the present that you have little inclination, and perhaps little strength, too, to think of the future, to plan; we were so completely occupied with the future in many respects that we made false judgments about the present. Now I believe that both will be equally necessary before long: men who see the present soberly, and yet still do not let the future – which is also part of reality – escape. Irresponsibility towards the future is nihilism, irresponsibility towards the past is enthusiasm.[21]

To Eberhard Bethge himself, he wrote shortly afterwards of the passengers on the train:

All they have for a couple of hours of leisure is a brooding to themselves, neither happily nor unhappily – it's like a more or less apathetic expectation of something in the future after one has done all that is in one's power; but at the same time it is neither surrender nor rebellion or defiance – their faces show a weary indifference instead. Their personal inner life has no more focus.[22]

In the *Ethics*, written during the same period as this correspondence, Bonhoeffer sets the national story firmly within the history of the west as a whole. All the western nations share a common heritage, a Christian heritage, and one may even speak of Christ as the unifying structure of the west. Other features also belong to the western tradition: classical antiquity (though made accessible to us only via Christianity), the concept of the democratic sovereign state (since the American and French revolutions), and technology. But as to the future, Bonhoeffer felt that the 'godlessness' of the modern west was a deliberate rejection of Christ as its unifying factor, and this rejection of the basis of its own life was bringing about a nihilistic rush to the 'void', engulfing 'life, history, family, nation, language, faith . . . the void spares nothing'. A major sign of that imminent void was the total lack of that sense of history which for Bonhoeffer was essential for true responsibility:

In the face of the peril of the void there is no longer any meaning in the question of the historical inheritance which requires of those who receive it that they shall both develop it in the present and hand it on to the future. There is no future and no past. There is only the moment which has been snatched from the void, and the desire to snatch from the void the next moment as well . . . The burden of yesterday is shaken off by glorifying the misty past, and tomorrow's task is evaded by speaking rather of the coming millenium.[23]

Similarly, in prison Bonhoeffer complains of the one who 'forgets', who 'feels neither responsibility towards the past nor desire to shape the future'.

Britain: flight from the future

The heritage, then, is not ours for superficial admiration or smug glorification; it is ours for examination and genuine appreciation. Nor is it simply to be enjoyed and preserved. It has to be developed and handed on. That is what is really required in loving our country – loving its story as it has been, but also as it might be in the future. For Britain this poses some severe problems today. What Bonhoeffer calls a sense of responsibility for history is conspicuously lacking in this country – indeed a sense of *history* is lacking. The word itself has come to mean simply the past, not the ongoing story through the present. In face of a confusing and disappointing present, and an un-thinkable future, the past seems solid, secure and reposed in its achievements. Britain, it seems, *had* a history which ended around 1945 and with the dissolution of the empire. Now, it seems, as though the history has completely disintegrated. There seems scarcely any hoping, or daring to believe, that although *one* strand in the story may have ended, there may be other strands which can be taken up and which carry a promise of a new day, for a Britain recognizably the heir of the old but true to the realities of the world as it is today. The 'void' of which Bonhoeffer speaks can find ample il-lustration today, in a society which seems bent on atomizing itself into individuals seeking fulfilment in their own private worlds. The urge for immediate and complete gratification of wants and desires (often calling itself 'fulfilment') will sweep through a society which has lost all sense of history, for if history means anything it means that fulfilment, gratification and satisfaction *cannot* come all at once. There has to be struggle and waiting in hope for what is really worthwhile. Most ominously of all, contemporary hedonism has not only its obvious secular forms, but some superficially highly attractive and exciting religious types as well.

It is not, however, just their 'ancient' history which occupies the attention of the British to excess, and at the expense of the future. A whole chapter could be written on the obsession with the Second World War. This is not in the least to deny that the war was a great and necessary struggle: Bonhoeffer's prayer, after all, was answered. It was moreover a great social experience for the British people, a tremendous display of solidarity. It has provided the paradigm of British fraternity, so that today whenever a minor affliction such as a 'flu epidemic or a blizzard disrupts local community life, yet people 'club together', older citizens say, 'Just like the war-time spirit.' Indeed, the war was the last great common positive experience of the nation as a whole, when, 'up against it', they knew who they were and what they were about.

Hence the fascination of it, even for those of us born too late to experience it. Yet therein too lies its danger. Rather than try to sort out what Britain should be committed to in the present-day world, which seems so much more complicated than even that of 1939, rather than try to sort out what the role should be of a Britain set firmly in the ranks of middle-order powers, it is just too tempting to fight the last good, clean, clear-cut war over and over again in books, documentaries, endless television soap-operas of prison camps and resistance movements and the like . . . and in the South Atlantic.

The Falklands episode was treated by government spokesmen and much of the media as a re-run of D-Day put on, it would seem, for the benefit of those of us who had missed the real thing in 1944. With General Galtieri himself not unlike a *Führer* in style, British politicans competed for the role of Churchill, with or without cigar. The re-call into active service of Dame Vera Lynn to record a syrupy number called 'I love this land' was the final confirmation, if any were needed, that an exercise in nostalgia for the emotional certainties of the past was taking place, rather than an encounter with the global realities of the 1980s. The reluctance to seek a long-term political solution which will recognize the aspirations of Latin Americans, instead of viewing the Falklands purely as a means of defying those aspirations and asserting British 'greatness', is a classic example of refusing to ask 'how the future generation will live' – both of the Falklanders and future British servicemen.

A sense of history means more than keeping the last Lancaster bomber flying. Historical awareness in the fullest sense comes with the responsibility of carrying on the *new* chapter of the old story. The main themes, the most deeply embedded themes of the story, are about cultural, religious and political diversity held together in what is truly a *commonwealth* (a word worth pondering on); about free-dom; about the equality of all citizens under the law, and their right to protection under that law; about the accountability of those in power to the representatives of the people; about representative democracy; about the inventive and creative use of scientific and technological knowledge; about producing goods *and* enjoying them. Loving Britain's heritage means deciding how *these* are to be used and handed down for the twenty-first century.

Bonhoeffer's challenge to us is to accept the future as part of our reality, rather than something that will simply come upon us as we walk backwards away from our past. It is a call for realism combined with inventiveness, a willingness to experiment with new ways of working in industry, new ways of representation of the people, new ways of allowing local communities to develop their potential and release their energies, new ways of relating to the outside world, especially the Third World. Britain's greatest need today is imagination.

6
Accepting Guilt

We are told that the economic achievement of the Western countries has been at the expense of the rest of the world, and has impoverished them, so that what are called the 'developed' countries owe a duty to hand over tax-produced 'aid' to the governments of the underdeveloped countries. It is nonsense – manifest, arrant nonsense – but it is nonsense with which the people of the Western countries, clergy and laity, but clergy especially – have been so deluged and saturated that in the end they feel ashamed of what the brains and energy of Western mankind have done, and sink on their knees to apologise for being civilised and seek to be insulted and humiliated.[1]

Enoch Powell's diatribe appealed powerfully to those who see a conspiracy by liberal opinion to induce a hang-dog mentality on the part of Britain in face of the 'Third World'. Of course practically every phrase in that statement begs basic questions of fact and interpretation. Caricature is one of the oldest weapons of political polemic, and world development campaigners should not take too much offence at taking their turn in the queue of victims. But our concern is with an implication in these words: that the last thing we should ever admit to, is that our country might have incurred guilt by its actions in the world. It is, apparently, tantamount to asking to be 'insulted and humiliated', and therefore the antithesis to loyalty to one's country.

Can we love the guilty?

Can one identify with a country that has been found responsible for acts of injustice and inhumanity? The answer to this cannot be glib. The moral sense will not permit a straightforward 'yes'. The trouble is that as human persons we do not consist solely of consciences, nor does life comprise moral decisions alone. Life involves relationships of *belonging* to others, in circles of family and friends, associates and wider social groupings including, of course, country. We feel a deep need to belong to such a wider whole; but what happens if the suspicion arises of dishonourable action by the group to which we belong? There is bound to be tension between the instinct of group solidarity, and the uneasy conscience. It is in the need to resolve this tension that patriotism faces its profoundest crisis. Indeed, it is just at this point that 'loyalty to country' comes to mean, for many people, the refusal to admit any guilt attaching to the nation whatsoever. One cannot readily belong to a community smeared by shame – therefore the slightest accusation against the nation must be ruled out of court from the start. Supporting one's country means protesting its innocence. Talking of its guilt is treason. Such 'patriotism' can take varying forms of expression, from aggressive self-justification, to a complacent blandness. If accused of misdeeds, the misdeed is bluntly denied; or excused by pressing circumstances; or put alongside the record of other nations' dark deeds in order to be shown creditable by comparison; or regarded as mere accidents unrelated to the 'real' life of the country. Taken out of context, two lines by Rudyard Kipling point up this attitude:

> If England was what England seems
> 'Ow soon we'd drop 'er. But she ain't!

As C. S. Lewis pointed out, true love never spoke that way. 'It is like loving your children only "if they're good", your wife only while she keeps her looks, your husband only so long as he is famous and successful . . . A man who really loves his country will love her in her ruin and degradation.'[2]

But can love of country actually survive the ruin and degradation, not just of military defeat or economic collapse, but the realization of great and awful guilt incurred by inhumanities committed in its name? Clearly, a love that is mere dotage on the beloved, a sentimentalizing or idealizing possessiveness, will recoil in horror – or would if it could. The difficulty is that loving a country is not like loving a friend, in that a friend can be 'dropped'. But, *pace* Kipling's soldier, we cannot 'drop' our country, even if we wanted to, for we are part of it. We cannot escape our national identity any more than slough off our skin. We cannot detach ourselves from it as we can from another person. We are in and of the country – we *are* our country. The reaction to real or imagined guilt must therefore take place differently: if we are not to belong to a guilty country, the country must never be allowed to appear guilty. Every opportunity must be siezed for its self-justification before the eyes of the world. If we cannot detach ourselves from our country – and indeed the instinct for solidarity will be so strong anyway – then we have to detach ourselves from any mention of guilt.

This is the crisis point of patriotism. Everything hinges on whether the urge to solidarity will crush the conscience – which means that the country must now be painted in false colours – or whether the conscience will be allowed to speak the truth to the nation. But if the latter, how can the nation survive its own condemnation? Are not solidarity and the recognition of guilt incompatible? Must not loyalty consist in affirming the national innocence, like a mother or father telling the police that the youngster being questioned 'would never do a thing like that'? Societies are at their most sensitive on this point. The reaction of the right-wing press and (apparently) of Downing Street to the low-key stance of the service in St Paul's Cathedral following the Falklands conflict in 1982, was almost exactly that of Horatio Bottomley, editor of *John Bull*, in 1916 when plans were announced for the 'National Mission of Repentance and Hope'. What need, thundered the mouthpiece of patriotism, was there of *repentance* when the nation was at war with evil? Least of all could the men at the front be called sinners – they were 'saints and heroes'. William Temple wrote reasoned letters in reply, but it was Studdert Kennedy, the most famous padre of the war, who had the plainest answer to Bottomley. Addressing troops in France he exclaimed: 'Saints! Well, eyes right and have a good look at the man next door to you.'[3]

The point of the Christian tradition is that it does not see the recognition of guilt and the affirmation of solidarity as incompatible. As has been made clear earlier, the Christian understanding of love is of a love that moves towards its object in all its reality. It has now to be said that this includes the sinful reality of the one who is loved. It is as grace for sinners that the love of God is revealed in the death of Christ (Romans 5.6–8). A true love will be prepared to face fully the shame of the beloved and, not minimizing in any way the reality of the guilt, to identify with the loved one in order that the guilt might not be borne alone. The gospel takes sin seriously – desperately seriously – because it can also announce the remedy for sin, which is the divine forgiveness. The message of the forgiveness of sins both demands and enables guilt to be brought fully into the light of day, recognized, confessed and repented of, that it may be removed. A true love of country will therefore include the readiness to admit its guilt in quite concrete terms and to intercede for the expiation of that guilt. It will be expressed not in a denial of loyalty, but in the deepest identification and solidarity with the country under the thunder-cloud of judgment upon it, not as an accuser, but as one of the accused oneself. If patriotism means love, this will be patriotism at its deepest.

Guilt and grace: Lutheran Bonhoeffer

If the story of modern Germany, of all the western nations, provides the severest test-case of the recognition of national guilt, it is equally true that the story of Dietrich Bonhoeffer – including his own reflections on his experience – offer us the most striking instance of a man who broke through to a new depth of love for his country, precisely by meeting unreservedly the reality of its guilt, and the need for its healing. At the end, this cost him his life. But as part of the coherence of life and thought in Bonhoeffer, it must be recognized that he was *theologically* prepared for this sacrifice from the very start of his career. Bonhoeffer was a Lutheran, and for him this signified not just an ecclesiastical label, but a deep theological commitment.

For Martin Luther, the forgiveness of sins through the cross of Christ was both the liberating breakthrough at the heart of Christian experience, and the basis of all theology. The doctrine of atonement was not just one among other doctrines in the Christian edifice, but that which alone made all true thinking about God possible. For how else could fallen man, his intellect no less than his other faculties warped by self-centredness, understand God except by God's gracious condescension even to the death on the cross? God, said Luther, 'is not to be found except in sufferings and in the cross'.[4] On such a view, sin and guilt are taken with desperate seriousness. Equally, no other theology can so gladly and assuredly announce the victory over sin and its consequences:

When sin is pardoned, and the conscience delivered from the burden and sting of sin, then may a Christian bear all things easily: because he feeleth all things within sweet and comfortable, therefore he doeth and suffereth all things willingly.[5]

The currents of later Protestantism in Germany did not always flow as deeply as this. Theological formulation was capable of becoming as rigid and abstract as the scholasticism which Luther rejected. At the other extreme, faith could become a matter of highly individualistic and self-indulgent pietism. More generally, as the centuries rolled on, Luther's 'Christian freedom' could be interpreted as a vague sanctioning of a complacent, bourgeois existence which felt neither the weight of the law nor the liberation of grace. But by the time Dietrich Bonhoeffer became a theological student a major revival of Luther studies was taking place; and a leader of this revival was Karl Holl of Berlin, whose seminar Bonhoeffer attended in 1925. From Holl Bonhoeffer particularly imbibed Luther's radical view of sin as the 'heart turned towards itself', and consequently the inability of man to love God even when most devout. At the same time, the young Bonhoeffer felt that Holl did not adequately stress what he saw as *the* cornerstone of Luther's theology, and the source of faith's assurance: the Christ who is *other* than us and *for us*.

Luther's radicalization of sin and grace runs through Bonhoeffer's theological writings, alongside Barth's emphasis on the hiddenness of God and the sovereignty of his Word. We meet it in his inaugural lecture at Berlin University in 1930, 'Man in Contemporary Philosophy and Theology', where 'man under sin' and 'man under grace' are the twin poles of a true concept of man in relation to God.[6] We meet it in his biblical expositions of creation, fall and temptation: 'It is not the purpose of the Bible to give information about the origin of evil but to witness to its character as guilt and as the infinite burden of man . . . As a creature of God I have committed a completely anti-godly and evil act, and that for that very reason I am guilty – and moreover inexcusably guilty. It will never be possible simply to blame the devil who has led us astray.'[7] To be human means to be exposed to the judgment of God, and no amount of devotion even for God's sake can exempt a person from this judgment. Any tendency simply to pay homage to Bonhoeffer as a hero-martyr is brought up short by his own words:

A suffering for Christ's sake which acknowledges no element of judgment in it is fanaticism . . . The *one* judgment of God which came upon Christ and will come upon all flesh in the end – the judgment of God on sin. No man can give himself to Christ without sharing in this judgment of God. For it is that which distinguishes Christ from the world, that he bore the judgment which the world despised and rejected . . . It is that which distinguishes suffering in the fellowship of Jesus Christ from suffering in the fellowship of any other ethical or political hero.[8]

We meet the same emphasis in the *Christology* lectures, where the incarnate and crucified Christ is seen as sinless precisely through his bearing the likeness of sinful humanity, that is, in being utter grace through identification. Christ entered human sinful existence 'past recognition', but because it was *Christ* who took sinful flesh upon himself, he was without sin:[9] 'He was really made sin for us, and crucified as the *peccator pessimus* the worst sinner.' We meet the same theme in *Cost of Discipleship*, with its sharp contrast between 'cheap grace' which justifies sin, and 'costly grace' which justifies the sinner who accepts the forgiveness of sins in fellowship with the suffering Christ.

It is, moreover, a theme met with continually in Bonhoeffer's personal and spiritual life. It was the basis of the practice of brotherly confession which he introduced into the community at Finkenwalde. It was, to the end, the mainspring of Bonhoeffer's own faith. In the last surviving prison letter to Eberhard Bethge he writes: 'My past life is brim-full of God's goodness, and my sins are covered by the forgiving love of Christ crucified. I'm most thankful for the people I have met, and I only hope that they never have to grieve about me, but that they, too, will always be certain of, and thankful for, God's mercy and forgiveness.'[10] On Low Sunday, 1945, Bonhoeffer's last act before being taken away for the final questioning was to conduct a service for his fellow-prisoners, at their request. The Old Testament text for the day was Isaiah 53.5: 'With his stripes we are healed'.

Bonhoeffer, then, was a Lutheran of the Lutherans. Sin and guilt must be faced but, even more importantly, *can* be faced and

overcome through grace. In the light of this, guilt can be acknowledged, and presented for removal. Repentance does not lead to
extinction in self-abasement, but to new life.

Corporate guilt: the nation

One of the most significant marks of Bonhoeffer is the way in
which he transposed the traditional Lutheran theme of guilt and forgiveness into a key other than that of purely individual salvation. His
doctoral thesis *Sanctorum Communio* is frequently described as a bold
attempt to unite theology and sociology in an understanding of the
church as community – and indeed it is. But it also contains some
striking observations on non-ecclesiastical community in general,
and on family, people and country in particular. Bonhoeffer agrees
that a society consists of individuals, but also states that it may be
thought of as a 'collective person'. The usual dichotomy between
man as a social being and man as an individual, is a dangerous
abstraction. Where men regard themselves as belonging together in
society, their sociality is part of their individuality no less than their
society being the sum of their individual existences. Bonhoeffer
therefore demands a theological understanding of human community as under sin and grace, in need of atonement and repentance,
no less than the individual. 'The call is to the collective person, and
not to the individual', he says, referring to the Israelite concept of the
people of God and the prophets' witness to that people. 'It is the
people that is to do penance as the people of God. It was the people,
and not the individuals, who had sinned. So it was also the people
who must be comforted' (Isaiah 40.1).[11] Then a few lines later comes
this passage:

It is not only individual Germans and individual Christians who are guilty; Germany
and the church are guilty too. Here the contrition and justification of individuals is of
no avail; Germany and the church themselves must repent and be justified. The community which is from God to God, which bears within it an eschatological meaning –
this community stands in God's sight, and does not dissolve into the fate of the many.
It has been willed and created, and has fallen into guilt; it must seek repentance, it must
believe in and experience grace at the limits of time.[12]

This passage is remarkable, not least for being written in the
Germany of 1927. 'Guilt' was then an explosive word to the mass of
Germans still smarting under the terms of the Versailles Treaty,
which attributed to Germany sole guilt for the outbreak of the First
World War. This clause hurt German sentiment at least as much as
the imposition of economic reparations; and the Bonhoeffer family,
no nationalists themselves, did not repress their own sense of
grievance. To speak of a 'guilty Germany' so directly as Bonhoeffer

does here, albeit in a recondite academic treatise, displays unusual theological objectivity.

Not long after writing this, Bonhoeffer spent his year in the United States, where on several occasions he addressed student gatherings on contemporary German attitudes and aspirations. Even today, his accounts of the sufferings of German people during and immediately after the war make deeply moving reading: the loss of life, family sorrow (not least his own), poverty, hunger, disease and despair. His own attitudes to the guilt question then emerge:

. . . Christian people in Germany, who took the course and the end of the war seriously, could not help seeing here a judgment of God upon this fallen world and especially upon our people.

Before the war we lived too far from God; we believed too much in our own power, in our almightiness and righteousness. We attempted to be a strong and good people, we felt too much satisfaction with our scientific, economic and social progress, and we identified this progress with the coming of the kingdom of God. We felt too happy and complacent in this world; our souls were too much at home in this world. Then the great disillusionment came. We saw the impotence and weakness of humanity, we were suddenly awakened from our dream, we recognized our guiltiness before God and we humbled ourselves under the mighty hand of God. When I was speaking of 'guiltiness', I added on purpose: 'guiltiness before God'. Let me tell you frankly that no German and no stranger who knows well the history of the origin of the war believes that Germany bears the sole guilt of the war . . . It seems to me that this is the meaning of the war for Germany: we had to recognize the limits of man and by that means we discovered anew God in his glory and almightiness, in his wrath and his grace.[13]

A few years were to pass, and Bonhoeffer could only admit that Germany's actions in the eyes of the world corresponded much more closely with the actuality of guilt before God. But even in this passage we see an open-eyed admission of what is unacceptable in his country. Notice, too, his use of the first person plural. He identifies with what his country and its leaders did while he himself was but a child, no less than with the country in which he is now an adult, participating citizen. If it is objected that many of his fellow Germans would refuse to be included in his 'we', refusing on nationalist grounds to identify with his repentant attitude, Bonhoeffer would reply that the Christian repents on behalf of the total community. We may refer back to *Sanctorum Communio* again:

The 'people' is to repent, but it is not a question of the number who repent, and in practice it will never be the whole people, the whole church, but God can so regard it 'as if' the whole people has repented. 'For the sake of ten I will not destroy it' (Genesis 18.32). He can see the whole people in a few individuals, just as he saw and reconciled the whole of mankind in one man. Here the problem of vicarious action arises . . .[14]

Perceptive interpreters of Bonhoeffer have commented on how his radical prison theology reaches back to some of the christological insights of these early years. But equally significant was the way in which the course of action which put him in prison and led to the gallows, was itself a living out of this youthful concept of the guilty nation, and the need for some to be the repentant, confessing ones who are drawn into the way of atonement for the sake of all. They are the ones who see, acknowledge, identify with and confess their people's guilt, and seek its expiation. They, of all people, love their country.

The church as the community of confession

Bonhoeffer was not completely alone in recognizing the call for confession of guilt during the Nazi years. On 27th September 1938, as the Münich crisis appeared to mean imminent European war, the Provisional Leadership of the Confessing Church produced an 'Intercession Liturgy' for use in the churches in the actual event of war. The work of Superintendents Albertz and Böhm, the proposed service was heavily weighted with penitential prayers on behalf of both the church and the nation, and with intercessions on behalf of all to whom war would bring upheaval and sufferings. The implication was clear enough, that the involvement of Germany in war was to be interpreted as divine judgment rather than the great breakthrough to national glory:

We confess before you the sins of our nation. Within it your name has often been blasphemed, your Word attacked, your truth suppressed. In public and in secret much injustice has been committed . . . Lord, our God, we lay before you in penitence these sins of ours and these sins of our people. Forgive us and temper justice with mercy.[15]

The liturgy was never used. Not only was the war postponed for nearly a year, but the service was condemned by certain bishops, and by the nationalist and militarist press: treachery, defeatism, a threat to national morale were allegedly its main features (readers may draw what parallels they wish with the anger directed at the St Paul's Falklands service in 1982). Not until after the Second World War was any similar statement of confession to be issued in the name of German Protestantism, and even then it was occasioned by the renewing of relationships with the churches from abroad. In October 1945, a delegation from the infant World Council of Churches met leaders of the German Evangelical Church in Stuttgart, and the following declaration was read to the visitors:

With great pain do we say: through us has endless suffering been brought to many peoples and countries. What we have often borne witness to before our congregations, that we declare in the name of the whole church. True, we have struggled for many years in the name of Jesus Christ against a spirit which found its terrible expression in the national socialist regime of violence, but we accuse ourselves for not witnessing more courageously, for not praying more faithfully, for not believing more joyously and for not loving more ardently. Now a new beginning is to be made in our churches.[16]

The Stuttgart Declaration helped significantly in the process of reconciliation between Germany and the outside world, and not only in the churchly sphere. It also aroused resentment within Germany, among circles for whom national defeat once again signalled the time for self-pity rather than self-assessment. But one can hardly help wondering what form the confession would have taken if Bonhoeffer had survived to take a hand in its drafting. In fact, strong clues are provided in parts of *Ethics* and other writings from his active conspiracy period, for one of Bonhoeffer's services to the resistance was to prepare a confession of guilt to be read from pulpits in the event of a successful *coup*. By comparison with the Stuttgart Declaration, Bonhoeffer's confession is far more specific, blunt and terse:

The church confesses that she has not proclaimed often and clearly enough her message of the one God who has revealed himself for all time in Jesus Christ and who suffers no other gods beside himself. She confesses her timidity, her evasiveness, her dangerous concessions. She has often been untrue to her office of guardianship and to her office of comfort. And through this she has often denied to the outcast and to the despised the compassion which she owes them. *She was silent when she should have cried out because the blood of the innocent was crying aloud to heaven. She has failed to speak the right word in the right way and at the right time.*[17]

The church confesses that she has witnessed the lawless application of brutal force, the physical and spiritual suffering of countless innocent people, oppression, hatred and murder, and that she has not raised her voice on behalf of the victims and has not found ways to hasten to their aid. *She is guilty of the deaths of the weakest and most defenceless brothers of Jesus Christ.*[18]

(Emphases mine, both quotations.)

In the light of this, we need not doubt that in the aftermath of the war Bonhoeffer would have insisted that the unmentionable fate of the Jews should be made explicit, and the church itself confess its guilty share in responsibility for the holocaust. Bonhoeffer's proposed confession in fact took as its programme the ten commandments, every one of which the church must admit to having violated. No pleas in mitigation could be allowed, no pointing to cases where resistance to evil *had* been offered (and his own actions would have had the highest claim here). Only a church confessing itself to be under judgment could rightfully intercede for a nation in its guilt. To make such confession was exactly the commission of the church:

By her confession of guilt the church does not exempt men from their own confession of guilt, but she calls them in into the fellowship of the confession of guilt. Apostate humanity can endure before Christ only if it has fallen under the sentence of Christ. It is to this judgment that the church summons all those who hear her message.[19]

The sharing of guilt

The way of solidarity with his country in its guilt was a course which Bonhoeffer deliberately chose to follow, and from which he had ample opportunity of escaping. The attempt to escape that solidarity did not necessarily entail physical flight from Germany. Bonhoeffer knew well enough that simply to be a pastor and teacher in the Confessing Church could in itself lead to a certain distancing of oneself from one's fellow countrymen. The cause of the one true Word of God could be turned into a means of sheer accusation of the people for their apostasy (the 'radical' critic of his society, church, club or whatever is always known for the way in which he stands just to the edge of his group, and always makes sure that if and when his fellows do adopt a more enlightened stand, he will again set up his stall a little further away – he can never be satisfied). Bonhoeffer's sensitivity here made his part in the church struggle fraught with almost unendurable tension, and he was made deeply uneasy by Karl Barth's reprimand when he left for London in 1933. Was it an attempt to escape? Maybe. But to Germany he did return two years later. The tension was even greater in 1939, for in almost every respect his journey to the United States was outwardly entirely legitimate. To avoid military call-up was not only a respite for his conscience, but safeguarded the Confessing Church. There was much that he could do for the ecumenical movement abroad, and much that he could do for theology in America. But once there, he again discovered that his way lay with Germany, suffering and guilty Germany. The ecumenical door was wide open, but to have gone through it would have meant a privilege he dare not take. Back in Germany, his entry into the conspiracy was an open-eyed venture in responsibility for his country's guilt – which he knew involved him in sharing in guilt in a way for which there was no clear theological or ethical guidance in his church tradition. It was not simply that Lutheranism laid great stress on obeying the powers that be as ordained of God, and allowed the course of tyrannicide only as a remote, hypothetical possibility. The *means* of removing Hitler demanded taking part in the masquerade of evil – serving in the *Abwehr*, camouflaging oneself as a Nazi, pretending to serve the country's war effort while scheming to bring it to an end. Bonhoeffer fully realized the ethical cost of the way of solidarity, as he wrote to some of his fellow-conspirators in the winter of 1942–43:

We have been silent witnesses of evil deeds; we have been drenched by many storms; we have learnt the arts of equivocation and pretence; experience has made us suspicious of others and kept us from being truthful and open; intolerable conflicts have worn us down and even made us cynical. Are we still of any use?[20]

He had discovered the paradox that responsible action in such an extreme situation meant not the avoidance of guilt in the interests of one's own purity, but doing that which is required for the sake of others regardless of the guilty contamination one may incur for one-self. One of the most profound themes of *Ethics* is that man becomes truly man in conformity with Christ, and because Christ is the bearer of divine judgment upon sin, conformity with Christ begins with the confession of guilt – one's own guilt and the guilt of all people. Because Christ entered into the guilt of others and took it upon himself, truly Christlike action will not flinch from bearing guilt if responsible action leaves no other course open. Personal innocence is a luxury by comparison, which a man may choose only at his peril, before God. 'He sets his own personal innocence above his responsibility for men, and he is blind to the more irredeemable guilt which he incurs precisely in this; he is blind also to the fact that real innocence shows itself precisely in a man's entering into the fellowship of guilt for the sake of other men.'[21]

In one of the most haunting of his poems written in prison, 'Night Voices in Tegel', Bonhoeffer allows the frightened, sleepless consciences of his fellow-prisoners – and, through them, all his compatriots – to find a voice.[22] But man's reproach against man is transformed by Bonhoeffer into a prayer, out of which a new hope arises:

> Only before thee, source of all being,
> Before thee are we sinners.
>
> Afraid of suffering and poor in deeds,
> We have betrayed thee before men.
>
> We saw the lie raise its head,
> And we did not honour the truth.
>
> We come before thee as men,
> And confessors of our sins.
>
> Lord, after the ferment of these times,
> Send us times of assurance.
>
> After so much going astray,
> Let us see the day break.
>
> Let there be ways built for us by thy word
> As far as eye can see.
>
> Until thou wipe out our guilt,
> Keep us in quiet patience.[23]

From this, it is but a short step to Bonhoeffer's final poem 'The Death of Moses', which perhaps enables us to guess some of the content of the prayer which he was seen to utter on the very steps of the gallows at Flossenbürg:

> To punish sin and to forgiveness you are moved,
> God, this people I have loved.
> That I bore its shame and sacrifices
> And saw its salvation – that suffices.[24]

Loyalty as martyrdom

Eberhard Bethge has described Bonhoeffer's relationships with his homeland in terms of the twin motifs of *exile* and *martyr*. Bonhoeffer can be seen to be an 'exile' in a physical sense at two stages of his life, during his time in London, 1933–35, and in his short visit to the United States in 1939. But in an inward sense he was also an exile in his commitment to the Confessing Church, and, insofar as it represented protest, as a member of the conspiracy. The exile is one who, finding his homeland intolerable, is constrained to protest and flee for the sake of his identity. But equally, Bonhoeffer felt constrained to identify with his country, and to fuse his sense of protest and exile with the summons to share in the process of its redemption, through martyrdom. Paradoxically, his choice to sink himself in the harrowing particularity of Hitler's Germany, when he could have chosen the straightforward route to ecumenical service in safety, has led to his posthumous status unrivalled in universal, ecumenical significance. 'Only when he proleptically took upon himself the guilt of his nation and confessed it, did the freedom of the Gospel unfold again.'[25]

Raymond Williams, the Cambridge social and literary historian, has catalogued several possible ways in which persons may be said to 'belong' to their society.[26] The *subject* is one who certainly regards himself as a member of society, but whose place is largely determined for him by authority, which he accepts with varying degrees of acquiescence. The *vagrant* is one for whom society has no place, and in whose drifting existence society has no place either. The *exile* is one repelled by his society and who opts out physically or mentally. The *rebel* is one who protests against the structure of his society as it is, in the name of an alternative which he desires and perhaps actively seeks to bring in. The *member*, finally, is one who is able to participate responsibly in the life and direction of his society. This is certainly an illuminating analysis. But Bonhoeffer reveals its incompleteness; for his own style of citizenship, while connecting with at least some of Williams's categories, does not finally fit into any one of them. As we have seen, he was certainly an exile at certain stages of his life. As a conspirator, he was, in Williams's sense, a rebel. Within the exigencies of Nazi Germany he even remained in some senses a member, for he never lost his sense of bourgeois responsibility. Perhaps he even experienced the world of the vagrant, as he joined the wretched riff-raff of prisoners in Tegel. But what of the *martyr*, the one who moves beyond membership, exile and rebellion, into willing acceptance of his country's shame and who feels the anguish of its guilt in his own soul, accepting it in spite of its unacceptability, and who bears in love the cost in his own death? There is something here which transcends the normal categories of citizenship, and which demands a new and deeper consideration of what 'loyalty to country' means.

Loyalty to guilty Britain

Bonhoeffer has shown us that there is a loyalty to country which includes recognition and acceptance of one's country's guilt, and intercession and action for its expiation. Since Bonhoeffer, patriotism can never carry quite the traditional sense again. Denial or excusal of the country's guilt is in the end not true love, not true loyalty, by Christian standards. The most damaging thing for a community, as for an individual, is that its guilt should not be treated. If it is not dealt with, there will be a continual flight from the past, a repeated attempt to paint the story in unreal colours, an exhausting attempt at self-justification. There is no chance of present realities being faced, no hope of responsibilities for the future being shouldered adequately, if the dread corners in the shadows are not illuminated and the demons exorcized. Those who really love Britain will therefore not avoid the question of her guilt, however much they may be accused of running the country down. They will do this, avoiding simplistic, ideological condemnations which suggest that there is nothing to be grateful for in being British, nothing to be justly proud of in her heritage. Indeed, they will use what is good in that heritage to expose all the more clearly where Britain has not been true to her best. But neither will they use the good as a pretext for avoiding or excusing the bad. They will utter their criticisms out of a basic identification with the country and a loyalty to it, and they will not avoid placing themselves with the accused.

They will look honestly and unflinchingly at Britain's record of behaviour as a colonial and imperial power. They need not subscribe to the childishly simplistic view that the whole of the story was a carefully planned capitalistic conspiracy to subdue and exploit the rest of mankind. They will know that the colonial expansion of the eighteenth and nineteenth centuries was for much of the time a haphazard and incoherent affair, and that not until the late nineteenth century did it ever achieve widespread and popular approval (Queen Victoria's diamond jubilee created as much as it expressed the imperial ideal). They will know that a good deal of personal idealism and sacrifice was channelled into the enterprise, in the sincere conviction that the spreading of British-born justice, education and health-care would make a better world. They will know that the nationalisms which it evoked in Africa and Asia this century have

themselves utilized the we tern goods which colonialism introduced. But they will also underline those episodes which show that
British people – or at least people who have left these shores – have
been as capable as any others of the most brutal acts of inhumanity.
They will speak of the opium wars against China as a thoroughly
sordid instance of fire-power directed for nakedly mercenary ends
and deliberately introducing a source of misery on a native population (and the Treaty of Nanking, foisted by such power on the
Chinese, may yet have repercussions on the future status of Hong
Kong, now looming on the horizon). They will not forget the deception of the Maories in the siezure of their lands; nor the persecution of the Australian aborigines, still less the actual extermination of
the Tasmanians (genocide did not begin with the Nazis). When
South Africa is mentioned, they will remember the horrors of the
Boer War, especially the concentration camps (yes, concentration
camps!) in which during just fourteen months over *twenty-thousand*
men, women and children died. Such episodes, and much else,
belong to the story.

If it is objected that all this is just past history, over and done with,
and that the present generation cannot be expected to feel any identification with the responsibility of their forbears, it has to be replied
that it is not as simple as that. What matters is how the story of the
past is handed on. If the story is used selectively, building up the
nation's idealized image of itself to the exclusion of such darker
episodes, then the present generation too is becoming guilty of those
sins of the past. Whenever Britain's 'greatness' is identified with a
glorified image of that past, and which suggests that greatness today
consists in similarly exercising such muscle-power on other inhabitants of the globe, without regard for the sufferings inflicted, then
we too are guilty. Whenever, in retelling the story of the past, the
guilt of former days is not recognized, it becomes contemporary
again.

Moreover, it has to be pointed out that the darker episodes are not
located only in that past which is beyond living memory for most of
us. Victory over Nazi Germany was vital for the sake of all Europe.
But it was not a guiltless victory. Until almost the outbreak of the
war, Britain was complacent to the point of indifference about the
plight of refugees from Germany. The story of the allies' failure to
respond even when Auschwitz was a known fact is only now beginning to emerge slowly and painfully. And still there are people in
Britain who refuse to believe that their political or military leaders
could ever actually order the deliberate massacre of helpless civilians,
despite the implications of the stated aim of the strategic bombing
offensive, which was to destroy the morale of the working popu-

lation of Germany. Nothing, but nothing, has yet been produced which even remotely justifies militarily, let alone morally, the holocaust released by the Royal Air Force and the United States Air Force on Dresden on 13–14th February 1945. An undefended city, known to be crowded with refugees from the east, became the funeral pyre of possibly as many as 135,000 people – on any count, far higher than the total number of British casualties from German bombing throughout the war.[27] The heinousness of Nazi crimes in no way mitigates the barbarism of this one, probably the most appalling incident in the whole history of British arms.

Those who truly love Britain will not try to pretend that such things did not happen, or excuse them, or claim that set alongside the brutal record of other nations these incidents pale into insignificance. They will accept the brutal part of the story, and reflect deeply on the fact of belonging to a country whose often-stated values of freedom and humanity have not always diverted her from cruelty. If they draw upon Christian perspectives, they will not be affronted by the suggestion that British humanity shares in the total fallenness of mankind, and that what has happened in the past may recur at any time. Indeed, they will not shrink from the recognition that as a result of past actions and policies certain attitudes and practices have virtually become endemic in British society. Whatever else the imperial dream produced of good and ill, it certainly engendered racism, the assumption that certain peoples are usable and, if occasion demands, disposable. We should not be offended by the claim that it is virtually impossible to be British *and* to be free from racism. Really to love the country does not mean regarding this accusation as an affront to our dignity, but as a diagnosis of a disease of which we need to be healed.

Nowhere was the racist assumption more evident than in the contrast between the heroism and sacrifice expended on behalf of the Falkland Islanders in liberating them from Argentina aggression, and the shameful treatment of the inhabitants of Diego Garcia in the Indian Ocean.[28] The latter island was until 1966 associated with Mauritius under British rule. Independence was granted to Mauritius on condition that the Chagos Archipelago, including Diego Garcia, was kept under British authority. The reason for this condition presently became evident, when Britain agreed to the United States using the island for a military communications facility – which in effect meant its transformation into a full-scale military base. The islanders, numbering about two thousand (about the same number as the Falklanders), were British subjects – but black. Hitherto they had lived an exemplary peaceful life, but their continued presence on the island was now deemed incompatible with

American military activities and interests. By a combination of
deception, cajolery, economic pressure and sometimes sheer force,
the population was compelled to transfer to Mauritius where they
effectively became refugees, many living in extreme poverty and
squalor. Few in Britain noticed or took up their cause, and not until
the spring of 1982 (virtually on the very eve of the Falklands conflict)
did the British government finally agree to anything approaching
reasonable financial compensation to the Diego Garcians. Both
Labour and Conservative governments were involved in this affair
which displays only too well how selective British concern for
'freedom' can be.

Meanwhile, victory in the Falklands released a euphoria hailing
the return of British 'greatness', with a Prime Minister telling the
armed forces that they had written a glorious chapter in the history
of liberty. That it was a remarkable instance of determination and
courage by the armed forces is not to be doubted. But to use it as a
diversion from cynical British behaviour elsewhere only adds to the
guilt which it would seek to hide. That guilt will not go away, and it
must be acknowledged by those who would love the real Britain,
which includes Britain with her own tale of disregarding people's
rights, past and present. It is here that attitudes to past, present and
future are impossible to separate out from each other. Writing in an
astringent secular vein, Donald Horne sets out part of the agenda for
a renewed British self-understanding:

There is a need for a re-writing of history, for a purging of some guilt by its contem-
plation. But English conceit is so much part of British history that it seems more likely
that at best it could only be purified, not destroyed. Not only because a nation, like an
individual, is likely to fall to bits if its only attitude to itself is one of contempt; and not
only because English conceit may be indestructible; but also because there is so much
in their history in which the British can still take pride – if they are prepared to be satisfied with goodness rather than uniqueness, with excellence rather than superiority.[29]

Those who are Christians can claim spiritual resources for a
venture in truthfulness, as they answer the call to stand with and for
their country under judgment, in intercession and repentant action,
Love to this extremity can be afforded, knowing that guilt is not the
last word. Superficial patriotism fears the admission of guilt because,
from the ordinary human perspective, it can only lead to inward
defeat and despair, the loss of all morale and hope. The issue of guilt
is therefore continually evaded, postponed, buried in the vain hope
that it might go away. But the Christian tradition knows that the
moment of acceptance of one's guilt can also be the moment of grace
and forgiveness, out of which a new hope can be born. What appears
to be a death, is a moment of new life. Reality is faced, the world as it
actually is can be accepted, and new energies released.

Dietrich Bonhoeffer demonstrated this way within Nazi Germany. It is relevant to all national contexts. Those who really love their country will neither evade the guilt of their country, protesting its innocence, nor will they evade their country in its guilt, despising its shortcomings. And in case this seems a particularly un-British idea, then it is worth pondering the lines of Britain's greatest imperial poet, written on the occasion of the empire's greatest display of grandeur:

> The tumult and the shouting dies—
> The captains and the kings depart—
> Still stands Thine ancient sacrifice,
> An humble and a contrite heart.
> Lord God of Hosts, be with us yet,
> Lest we forget, lest we forget!
>
> Far-call'd our navies melt away—
> On dune and headland sinks the fire—
> Lo, all our pomp of yesterday
> Is one with Nineveh and Tyre!
> Judge of the Nations, spare us yet,
> Lest we forget, lest we forget![30]

7
Might and Right

The issue of armed conflict towers over the present hour like an alpine crag behind which the sun is sinking, leaving the world beneath in deepening shadow. In Britain, particularly, anxiety has been mounting rapidly. The Falklands conflict suddenly and unexpectedly resulted in a clash of arms which, though minor by modern standards and mercifully brief, brought home to the public consciousness the instability of the international scene – a scene in which the legacy of Britain's colonial past continues to play no small part. But towering above all, dark, jagged and forbidding against the reddening sky, is the threat of nuclear war. The near breakdown in detente between east and west, the British government's decision to replace Polaris with Trident, and the siting of Cruise missiles on British soil, have brought the issue back into public debate with an intensity likely to surpass even that of the days of the Aldermaston marches in the 1960s. The peace-movement of today is a more multifarious affair than its predecessor of a generation earlier, not least because the mainstream churches in Britain and on the continent are now much more deeply involved. The Anglican report *The Church and the Bomb*[1] may not represent 'official' Church of England thinking, but it is equally true that there is now more questioning of stated British defence policy at all levels in the established and other churches, than ever before.

In this debate, the word 'patriotism' will inevitably crop up repeatedly, whether used as a 'good' or a 'bad' term, because patriotism and the defence of one's country have always been so closely linked. In normal understanding, the minimal meaning of patriotism is precisely the sense of duty to rally to the armed defence of the territory, lives, freedom and values of one's people. In the sacrifice which this may entail, patriotism is thought to find its ultimate and absolute expression: dying for one's country. For many people, therefore, patriotism *is* the willingness to defend one's country, and any posture which appears to weaken the capability of resistance against an aggressor is automatically 'unpatriotic'.

The introduction of Dietrich Bonhoeffer into this debate can only challenge the terms in which it is set. He prayed for the military defeat of his country, and shared in the conspiracy against its leadership. His participation in that conspiracy made him an accomplice in violence, which was an ethical sacrifice after his staunch advocacy of peace and non-violence during the 1930s. The man who told his friends in 1934, that if war came he would pray that God would give him the strength not to take up arms, *did* effectively take up arms when war came – against the German state of the time. Neither Bonhoeffer the pacifist nor Bonhoeffer the conspirator wear the normal patriotic colours, a fact which still makes him *persona non grata* for many Germans today, whatever their views on the Nazi period. Certain British assumptions are likely to be disturbed also.

But care is needed when seeking to relate Bonhoeffer to situations far removed from his own context. Bonhoeffer certainly supplies a rich quarry of quotations with which to buttress an internationalist, non-violent stance. 'Peace on earth is not a problem, but a command given at Christ's coming.'[2] What could be more forthright than that? Yet as we shall see, Bonhoeffer was as deeply critical of certain aspects of the peace-movement of his time, as he was opposed to the resurgent nationalism of his native Germany. Pacifists and peace-campaigners no less than others will therefore be challenged by Bonhoeffer on some of their fundamental presuppositions and underlying motives. Further, while Bonhoeffer was certainly prophetic in much of what he said on the peace issue as on so much else, we need to remind ourselves that in one crucial sense he cannot be our contemporary. When the Hiroshima bomb exploded on 6th August 1945, Bonhoeffer had already been dead nearly four months. That explosion marked a watershed in human history – and Bonhoeffer remains on the other side of it. The mushroom cloud did not loom on his horizon, as it does perpetually on ours.

This chapter is not intended to be yet another appraisal of the moral and political issues presented to Britain today, and to Christians in particular, by the manufacture and possession of nuclear weapons. It is rather an attempt to let Bonhoeffer challenge us, whatever particular position we hold, on what we think is ultimately at stake in the debate – and particularly when the word 'patriotism' is put on the table. However, since the area we are considering is so polemically charged at the present time, it is only fair that the reader be given an idea of where the writer stands on the issue of war in general, and nuclear weapons in particular. I am not a pacifist. I hold that, highly regrettable though it may seem, ever since the Constantinian era the Christian church has been able to excercise historical responsibility in the affairs of nations only by a recognition of the role of power in those affairs, which at times must include the possibility of military force. I do not regard the theory of the just war as a cynical theological device to keep the church subservient to the state, but as an honest attempt to prevent the use of force becoming an end in itself, and to preserve moral ends in a world where sinful power-structures will not simply disappear because we do not like them. Equally, I hold that the use, or the threatened use, or the possession of nuclear weapons, is incompatible with the just war tradition, and the biblical ethic forbidding the wanton destruction of life. My position is broadly in line with that of the authors of *The Church and the Bomb*, in advocating that Britain should give up its independent nuclear deterrent as a stage in the process of multilateral disarmament. I equally wish to stress that I believe that such a process will be formidably difficult, and like all creative political enterprises, compounded of risks and compromises. Nor do I wish to pretend that I derive these views from Bonhoeffer. He cannot be brought into the discussion simply to support one's case. Once again, he must be allowed to make his own contribution.

Britain – a militaristic nation?

Whereas Bonhoeffer spoke out of a situation of the most extreme nationalist militarism, it may be felt that Britain has never offered, nor is ever likely to offer, any parallels to either the Prussian or Nazi sabre-rattling mentality. Indeed the British habitually refute any charge of being a 'militaristic' people, and there is much in their tradition to support their case. The British have customarily seen their world-power status as based upon trade and commerce rather than upon arms. Napoleon's jibe about the nation of shopkeepers has been gratefully received and worn as an ironic compliment. Perhaps due more to complacency and inefficiency rather than to conscious opposition to arms, Britain entered two world wars this century grossly unprepared both in men and equipment. Conscription has only been applied in emergencies. National service, which lasted until about fifteen years after the Second World War, was accepted by most men as an unfortunate necessity interrupting personal life and careers – something to be gone through without too much complaining but no excess of enthusiasm either. For deep in the British psyche lies the yeoman image, the man who wants nothing more than to be quietly busy about the affairs of his shire, who will at the call of duty leave hearth and plough to fight a foreign foe, but will return to the fields where his heart really lies. The soldiering life is discarded as easily as the uniform itself (and in Britain, uniforms worn in daily life, with the exception of the police, mostly signify positions of servitude rather than status and authority). Moreover, there is in Britain a well-established tradition of separation between the military establishments and political leadership. This is in marked contrast to the United States, for example, where the voice of the military may frequently be heard loud and clear on matters of national policy to a degree which would be thought quite improper in Britain. There is indeed in Britain a deeply-embedded tradition of keeping arms in their proper place.

Against this particular element, however, other features must be brought into view. That Britain's trade and manufacturing industry grew to the extent that it did, owed much to her *naval* power. Sea-borne power enables the reality of armed force to be disguised to some extent, partly because so much of the action takes place far over the horizon, partly because naval warfare seems a less muddy and wantonly destructive form of combat compared with that waged across farms and towns by tanks and flame-throwers, and partly because a certain romance is attached to sea-faring in any case. In addition, naval power can be extremely effective without an actual shot being fired. Yet in human terms, of suffering and hardship and death, the long-term results of a blockade can differ very little from those of an actual bombardment – a fact which provoked bitter German resentment against Britain at the end of the First World War. Those who had seen their children die from malnutrition did not feel inclined to listen to questions about what might or might not have happened in Liege and Louvain. Basically, guns afloat seem less sinister than guns on wheels, and 'Rule, Britannia!' can be sung lustily with little realization that its actual sentiments are virtually those of nationalized piracy.

Britain, then, is open to militaristic influence, even if the ethos has never been so aggressive as that of the Prussian empire which, after the victory over France in 1870, put military power and ideals at the centre of the self-understanding of united Germany. It may be said that Germany's mistake in the nineteenth century was to adopt militarism as the means to advancement in the world, to compensate for relative economic immaturity. That could signify that it would be a similar mistake for Britain, a century later, to adopt overt militarism as a compensation for economic senility, a short-cut to renewed self-esteem and international standing. A spasm of military muscle may well offer a momentary distraction from the frustrations of industrial stagnation and social unrest at home, and loss of significance abroad. That is why the chief doubts about the Falklands conflict concern the political exploitation of it at home, its portrayal as a revival of British greatness, a demonstration of British grit in face of a doubting world. That the victory was a remarkable achievement in terms of the skill and valour of those who took part, is not in doubt. On the other hand, that Britain had to resort to arms at all was a condemnation of the prolonged refusal – ultimately in Parliament itself, the same Parliament which yelled for action when the crisis finally broke – over the years, to find a realistic and viable future for the islands in relation to Latin America. War is a signal of failure in relationships. Theologically, however unavoidable it may be politically, it has to be interpreted as a judgment upon all the parties concerned. Self-righteous boasting only compounds the guilt.

To say that a nation is militaristic means that military power, instead of being viewed as *instrumental* in safeguarding the nation's interests and values, comes to be *identified as those values*. The nation's strength – even its identity – are seen to lie in its armaments, the acquisition of which takes on a determining power of its own in affecting national policy. It could well be that when all the strategic, rational and moral arguments against the British independent nuclear deterrent have had their say and even carried the day, the biggest obstacle to disarmament will still remain to be tackled: the gut psychology of the status symbol. Margaret Gowing characterizes the way in which the post-war (Labour) government's decision to manufacture atomic weapons was taken in 1947:

It had not been a response to an immediate military threat but rather something fundamental and almost instinctive – a feeling that Britain must possess so climacteric a weapon in order to deter an atomically armed enemy, *a feeling that Britain as a great power must acquire all major new weapons,* a feeling that atomic weapons were a manifestation of the scientific and technological superiority on which Britain's strength, so deficient if measured in sheer numbers of men, must depend.[3]

(Emphases mine.)

The original decision having been made on the basis of such massive assumptions about national greatness and prestige, a decision to relinquish nuclear weapons will require a huge adjustment in those assumptions which are still current. Can a nation which renounces the possession of the most technically effective weapons available, really be taking itself seriously? Would not the abandonment by Britain of its independent nuclear force be the most definitive admission of decline and fall? And would not that be the very antithesis to 'patriotism'?

Bonhoeffer: peace as God's command

In Chapter 2 we noted Bonhoeffer's commitment to the peace cause, which was crystallized by his encounter with Jean Lasserre in New York during 1930–31, and took its theological stand on a concrete interpretation of the Sermon on the Mount. Eberhard Bethge writes: 'Not that Bonhoeffer immediately became a convinced pacifist – in fact he never did so – but after meeting Lasserre the question of the concrete answer to the Biblical injunction of peace and that of the concrete steps to be taken against warlike impulses never left him again.'[4] Bonhoeffer's commitment, as has been seen, found expression in his work for the World Alliance.

Bethge's qualification about Bonhoeffer's 'pacifism' should be carefully noted. On the one hand, in *Cost of Discipleship* he could write:

The followers of Jesus have been called to peace. When he called them they found their peace, for he is their peace. But now they are told that they must not only *have* peace but *make* it. And to that end they renounce all violence and tumult. In the cause of Christ nothing is to be gained by such methods . . . His disciples keep the peace by choosing to endure suffering themselves rather than inflict it on others.[5]

But Bonhoeffer never tried to force this position upon his Finkenwalde students, most of whom were surprised when one day he gently queried their enthusiasm for the military call-up. He simply wished the pacifist view to be considered on its own theological merits. Nor did he, in the name of peace, despise the experience of those who had fought in the First World War, and those who had suffered through it whether as wounded or as bereaved. His reflections on *Volkstrauertag* – the German equivalent of Remembrance Day – delivered to his ordinands, are models of pastoral sensitivity.[6] These notes were in part prompted by the change of name of the day ordered by the Nazi government from 1936 onwards, from *Volkstrauertag* (literally, 'People's Day of Mourning') to *Heldengedenktag* ('Heroes' Remembrance Day'), signifying a marked change in emphasis from grief to pride. Pastors ought not to behave as though the occasion did not exist, states Bonhoeffer, nor should they speak of it casually. It is a deeply serious occasion (and Bonhoeffer was doubtless speaking out of his own family's distress at Walter's death in 1918) on which people have a right to expect the Word of God from the Church – the gospel of consolation for the afflicted, and the answer to the question 'How could God permit all this to happen?' Two million died in the war, and many survivors bear the marks of death. And Bonhoeffer can even commit himself to the remark: 'Dare we forget that the soil on which we live was preserved and fought for on our behalf through our brothers' blood? Dare we cease to be thankful today?' There is then a necessity – an unequalled necessity – for solidarity with people in their genuine feelings at this point. 'Whoever speaks only mockingly or moralistically about 1914–18 makes his words not worth believing.'[7] The focal point of the occasion must be repentance, for war must always in the end be seen as a sign of rebellion against God, an omen of the break-up of the godless world. Yet the world in its godlessness is borne on the cross by God's love.

In *Ethics* Bonhoeffer writes in a surprisingly detached manner about war – perhaps the only way in which it could be spoken of now that it was the fact of life in Europe.[8] He can also cite war as an example of the paradox that on occasion the law can only be made effective if it is momentarily broken. 'In war . . . there is killing, lying and expropriation solely in order that the authority of life, truth and property may be restored.'[9] But such violation, for however high a motive, incurs guilt which must be born in responsible freedom before God. For Bonhoeffer the onus always lay on the advocate of force to prove his case against non-violence, and even if that case were to be proven – as in effect happened when Bonhoeffer actively joined the conspiracy – the action could never be guiltless, and could only be accompanied by confession and undertaken in penitence. The door is bolted against all self-justifying parading of virtue when force has been used and blood has been shed. 'Why does the Christian Church so often have to look on from outside when the nation is celebrating?' asked Bonhoeffer in *Cost of Discipleship*, and gave the answer in terms of the church's viewing the world in vicarious sorrow 'for its guilt, its fate and its fortune'.[10]

Bonhoeffer took his constant emphasis on guilt and the forgiveness of sins right into the heart of the church's proclamation of peace. Failure to take seriously – that is, to stake one's life upon – the forgiveness of sins was perceived by Bonhoeffer to be at the root of much of the church's reluctance to issue a clear and precise word of peace as the command of God. There was always the dilemma of the lack of adequate knowledge of the situation being addressed. Two responses were possible:

first, there is that of evasion and turning aside to general principles. That is the way the churches have almost always gone. Or alternatively, we can look at the difficulty squarely and then despite all the dangers we can venture to do something *either* by keeping a qualified and intentional silence of ignorance *or* by daring to put the commandment, definitely, exclusively and radically. In that case the church will dare to say, 'Do not engage in this war', 'Be socialists', uttering this commandment as the commandment *of God* in the clear recognition that this can be so. In so doing the church will recognise that it is blaspheming the name of God, erring and sinning, but it may speak thus in faith in the promise of the forgiveness of sins which applies also to the church. Thus the preaching of the commandment is grounded in the preaching of the forgiveness of sins.[11]

We must recognize this insight as fundamental and permanently valid for the way in which the church, in any of its manifestations, pronounces on contemporary issues. A church which in the act of proclaiming what it believes to be the concrete will of God admits also its fallibility, culpability and need of grace, will be saved from that pretentiousness and self-righteousness which so often accompanies the would-be 'prophetic' voice. The moralizer accuses and despises those who do not (yet) see things as he does, be it on the matter of overseas aid, race relations or disarmament. By so doing he prompts his 'opponent' to be yet more defensive and entrenched, and secretly comes to admire himself as a martyr for truth and justice by virtue of the obloquy he receives. A Christian contribution to the current debate on peace and desarmament will be made not simply by what is said, but how it is said.

Peace: the danger of idealization

We saw in Chapter Two that Bonhoeffer's chief concern for the World Alliance during the early 1930s was that it should understand itself in a fully theological sense as representing the church of Christ before the nations, and that as such it should try to deliver a definite command of peace to the world. Negatively, his anxiety centred on the looseness of 'Anglo–Saxon' thought in this branch of the ecumenical movement, which approached the peace question in a purely pragmatic way. It saw peace as a 'problem' requiring for its solution some means of preventing the nations going to war with each other. In the summer of 1932, at the World Alliance youth conference in Czechoslovakia, Bonhoeffer delivered his long paper 'A Theological Basis for the World Alliance?'. In it he criticized the way in which this pragmatism views 'peace' as an absolute ideal, in effect as an 'order of creation' which is identified with the gospel itself 'and as such must be preserved unconditionally'. But peace, says Bonhoeffer, is not an end in itself but 'a command of the angry God, an order for the preservation of the world in the light of Christ'. The next few sentences deserve quoting in full:

International peace is therefore no ideal state, but an order which is directed towards something else and is not valid in itself. The making of such an order of preservation can of course obtain absolute urgency, but never for its own sake; it is always for the sake of him to whom it is directed, namely for the sake of the receiver of the revelation. The broken character of the order of peace is expressed in the fact that the peace commanded by God has two limits, first the truth and secondly justice. There can only be a community of peace when it does not rest on *lies* and *injustice*. Where a community of peace endangers or chokes truth and justice, the community of peace must be broken and battle joined.[12]

It is startling to hear Bonhoeffer criticizing some of his fellow peace-workers on the very same grounds as he rejected the views of the Nazifying 'German Christians'. The pacifist insistence on peace as an absolute end in itself, and the nationalist insistence on the absolute claim of the nation, were alike guilty of elevating certain conditions of human society to eternally valid significance as 'orders of creation'. Peace and the nation should both be seen as *orders of preservation,* pointing beyond themselves to the lordship of Christ who requires human community for his word to be proclaimed and received. God's claim comes upon peace and the nation alike, in the call for truth and justice. Bonhoeffer continues:

For Anglo-Saxon thought, truth and justice remain constantly subordinate to the ideal of peace. Indeed, the existence of peace is virtually itself the proof that truth and justice have been preserved; because the order of peace is a reality of the Gospel, of the kingdom of God, truth and justice can never be contrary to it. But it has become clear that precisely this conception is illusory. The reality of the Gospel is not the external order of peace, nor even the peace of the battle for the same cause, but only the peace of God, which brings about the forgiveness of sins, the reality in which truth and justice are both preserved.[13]

This, it should be noted again, was said in 1932 and therefore before the advent of Hitler to power. It is the language of a representative of Weimar Germany – defeated Germany, Germany still feeling forced to act in the role of under-dog. What Bonhoeffer states in criticism of 'Anglo-Saxon' thought is very similar to voices from the Third World and underprivileged groups in more recent years, who complain that when the rich call for 'peace', to the under-dog it sounds more like the maintenance of injustice.

It is clear that Bonhoeffer was no starry-eyed idealist yearning for peace at any price, and his remarks challenge the motivation of our contemporary peace-movement as sharply as that of the movement fifty years ago. He is providing one illustration of the perennial paradox of life, that we are only likely to reach a good, when we aim for an even greater good. Is even our desire for peace in the world today more than a self-centred wish for preservation? It may be argued that in the nuclear age that is indeed what it has come to, and must come to, for the choice is between peace at any price and total annihilation. But we are unlikely to achieve even that peace if we act only with our survival as our impulse. We need to be challenged on what we wish to survive *for,* however daunting a question that may seem, or irrelevant to the immediate task.

There can then, according to Bonhoeffer, be no simple, direct path to peace conceived as an absolute ideal. The route must lie through the thickets of truth and righteousness between people and nations.

This requires a further point to be spelled out:

If the ordering of eternal peace is not eternally valid, but penetrable at any time, simply because the complete oppression of truth and justice would threaten to make the hearing of the revelation in Christ impossible, then *struggle* is made comprehensible in principle as a possibility of action in the light of Christ. Struggle is not an order of creation, but it can be an order of preservation for Christ's new creation. Struggle can in some cases guarantee openness for the revelation in Christ better than external peace, in that it breaks apart the hardened, self-enclosed order.[14]

Implicit here is the recognition that for the sake of peace we cannot simply shed our nationhood, we cannot abandon the communities to which we belong. The issues of truth and justice and world order are issues between peoples and groups actually in existence, and to imagine that these issues could be dealt with by dissolving the distinctions in some amorphous whole of humanity is facile. That would be rather like attempting to bring peace to a fractious group of individuals by telling that because they are all equally human, and equally part of the one group, they can and should stop quarrelling. The possibility of real difference and grievance is thereby denied, and likewise of actual attempts to dominate and exploit. Peace is only likely to be achieved if the issues of the struggles are made still clearer, and possibly only through a sustained struggle by those whose dignity has been denied, to the point where that dignity is at least acknowledged by the hitherto dominant ones. It will be a process in which the individuals, far from submerging their identities, discover more deeply who in fact they themselves are, and why they are as they are. To move from this analogy (imperfect as all analogies are) back to the world of nations, it means that the struggle for truth and justice as the prerequisite for peace requires not the abandonment of one's nation for the sake of some as yet un-defined 'total community', but a deep and sober identification with one's nation in the context of the search for that greater community. One cannot simply jump out of the tensions of the situation be-tween one's own and other peoples, into an abstract realm above them. Truth and justice are not abstract principles, but the truth of a particular situation and the justice for a particular people in a specific place and time. The struggle for truth and justice therefore demands identification with one's people, either in their liberation from in-justice and oppression, or in the responsibility of exposing and bearing their guilt if they are in any way the oppressors or exploiters. There is therefore a powerful sense in which the cause of peace demands a truly 'patriotic' loyalty. Bonhoeffer's courage in naming struggle alongside peace as an order of preservation must be taken seriously by any who today would see themselves as part of a 'peace-movement'. It is necessary to declare the threat posed by the very presence of massive armaments, but it cannot be pretended that even if these were to be magically removed the issues of conflict between east and west would also have disappeared. One of the prime needs of our age is to learn how to live with struggle and conflict, and one of Bonhoeffer's major contributions was to force the fact of struggle under the noses of his fellow-Christians, and to point towards the ultimate theological frame of reference within which it can be handled, namely the doctrine of the forgiveness of sins as the ground of true community.

War as total annihilation

By *struggle,* however, Bonhoeffer did not mean *war.* The justifi-cation of struggle does not sanction war.

The right of war can be derived from the right of struggle as little as the use of torture may be derived from the necessity of legal procedures in human society. War in our day no longer falls under the concept of struggle because it is the certain self-annihilation of both combatants. It is in no way to be regarded as an order of preservation in the light of revelation, simply because it is so destructive.[15]

'The certain self-annihilation of both combatants': such words have a contemporary ring half a century later of which Bonhoeffer could never have dreamt. If the Second World War did not realize this full horror, it is now a fact of life that 'mutually assured destruction' is not only a possibility, but an actual, planned ingredient in the strategy of deterrence. With this in mind, we may listen to Bonhoeffer's next words:

The power of annihilation extends both to the inner and the outer man. War today destroys both soul and body. Now because we can in no way understand war as one of God's orders of preservation and thus as the commandment of God, and because on the other hand war needs idealising and idolising to be able to live, war today, and therefore the next war, must be utterly *rejected* by the church.[16]

It is often claimed on behalf of nuclear deterrence that it has preserved the peace between east and west for over thirty years. Might it not, then, represent an 'order of preservation'? Does it not at least preserve some kind of stability among the nations, in which life can at least continue? Two points may be made in reply to this.

The first is on a pragmatic level. It might be possible to conceive of mutual deterrence as a preserving force, if the 'balance of terror' was static. But it is not. What we have is not a steady equipoise, but a constant effort by each side to outweigh the other's capability. The 'balance' is at the mercy of the technological thrust on each side and could become highly unstable.

The second objection is theological, but no less practical in its implications. An order of preservation, in Bonhoeffer's sense, is valid only if it preserves human life for the advent of the word of Christ, only if it keeps life open towards the recognition of its true significance in God. It is highly questionable whether nuclear deterrence, by its very nature, can do this. Already, it represents the beginning of the 'inner' as well as 'outer' annihilation. Because nuclear weapons (even bearing in mind the doctrine of 'flexible response') raise destruction to an absolute level, they both require and consolidate the absolutization of the claim of the nation. Theologically, this is idolatry, the assumption by a human community of attributes which rightly pertain only to God. The nihilistic, self-contradictory consequence of all idolatry is immediately apparent – the invitation to self-destruction. The nation, raising itself and its existence to absolute and ultimate significance, opens the way to its total obliteration. Grasping at becoming an order of creation, it becomes an order of chaos. This is the ultimate theological ground for rejecting nuclear weapons as ethically unacceptable.

Bonhoeffer was at his most outspoken on the peace question at the Fanö conference of the World Alliance in 1934, where he delivered a paper and preached a sermon. The latter has survived, and is based on Psalm 85.8: 'I will hear what God the Lord will speak, for he will speak peace unto his people, and to his saints.' Peace, states Bonhoeffer, is not a problem, but the command of God. It is concretized in the church of Christ, transcending all national and racial boundaries which are relativized under Christ.

How does peace come about? Through a system of political treaties? Through the investment of international capital in different countries? Through the big banks, through money? Or through universal peaceful rearmament in order to guarantee peace? Through none of these, for the single reason that in all of them peace is confused with safety. There is no way to peace along the way of safety. For peace must be dared. It is the great venture. It can never be safe. Peace is the opposite of security. To demand guarantees is to mistrust and this mistrust in turn brings forth war. To look for guarantees is to want to protect oneself. Peace means to give oneself altogether to the law of God, wanting no security, but in faith and obedience laying the destiny of the nations in the hand of Almighty God, not trying to direct it for selfish purposes.[17]

These words, spoken four years before Munich, inevitably invite the charge of naivety. The late Richard Crossman who attended Fanö evidently thought so at the time.[18] But it is to be noted that Bonhoeffer is not laying down a pacifist line as a prescription to ensure safety. Nothing in this world can ensure survival, and once the question of safety becomes determinative, Bonhoeffer is arguing, we are on the wrong track altogether and chasing a will o' the wisp. The way of 'security' is in fact highly insecure, as is all too evident at the present time, for it is essentially self-contradictory. The desire to 'negotiate from strength' means that in order to have something to bargain with, one must go to the conference table ostensibly desiring peace but all the time trying to ensure that one *is* more powerfully armed than one's opponent. One cannot adopt that position without conceding to one's opponent the right to play the same game. The escalation of the arms race is therefore inevitable. The search for security through strength is, paradoxically, the certain road to utter vulnerability. At some point, some step which is a venture of trust must be made if the vicious spiral is not to continue indefinitely. Bonhoeffer's words need far less justification today than they did when he originally spoke them at Fanö.

There is another paradox in seeking security for one's country through the capacity for absolute destruction. It is that the greater the commitment to the military capability, the actual country which is supposed to be defended retreats progressively from view. Nuclear weapons, by their very enormity, introduce a momentum of their own into a nation's perception of itself in the world. They demand and create their own justification. As stated earlier in this chapter, Britain adopted atomic armoury virtually through an assumption that as a 'great power' it was natural to do so. And equally, to divest ourselves of such weapons now may seem a masochistic exercise in telling ourselves and everyone else that we are no longer such a power, nor wish to be so again. In the search for justification, the threat posed by the east now becomes a dogmatic, unquestionable conviction to the extent of denying that *anything* which the Soviet Union may do or propose or ask for can be anything other than sinister in purpose. There is surely a line, somewhere, between 'realism' concerning Soviet (as any other national) intentions on the one hand, and paranoia that can *only* view the Soviet Union as a threat. By now, anything that deserves to be called 'patriotism', any real positive regard for what one's country is and represents, has long since disappeared. By now, one's country no longer has any identity or definition of its own. It is seen only negatively in terms of the 'enemy', indeed the 'enemy' is actually now required for a true self-understanding and sense of value. If we had no enemy threatening us, wouldn't that mean there was little in us worth the envy of others? We end up more concerned to be anti-Russian than positively British. Because this is the psychologically diseased path of 'inner annihilation' which we are treading, Bonhoeffer's words come back at us as we try to visualize the progressive narrowing of options which will ensue unless the route is changed: 'The ultimate question for a responsible man to ask is . . . how the coming generation is to live. It is only from this question, with its responsibility towards history, that fruitful solutions can come, even if for the time being they are very humiliating.'[19]

   If patriotism of any sort means the love of country, to enter the country in the nuclear competition is hardly patriotic. Such war is not that of an earlier kind, where a number of people are called to risk or lay down their lives for their country, which will continue through the majority who survive. There can be no nuclear patriotism, for nuclear war risks the obliteration of the country as such. Bonhoeffer, for his part, scarcely ever even mentions the 'just war' theory, but in *Ethics* he is quite clear that 'total war' completely changes the significance of international conflict:

Western wars have always distinguished between means of warfare which are permissible and rightful and those which are prohibited and criminal. It was belief in a just, divine government of the world which made it possible to dispense with the perhaps effective but certainly un-Christian practices of killing the innocent – torture, extortion and the rest. War now always remained a kind of appeal to the arbitration of God, which both sides were willing to accept. It is only when Christian faith is lost that man must himself make use of all means, even criminal ones, in order to secure by force the victory of his cause. And thus . . . there comes total war, war of destruction, in which everything, even crime, is justified if it serves to further our own cause, and in which the enemy, whether he be armed or defenceless, is treated as a criminal.[20]

Nuclear weaponry demands that we place so high a value on our particular community, its distinctiveness (however ill-defined) and values (however relative) that we should be prepared for its sake either to inflict mass slaughter on others, or risk total obliteration ourselves, or both. And is there not something noble in wishing to be extinct rather than under the heel of an oppressor ('We must be free or die . . .'), to be dead rather than red? Lord Chalfont stated this view bluntly in December 1980: 'there can be nothing – *nothing* – worse than a life in which, by the exercise of relentless tyranny, the precious gifts of liberty and dignity are denied'.[21]

The grim scenario of subjection and occupation must indeed be faced as the ultimate backcloth of responsible decision on these issues. Lord Chalfont, however, is simply wrong. There *is* something worse than to live under such tyranny. It is to exist without faith and hope. An occupied Britain would still be Britain, and the example of eastern Europe does not counsel despair. It is a massive fact, and highly uncomfortable for the Kremlin itself, that communism has *not* been successfully imposed on the peoples of eastern Europe. Beneath the military and bureaucratic machinery the highly distinctive national characteristics of the peoples live on because *this is what these people are,* and these characteristics are genuinely owned by them. They simply cannot be removed. And any who talk of the end of 'Christian values' in such a situation do not know what such values are. In fact in the east much lively Christianity survives, with a good deal to teach the churches in the west about living without privileges. And Dietrich Bonhoeffer himself is among the greatest standing witnesses to the fact that even if the believer is in prison, his or her faith need not be. It is no accident that it was in his prison cell that Bonhoeffer tried to discern the outlines of a Christianity without 'religion'. With Karl Barth, he believed that because God really is God, and not a part of the world, he is not to be identified with any one structure, ideology, culture or social form, not even a 'religious' form of it. But God is not apart from the world. Christ crucified is the witness to God's strange presence in the heart of the world, and our encounter with God becomes real in sharing Christ's life for others – whoever and wherever those others may be. There is literally no place, no situation, where this faith in Christ is impossible, and where this responsibility may not arise. On the darkest day of this life thus far, 21st July 1944, the day after the great and noble conspiracy had at last been attempted and had failed, Bonhoeffer turned again to his favourite prophet Jeremiah, to the words he spoke to his scribe Baruch, on the day when Jerusalem's end seemed certain:

And do you seek great things for yourself? Seek them not; for behold, I am bringing evil upon all flesh, says the Lord; but I will give you your life as a prize of war in all places to which you may go.[22]

In the end, all that faith asks for is a foothold in human history. It does not ask for that history to be ended. The man of faith will want his country to continue its history, however dark the scene may appear to be for the moment. True patriotism, if faced with the ultimate choice, would rather the country continued in weakness than be obliterated in a trial of strength. That is not to make the existence of the country an end in itself, but to keep it as an order of preservation, a matrix of human community in which the one Lord, Christ, can be present.

The arms race as divine judgment

One last point must be made regarding how we interpret the fact that nuclear weapons actually exist. It is difficult to believe that, had Bonhoeffer survived, he would have done other than regard them as signs of the ultimate human apostasy, in face of the divine command to preserve life and not to kill. Quite what his views would have been on the means to remove or control them, we cannot speculate. But one suspects that he would not have been satisfied with a stance which, seeing such weapons as unacceptable, simply called for their abolition.

The previous chapter dealt with Bonhoeffer's heavy emphasis on human guilt and divine judgment, and on redemption as involving the acknowledgment of that guilt and judgment. We have also noted his suspicion of 'moral crusades'. It is at this point that the contemporary peace-movement should listen to Bonhoeffer as a critical ally, for there is an attitude which, naturally revolted by the appalling consequences of a nuclear holocaust, simply seeks to protest. The weapons are regarded as evil incarnate, an alien cancerous growth on humanity which must be excised by some means or other. But the danger of such moral crusades is that the evil is located almost entirely in certain tangible objects or persons outside oneself. Indeed it could be that such crusades are partly motivated by a deep yearning of the human mind to come to terms with the darker and destructive impulses of human nature, by projecting all sense of evil onto some external, objectifiable item. As is well known, that can readily happen in war when the enemy is made to embody all that seems dark and threatening, all the subterranean fears lurking in the soul. Those who throw themselves into a campaign against the bomb must face this question for themselves, for the sake of the campaign itself. If nuclear weaponry is regarded as simply alien to us, our efforts will be futile. The bomb is, after all, a human creation. As such, might it not be an expression of what we ourselves are, all of us, campaigners included? A desire to abolish the bomb, pure and simple, might easily be an attempt to repress and bury the unmentionable fact of our depravity. If so, it will be a futile attempt.

In this respect one must welcome Jim Garrison's highly original and disturbing thesis *The Darkness of God. Theology after Hiroshima.*[23] I do not pretend to agree with, or even comprehend, the whole of his argument which owes at least as much to the depth psychology of Jung as to Christian theology. But one must be grateful for a book which asks whether the western Christian tradition has so moralized its view of both God and man that it cannot now fully grasp the reality of evil as represented by nuclear weaponry. In the biblical tradition, especially the Old Testament and apocalyptic writings, God himself is seen bringing about 'evil' for the sake of his ultimately good purpose. Is there, then, an 'evil' side to God as well as a good? Yes, states Garrison, as there is in ourselves. What is lacking in this argument, however, is an adequate treatment of the biblical notion of *judgment,* a judgment which because of its implacability can only appear in human experience as 'evil'. Garrison speaks of God and man 'co-creating' evil. But does not the Bible speak rather of human bondage to sin and the divine judgment being two aspects of the same process? Thus Paul:

Therefore God gave them up in the lusts of their hearts to impurity, to the dishonouring of their bodies among themselves, because they exchanged the truth about God for a lie and worshipped and served the creature rather than the Creator . . . For this reason God gave them up to dishonourable passions . . .

(Romans 1.24f)

That man is caught in the products of his own sinfulness, corrupting his history, is itself a manifestation of divine judgment and wrath. One may extend this to the perversion of nationhood when seen as an end in itself, expressed in the means of mutually assured destruction. Karl Barth's comments on these same verses then sound especially fitting:

The confusion avenges itself and becomes its own punishment. The forgetting of the true God is already the breaking loose of his wrath against those who forget him. . . Our conduct becomes governed precisely by what we desire. By a strict inevitability we reach the goal we have set before us. The images and likenesses, whose meaning we have failed to perceive, become themselves purpose and content and end . . . And now there is no higher power to protect them from what they have set on high . . . They have wished to experience the known god of this world: well! they have experienced him.[24]

Barth himself, incidentally, came to be a vigorous opponent of atomic weapons when, thirty years after he wrote these words, they emerged on the world scene.

Bonhoeffer, for his part, shared this deep consciousness of judgment which, as we have seen already, meant that condemnation of sin begins with confession. From a Christian standpoint, opposition to nuclear weaponry must be a confessing, repentant opposition. That we are landed with nuclear weapons is itself a judgment upon us, and we cannot expect them to be removed without a confession of our guilt, without a recognition that the source of their production lies not only in the Pentagon, or the Kremlin, but in the fears and aggressive impulses within ourselves.

8
This People

Earlier in this book, we have attended to Dietrich Bonhoeffer's insights into the 'real', the actual life and humanity to which any authentic loving must attach itself, and we have attempted to apply this to 'love of country'. Since then we have explored further the necessity to take account of certain elements within this 'reality', which includes both the good of the inherited tradition and the guilt which has been incurred in the nation's history. But all along we have been carrying an assumption which may seem almost too obvious for stating, namely, that by 'country' we essentially mean its people: in our case, the people who happen to live in the place called the United Kingdom.

To bring this assumption out into the open can have somewhat subversive consequences, for all too often the people are encouraged to think of 'the country' as somehow different from and elevated above themselves. 'Your King and Country Need You', stated Kitchener's famous recruiting poster of the First World War. '*Your* resolution, *your* courage, *your* cheerfulness, will bring *us* victory', ran a Whitehall-produced poster in the autumn of 1939 – which puzzled many folk who until then had thought it was their own freedom they were fighting for. Perhaps it sounds as if people are being asked to be blatantly selfish if they are urged to make an effort bringing benefit to themselves, and therefore 'the country' must be held aloft as a personalized ideal. But in the end the country exists only in the people and as the people. We may talk of the country's traditions, but traditions can only live within people's minds. We may talk of the country's needs and interests, but whose needs and interests are they if not 'the people who live here'? Britain is more prone than other western nations to this verbal de-populating of itself, partly because of its highly symbolic constitution centred on the monarchy. Despite all the talk of democracy, there is still a powerful impetus in the British imagination which locates the essence of nationhood in the sovereign, with the people defined as his or her 'subjects'. The notion of 'citizenship' has still not fully percolated through British awareness, two hundred years after Tom Paine stated the charter of modern democracy in terms of the sovereignty and rights of *the people,* and despite the fact that the sovereign strictly reigns only by consent of Parliament which represents the people. One commentator goes so far as to suggest

that in Britain monarchy 'is used not, as can be the case in
Scandinavian countries, as a symbol of the people, but as a symbol of
the lack of value of the people'.[1]

The traditional reluctance of many British people to identify
Britain with themselves is also partly a product of one of the
outstanding features of the country's history – its continuity through
evolution. For centuries, the people have not had to pick themselves
up after either radical revolution and its aftermath, or defeat and
occupation by a foreign power, to ask 'Where do *we* go from here?'
The sense of being looked after by 'them' is deeply ingrained, and
hence that propensity to look for representations of 'England' in
figures and scenes far removed from daily existence, which was
noted in the first chapter. And of course some will wish to argue that
it is just because the people have, on the whole, been so well looked
after by those born to govern, that they have remained so cohesive a
unit in an age when much of Europe was shaken to the very
foundations.

Be all this as it may, the view to be taken here is that the reality of
the country is concentrated in the people who live here, in what they
actually experience, do, and suffer. High Tory feathers were ruffled
by well-meaning attempts at 'revising' the National Anthem recently. But no trendy tinkering can compare with Ebenezer Elliott's
truly radicalized lines composed well over a century ago during the
Chartist struggles:

> When wilt Thou save the people,
> O God of mercy, when?
> The people, Lord, the people!
> Not thrones and crowns, but men!
> God save the people; Thine they are,
> Thy children, as Thine angels fair;
> From vice, oppression, and despair,
> God save the people!

Love of country therefore means love of the actual people. But just
what does it mean to talk of 'a people'? Granted there are something
like 60 million people living in the United Kingdom, what makes
them *a* people? Is not this yet another convenient abstraction, an
effort to impose pattern and order on the untidiness of life? What
makes people into 'a people' is indeed very hard to define, although it
need not be the less real for eluding precise analysis and definition.
Society does not exist for the convenience of social theorists any
more than God exists for the benefit of theologians. Put crudely,
when people feel themselves to be a people, then they are so. Of
course there are certain more objective constituents of this sense of
community. People cannot be expected to feel part of the same com-

munity unless, as well as living in the same territory, there is a measure of shared language, tradition, historical experience and commitment to common political institutions and objectives. That this is *not* the case with large segments of the population in Northern Ireland highlights the fact that elsewhere in the United Kingdom the inhabitants do by and large feel that they belong together, and feel moreover that a sense of 'national unity' is a good thing.

National community

The word 'community' has quietly slipped into this chapter already, and taken its seat as if by right. It has become the catch-all in modern talk about human society, and shares the fate of all such terms by becoming as ill-defined as it is well-used. We speak of 'the community' meaning, rather vaguely, the wider society beyond the immediate context of home, school, church or place of work. But we also speak of 'community' in the abstract, referring to some absolute ideal of human society. Much talk about 'community' as such an ideal has been provoked by a sense of loss, of nostalgia for a former way of life believed to have been disrupted by industrialism. The outlines of that ideal may be derived from a variety of sources. German social theorists of the nineteenth century tended to take as their reference-point the Greek city-state. British social critics, especially socialists, looked to rural England and the supposedly 'organic' life of the village. Loving one's country will at least mean cherishing this ideal of community for the whole people, appreciating it where it actually exists, fostering it where it is in process of development, and striving to bring it to birth where it is presently lacking.

But this is also the point of divergence and conflict. Perceptions as to what constitutes the true community of the nation, and how it ought to be realized, vary considerably especially in conjunction with social perspective. The Etonian who migrates through Balliol into the Tory-and-city corridors of power views the nation as working according to a system which, if not perfect, has been tried and tested by time. If there were a better one, no doubt it would have appeared by now. Minor adaptations may be needed here and there, a slight trimming of the sails according to the weather, but by and large the ship is sound. All that is needed is for the lower decks to pull their weight. Members of a middle-class family will judge society in terms of the prospects it offers for personal fulfilment and achievement, with a great deal of emphasis on 'freedom' and 'incentive'. Working-class aspirations may be no less reward-orientated but with a much more corporate emphasis. The understanding of what national loyalty means will shift according to these social perspectives, and no one class or political outlook has a monopoly of it. The Conservative Party annual conference, bedecked in red, white and blue, certainly tries to sell itself as guardian of the nation's pride. But socialism also has its own patriotic tradition, apart from some highly intellectualized elements who affect to despise it in favour of a rarified type of internationalism. No more patriotic piece of writing has appeared this century than George Orwell's war-time essay *The Lion and the Unicorn*,[2] much of which is an attempt to rescue the word 'patriotism' itself from the right-wing embrace:

Patriotism has nothing to do with Conservatism. It is actually the opposite of Conservatism, since it is a devotion to something that is always changing and yet is felt to be mystically the same. It is the bridge between the future and the past. No real revolutionary has ever been an internationalist.[3]

Orwell was as certain as any that Hitler had to be defeated. At the time of writing (1940–41) he was equally certain that victory required a socialist revolution in Britain, since only then would the economy and industrial base be put on a sound enough footing for the war-effort to succeed. And only when the people themselves took charge and dismissed the 'old and silly' who had been mismanaging affairs for so long, would progress be made. With the wisdom of hindsight, we can see how Orwell reckoned neither with the ability of a coalition government to organize a war-economy, nor with the significance of the United States both before and after its entry into the war. But much of what he says is not devalued by his polemical shortcomings. Above all his book is marked by a lively sense of what is distinctively British at a commonplace, everyday level. He describes the sensation of arriving back in England after foreign travel:

Even in the first few minutes dozens of small things conspire to give you this feeling. The beer is bitterer, the coins are heavier, the grass is greener, the advertisements are more blatant. The crowds in the big towns, with their mild knobby faces, their bad teeth and gentle manners, are different from a European crowd.[4]

It is the 'gentleness' of English manners and civilization which Orwell identifies as the key national characteristic. It was this characteristic of ordinary folk which gave him hope for a revolution as humane as it was just. Such people could be entrusted with power:

The heirs of Nelson and of Cromwell are not in the House of Lords. They are in the fields and the streets, in the factories and the armed forces, in the four-ale bar and the suburban back gardens; and at present they are still kept under by a generation of ghosts.[5]

Orwell hardly seems to reckon with the difficulty that a people so 'gentle' are unlikely to work themselves into the ruthlessness required for a genuine revolution. But Orwell has made his point.

The country is for the people, not vice-versa, indeed the country *is* the people. Patriotism therefore need not mean a commitment to keeping things as they are, a reverence which drapes the Union Jack over privilege and inequality. It can equally mean a commitment to change, if one's love of country really is a love of its people, and especially of those whose plight gives them little outward cause to be grateful for living here.

Indeed it is all too clear that by 'patriotism' many people do *not* mean a commitment to the welfare of the people of Britain, but an attachment to its present appearance which includes some massive and growing inequalities. When health workers campaign for a wage appropriate to their effort and importance in the community they are accused of 'holding the country to ransom', and their behaviour is contrasted by Mrs Thatcher with that of the troops returning from the South Atlantic. It is hard to see how they are 'letting the country down' any more than those who invest overseas the profits of industry in Britain.

Britain: inequality, diversity and unity

The degree to which a population feels itself to be 'a people' will vary with time and circumstance. The British have characteristically felt themselves to be most intensely one with themselves when faced with a danger common to all, as supremely happened in 1940. Out of that time of common danger and common sacrifice was born a hope for a social equalization and integration unknown in Britain before. Daniel Jenkins suggests that 1940–60 may well be judged the *only* period in their national history when the British have been a substantially united people.[6] Since then, with steepening economic decline, diverging political stances and interests have again become more sharply defined. There are of course those who are only too glad to see the end of 'consensus', equating it with a commitment to nothing in particular except a painless existence for the floating voters.

On a Marxist analysis, conflict is necessarily of the essence of the present social order, and if it is not immediately apparent, that is only because one of the subtle tactics of capitalist society, especially in Britain, is to disguise it as far as possible. On this view, Britain's ills stem from the indefinite postponement of the social revolution which began in industrialization. The industrial revolution saw the emergence of a new race of bourgeois, entrepreneurial capitalists. Had they been faithful to their own instincts, they would have completely wrested power from the old aristocracy, and in turn paved the way for the proletarian revolution. As it was, the new capitalists compromised with gentility, adopting its manners, ideals and education. What has resulted, therefore, is a society still highly stratified, essentially governed by a patrician élite, with an alliance of old and new rich against the proletariat. Britain is governed by an élite, sometimes Conservative and sometimes Labour, which is not really interested in the economic development of the nation as a whole, so much as the preservation of the comfortable distinctions between middle-class and working-class life.[7] Until *power* really changes hands, and is grasped by the working people, conflict is inevitable and right.

The importance of the Marxist analysis is its ruthless exposure of the fracture-lines in society. Conflicts of interest between social classes are real, and any talk of the nation as a community, or family, or even as 'the people', which has not passed through the Marxist grid, is liable to be deemed superficial and sentimental. Not that at present it should be necessary to have a course in Marxism to be made uneasy with the thought of the nation as a unity. The 'two nations' theme has returned as grim-faced as ever, in terms of relative deprivation. In fact it never really disappeared, for despite all the post-war efforts at income redistribution and taxation policies, Britain remained a profoundly unequal society in terms of personal wealth and command of resources, even in the welfare state. Now, with about four million unemployed, simply to have a job is to join the privileged. At the bottom of the pile, a new Dickensian society is emerging in our cities among the homeless and jobless. Worst of all, much of the black population, already inhabiting much of the worst housing and suffering the most blatant discrimination in employment, has been made to feel virtually disowned by the nation. Small wonder that to young Rastafarians Britain is not home, but Babylon, the alien place of exile.

How then, in the midst of such inequality, can we speak of 'the people'? We can speak of it because it would seem that in the consciousness of most people, in Britain at any rate, a surprising sense of national solidarity still seems to surpass the consciousness of class division and conflict. This is not to deny the reality of class consciousness and class interest, but it is to question whether this is of such paramount, determinative significance as some social theorists consider it is, or ought to be. One suspects that most of the inhabitants of this country, including those who are suffering most acutely from present iniquities and inequalities, *do* regard the nation as in some sense a family – a quarrelling one maybe, but a family nonetheless (most quarrels, after all, take place in families). The quarrelling may run very deep, may well be about how the family should be run, may even be about power and for power (again, as often happens in families). But for most people a sense of total solidarity is hard to displace, which is one of the reasons why some who in theory have every reason to vote communist just do not do so. In the 1979 General Election, even the Glasgow Gorbals gave only 1.1% of its votes to the Communist Party candidate. To fail to recognize the felt importance of cohesiveness because it seems counter to one's theory of how things *should* be, is simply another instance of the tendency to show more concern for one's ideology than for the reality.

As well as inequality, diversity confronts the notion of 'the people'. Of course diversity and inequality are frequently entangled with each other. To talk of race in Britain at the moment, is to talk both about ethnic or cultural differences and about gross inequality of treatment. In a crude but telling simile, race has been likened to the barium meal which shows up to the extent of inequity and exploitation already there in the body. But it is not just privilege and deprivation that are highlighted by the arrival of the ethnic minorities in Britain. There has always been diversity within British society as well, and what is now styled the 'multicultural' society can be interpreted as a peculiarly heavy emphasis of this fact. There is not just one culture, one social norm, in Britain, but a matrix of subcultures. Those whose objection to black immigration is that it introduces an 'alien' culture into this country have a grossly oversimplified view of 'British culture'. It is an understandable tendency to regard what we are used to as 'normal' or even 'proper', and what is new and different as abnormal or even a threat. But it is not at all clear that the 'alien' cultures now in Britain threaten what is good in British life. In what way does the often authoritarian family style of some West Indian communities threaten British domestic mores? How does the emphasis on tolerance and hospitality so characteristic of Indian religion subvert 'British values' of decency? Or in what sense is the Islamic duty to provide for the relief of the poor in one's neighbourhood an insult to the British way of life?

We need reminding, as was said in Chapter Five, that British culture has never been static, never monochrome. If it has a genius or characteristic, it is to be always experimenting – albeit cautiously – with a variety of styles and modes of life which interact or compete in many different ways with enriching effects. It is a place of tensions between elements which may indeed represent quite different interests and convictions, but which rarely seek to annihilate each other. Oliver Cromwell was hardly weak on convictions yet it was he, of all people, who told the feuding dogmaticians of the Church of Scotland, 'I beseech you, in the bowels of Christ, think it possible you may be mistaken.' Indeed, it is in matters of religion that Britain has had one of her most effective lessons in accepting plurality as a positive gain. Those who dissented from the Church of England in the seventeenth and eighteenth centuries were regarded as alien and probably suspect in their national loyalty (as ethnic minorities now, in some eyes). It took a very long time indeed to convince Britain's governing classes that one *could* disengage from the national church yet be as devoted as any to the realm. Nor has the full contribution of religious dissent to the life and vitality of Britain even yet received its full due. Much so-called church history is in fact Anglican history, that is, not only written about the Anglican Church, but from its perspective. The Victorian chapel is still frequently dismissed as a sectarian, puritanical and self-righteous home of cant. Yet in its heyday, especially in the northern towns, chapel provided many ordinary people with one of the richest textures of personal and communal life which the local scene has ever offered. It was not only the gathering of the faithful on Sundays. In its weekday activities, as varied as study and craft circles, choral societies, educational institutes and literary societies, social service projects, political debating circles and savings schemes, it brought together religion and recreation, liberal education and political awareness, social responsibility and self-improvement – all within a network of close ties of friendship and kinship (and the often intervening courtship). Perhaps its very success was its own undoing, for chapel life released into the wider world so many gifted and newly confident people from the lower middle-classes who often cast around for still wider opportunities of initiative and leadership, unable to be confined by the local scene which nurtured them (so, for example, Welsh nonconformity and such as David Lloyd George). That it all took place independently of the establishment, which indeed often regarded it with active distaste, and yet had such an enriching effect on national life, is but one instance of the positive benefits of allowing distinctive groups to be themselves and thereby contribute to the whole.

This requires that we acknowledge a certain competitiveness in different cultural stances, and that we should be prepared to ask whether a mode which happens to be dominant at the moment has any divine right to be the assumed norm for the national character. Donald Horne has written provocatively of the ambivalent attitudes to the industrial revolution in Britain, represented by what he calls the 'northern' and 'southern' metaphors. Each has its own perception of 'Britishness'. According to the northern metaphor, Britain is pragmatic, experimental, Puritan and bourgeois, and believes in struggle. According to the southern metaphor, Britain is romantic, illogical, muddled and 'divinely lucky'; also essentially Anglican, aristocratic, traditional. Both metaphors tend to a sinful excess – the northern to avaricious self-interest, the southern to pride and a belief that men are born primarily to serve. But, argues Horne, many of the ills that have led to Britain's present problems are to be laid at the door of the southern metaphor and its overall dominance over those who govern. 'The Southern Metaphor led the British to conclude that their success was due not to their own efforts but to the whimsicalities of their superior nature. It was not for what they did but for what they were that destiny had rewarded them so lavishly.'[8] Horne's eventual conclusion is that real change in Britain will only occur 'to the extent that the two-nation system disintegrates into a more diverse society, with a multiplicity of conflicting values and snobberies in which diverse groups of people can follow their diverse purposes with sustaining belief and the ability to support their diverse images of society and of social values.'[9]

   William Waldegrave, a representative of intellectual Toryism in the Disraelian tradition, writes very effectively of the need for community, and *particular* communities, in sustaining human life.[10] Conservatism, he argues, sees the natural object of allegiance not in the 'politically delineated state, but the naturally grown community – village, district, college, factory, town or fraternity'. In such 'natural' communities is where development over time generates a sense of belonging and allegiance. 'What the Conservative sees is that those who thought that such allegiance must only and always attach to the nation, let alone the organs of the State, were making the mistake of equating nation and community. The two are far different creatures.'[11] Waldegrave sees modern British history as a finally *unsuccessful* attempt at creating a 'national community', not least because of the re-emergence of regionalism.

   One may readily admit that 'community' must in the first place mean something more local and immediate than 'nation', as something with which people may naturally identify. And in fact a strong sense of local solidarity has been one of the traditional strengths of British life. But to conclude that because the nation as a community is hard to define, or has not so far been completely realized, nor is ever likely to be perfectly achieved, we should therefore drop the notion altogether, is a dangerous counsel of despair. For under the cloak of diversity, and in the name of 'community', savage inequalities can shelter *ad infinitum*. Declining Welsh valleys and decaying inner-cities can be written off as separate 'communities' of no real concern to the rest of society. Some sense of an overall belonging together, and of mutual responsibility, is necessary for the people as a whole. It need not be a bleak vision of monolithic sameness nor – and here one agrees heartily with Waldegrave – need it mean allegiance to the state or its organs. But somehow we need both a loyalty to the best of the particular inheritance and culture by which we distinguish ourselves, and an exposure to what is happening elsewhere and among the people as a whole. A. H. Halsey unashamedly applies the image and value of the family to the nation as a whole, as the desirable ideal. *Fraternity* is required in addition to liberty and equality, and as providing a third way between capitalism and communism:

Past failures to achieve fair and equal social distribution have driven some to apathy, others to belief in a violent seizure of power and the imposition of an authoritarian social order, and still others to denial of the possibility or even desirability of an egalitarian society. These are the roads to tyranny. Our experiences of industrial, nationalist, and racial conflict continually demonstrate the need for a new sense of equality to replace old class-restricted liberties and status-crippled fraternities. We have still to provide a common experience of citizenship in childhood and old age, in work and play, and in health and sickness. We have still, in short, to develop a common culture to replace the divided cultures of class and status.[12]

Halsey realistically perceives that fraternity cannot be imposed or legislated, but, in the end, only fostered and encouraged where it is actually growing. Liberty, equality and fraternity as a whole can only come through persuasion, not dictatorship. To that end, we should encourage those institutions which require and foster those values and enable themselves to prove their worth.

But liberty, equality and fraternity can disappear in abstractions. We need to ask not only what the better society will be like, but what we ourselves shall be like as persons actively involved in the discovery of a common humanity, making ventures in fraternity across the lines of privilege and social class.

Dietrich Bonhoeffer: a bourgeois theologian?

It is just at this point that a certain aspect of Bonhoeffer's life and thought which has until recently received relatively little attention, is very pertinent. At certain stages of his life Bonhoeffer was deeply concerned about how a person of his own social standing should relate to other groups, and indeed what it meant for both himself and these others to be 'German'. Today of course one of the liveliest issues in theology concerns the degree to which a theologian's outlook reflects his or her social background. One of the main tenets of 'political theology' is that, since the bias of the gospel is towards the poor, authentic theology is a theology not only for but *of* the poor and any theology produced from a middle-class background (especially white and male), is *ipso facto* suspect. From this perspective, Bonhoeffer himself must be highly suspect, for all his supposedly 'radical' influence in post-war western Christianity. His concern for modern, secular man who has 'come of age' may be understandable for a highly intellectual mind seeking to come to terms with the scientific milieu of the industrialized west. But the question of 'religion' is not the most crucial one. First and foremost is the question asked by the poor, how man can be *human* today. So runs the contemporary critique, and the modern political theologian will have little difficulty in showing how Bonhoeffer seemed relatively naive and partial in his social judgments and, lacking the sociological tools to analyse the structure of his society, worked with un-examined bourgeois presuppositions. *Ethics* for instance provides passage after passage where Bonhoeffer seems to advocate a highly stratified, patriarchal society as most nearly conforming to 'Christian' order. He sees the emancipation of man and the emergence of the notion of 'the rights of man' in the eighteenth century highly ambiguous in their consequences:

Bourgeoisie and reason were henceforward inseparable. But behind the bourgeoisie there loomed the dark menace of the masses, the fourth estate. All it stood for was simply the masses and their misery. The masses have equal contempt for the laws of blood and for the laws of reason. They make their own law, the law of misery. It is a violent law, and short-lived. We today are standing at the culmination and crisis of this uprising.[13]

Here, it may well be felt, we have a typical bourgeois perspective which views the ominous, faceless conglomeration ('masses') of society beneath the sphere where truly civilized living takes place. Then, also in *Ethics,* we have Bonhoeffer's theological arguments for a necessary relationship of 'superior' and 'inferior' (albeit under the overall superiority and lordship of God). Moreover it may be argued that Bonhoeffer's central ethical notion of responsible action or 'deputyship' reveals the bourgeois assumption that ethics is about *individual* action and ignores the corporate dimension.

Are we then left with a bourgeois, conservative and elitist Bonhoeffer, whose later thought simply reflected the fact that he was becoming affianced to an East Prussian *Junker* family? A German equivalent of T. S. Eliot and his *Idea of a Christian Society*? If this were in fact the sum total of his social consciousness we would indeed have to consign him regretfully to his particular historical context for good. But that is not the whole story. There is another side to Bonhoeffer, namely, the way in which he *was* conscious of social perspectives other than his own, and further, the way in which he attempted, more seriously than with most people of his back-ground, to see the world through the experience of people very different from himself. He gives us a demonstration of one who, while not disowning his social tradition and upbringing, was able to transcend its limitations to a remarkable degree through encounter with others. As such, he does not offer us a blue-print for the new society, but he does show us how it is possible to make personal ventures in fraternity. Such ventures, with the particular experience and new understandings of life which they open up, may seem trivial by comparison with the overall grand vision of the new order. But without them social transformation towards a national community of 'the people' is hardly possible.

Bonhoeffer and the proletariat

As was seen in Chapter Two, Bonhoeffer's upbringing was in a family which embodied the highest standards of upper middle-class German life, combining elements from both the liberal and aristo-cratic traditions of nineteenth-century culture. It was a privileged environment, and Dietrich was not the only member of the family to be highly conscious of this. His older brother Karl-Friedrich returned from the trenches an ardent socialist, and from that point on the Bonhoeffer home frequently resounded to lively social and political debate. Dietrich himself never exchanged the liberal perspective for the socialist, but early in his career there are more than hints of a desire to come to terms with the fact of the urban working-class. In *Sanctorum Communio* (of all places, one might say) there is a remarkable section on 'Church and Proletariat' – and so provocative did it appear to Bonhoeffer's teacher Reinhold Seeberg that the latter insisted it be excluded from the thesis as presented for examination.

In this section, Bonhoeffer states that *everything* for the church of the day depends on a new approach to the masses who have turned away from it. Indeed the very future of the bourgeois church and its renewal depends on this, for the bourgeois church is threadbare.

It seems to me as if, despite outward opposition in the proletariat, there is no modern power which is basically more open to the Christian gospel than the proletariat. The living proletariat knows only one thing, affliction, isolation, and cries out for one thing, community. These ideas are of course entangled and confined in class consciousness. Nevertheless they are seeking something more intensively than the bourgeoisie ever did.[14]

The root of the problem, Bonhoeffer suggests, is that the bourgeois church itself, for all its admirable efforts at social service and the like, does not know what true community is. Proletarians must be brought into the actual service and *leadership* of the church. 'The church of the future will not be bourgeois.'[15] Bonhoeffer makes clear that he is not equating Christianity with socialism. Socialization does not mean the coming of the kingdom of God on earth. 'All the same there seems to us to be a certain "affinity" between socialism and the Christian idea of community, which we must not neglect.'[16]

Significantly, having said that the future church will not be bourgeois, Bonhoeffer immediately goes on to say 'We cannot tell what it will look like.' Thus to be committed to the growth of true community requires a certain openness, an agnosticism about the exact shape of the future. Community does not come through the imposition of some pre-determined blue-print. Precisely because it comes through the interaction of persons in greater freedom and equality than exists at present, it cannot be fully anticipated. Yet we must be committed to it! With this recognition of the necessity to strive for what cannot yet be fully comprehended, we come very close to one of the secrets of Bonhoeffer's whole spiritual and intellectual pilgrimage. It emerges again powerfully in his wrestling, while in prison, with the form of Christianity and the church in an age without religion, and also, as we shall see shortly, in his prison writings on social and national identity. But it is important to note how early in his career it was an important ingredient in his thought, in these attempts to state a doctrine of the church in its social context.

Nor was this purely an academic question for Bonhoeffer. During 1931 he chose not to confine his activities to the academic lecture room, and conducted a confirmation class of forty boys in the working-class district of Wedding, in Berlin. He made at least one unsuccessful effort to secure a parish ministry in such an area. Despite the huge gulf between the social backgrounds and experience of the boys and himself, Bonhoeffer related to them extraordinarily well. One of them recalled years later:

To be near us, our pastor rented a furnished room in the north of Berlin. His landlady was explicitly instructed by him to allow us into his rooms in his absence – an expression of great confidence such as we had hardly experienced before, but which we certainly appreciated.[17]

Bonhoeffer seems to have had an innate gift for creating such relationships by his openness and respect, which took persons with utmost seriousness, giving and inviting trust. Such is the stuff of community. Not that Bonhoeffer pretended to himself or others that it was easy work. Pastoral visitation of the boys' homes was peculiarly challenging and disturbing as he confided in a letter to a friend:

To think of those excruciating hours or minutes when I or the other person try to begin a pastoral conversation, and how haltingly and lamely it goes on! And in the background there are always the ghastly home conditions, about which one really cannot say anything. Many people tell me about their most dubious way of life without any misgivings and in a free and easy way, and one feels that if one were to say something then they simply wouldn't understand.[18]

Many pastors in such circumstances might feel it was a noteworthy achievement even to have people talking to them in such a way.

In the light of these early concerns, one is tempted to ask why the Bonhoeffer of *Ethics* appears in such patrician or even elitist guise.

Had the intervening church struggle driven the proletariat from his mind? Not entirely, but with the advent of the Nazi regime one issue above all others was thrust to the fore: race.

Bonhoeffer and race: the Jewish question

Bonhoeffer had become interested in racial issues during 1930–31 in America, through his involvement in the black communities of New York. When he returned home he could hardly have imagined that the 'Jewish problem' was soon to become *the* issue demanding a personal, political and theological response. Bonhoeffer was of course adamant that the 'Aryan' issue as it applied to the church was of crucial theological importance. The church forfeited all claims to be the church of Jesus Christ if it allowed race, or anything else other than faith in Christ, to be the basis of either its membership or pastoral offices. But equally, and more clearly than most church-men, he saw too the evil of introducing a racial basis into 'the people'. This was not just a matter of abstract principle, for the effects of measures against the Jews bore in on him personally. His friend and fellow-minister Franz Hildebrandt had to leave Germany, as also his brother-in-law Gerhard Leibholz and family.

We do not find any single straightforward statement from Bonhoeffer about the wrongness of racism in general or anti-semitism in particular. To speak in abstract generalizations was not Bonhoeffer's style. What he vainly hoped for, was that the Confessing Church should speak quite concretely on behalf of the oppressed. As early as 1934, Bonhoeffer wrote to a friend about the need for the church to break its theological reserve over the state's actions and quoting Proverbs 31.8: 'Open your mouth for the dumb.'[19] 'Only he who cries out for the Jews has the right to sing Gregorian chant' is almost certainly an off-the-cuff remark of Bonhoeffer, though its occasion has never been precisely identified. But even after the notorious Crystal Night of 1938 the church maintained its silence. As we saw in Chapter Six, had Bonhoeffer survived the war he would certainly have wanted the new church to include in its act of repentance an admission of its tragic failure here. And 'Operation 7', more directly than the conspiracy itself, led to Bonhoeffer's arrest in 1943.

In 1933, Bonhoeffer delivered a paper to a group of pastors in Berlin, 'The Church and the Jewish Question'.[20] It is essentially a cautious and not entirely consistent questioning of the traditional Lutheran doctrine of the separation of spheres of church and state, and of acquiescence in the state's measures. But the implication is always there, that the Jews are being subjected to oppression, that the state has to be questioned by the church as to the moral legitimacy of its actions and – most clearly of all – that the Jews *are* part of the German people. There is always the possibility, states Bonhoeffer, that the State might, in the interests of law and order, enact too much or too little law. 'There would be too little law if any group of subjects were deprived of their rights.' Nazi ideologists, on the other hand, would not even have accepted that Jews were 'subjects' having any 'rights' at all in Germany. Bonhoeffer thus worked with the presupposition that 'the people' was racially inclusive.

The conspiracy and the 'view from below'

With the onset of war and the entry into the conspiracy, Bonhoeffer was led more deeply than ever into an exploration of the character and future of his country. As was seen in Chapter Five, the concept of the inherited tradition became ever more important to him. Further, the very fact of acting to remove the present tyranny demanded of him and his fellow-conspirators that they think responsibly about the features of the nation that would have to be rebuilt afterwards. Until then, Bonhoeffer, his family and close associates, had been able to view themselves as secure, responsible servants of society by virtue of their privileged upper-class background, as men of rank and profession: academics, senior civil-servants and the like. But conspiracy brought with it a sense of alienation and isolation from the present order, and the ever-present knowledge of their fate in the event of being discovered. During the winter of 1942–43 Bonhoeffer wrote his little essay 'After Ten Years' as a Christmas present to his closest friends. To this piece Eberhard Bethge has appended an unfinished paragraph, 'The View from Below', written in similar vein and probably at the same time:

We have for once learnt to see the great events of world history from below, from the perspective of the outcast, the suspects, the maltreated, the powerless, the oppressed, the reviled – in short, from the perspective of those who suffer.[21]

The important thing is that this 'experience of incomparable value' should be allowed to foster an enlarged generosity and humanity.

We have to learn that personal suffering is a more effective key, a more rewarding principle for exploring the world in thought and action than personal good fortune. This perspective from below must not become the partisan possession of those who are eternally dissatisfied; rather, we must do justice to life in all its dimensions from a higher satisfaction, whose foundation is beyond any talk of 'from below' or 'from above'.[22]

So Bonhoeffer was discovering that new social perspectives – not new theories or ideologies about society, but actually seeing life through the eyes of the oppressed – could be deeply positive and enriching, leading towards a new wholeness of character. Perhaps the fact that he was already making this discovery, together with his natural openness towards all sorts and conditions of people, is what enabled him to make such an impression on warders and prisoners alike in Tegel prison. Again, he made no attempt to discard his background. He did not artificially adopt the pose of a proletarian. He remained himself, and allowed others to be themselves while seeking to stand where they stood. That saved him from either despising the working-class, or sentimentalizing them. Very revealing is an aside in one of the prison letters to Eberhard Bethge in December 1943:

Some people have been so violently shaken in their lives from their earliest days that they cannot, now, so to speak, allow themselves any great longing or put up with a long period of tension, and they find compensation in short-lived pleasures that offer readier satisfaction. That is the fate of the proletarian classes, and it is the ruin of all intellectual fertility. It's not true to say that it is good for a man to have suffered heavy blows early and often in life: in most cases it breaks him.[23]

This is still the language of the aristocrat, but neither a patronizing nor a moralizing one. It is the recognition that a good deal of what people are, has to do with what they have been through, especially the experience of suffering. In prison, especially among the younger inmates, Bonhoeffer recognized the casualties of social deprivation typical of any urban, industrialized society.

In the prison writings, it also becomes clearer that in advocating a necessary stratification of society under the leadership of some kind of elite, Bonhoeffer was *not* envisaging the continuance of social and economic class-systems as known hitherto. Government and leadership should be exercised by those who had the appropriate moral and spiritual qualities.[24] This obviously invites the retort: are these values so self-evident to all? Will not the claim to such values provide yet another hypocritical justification of power and privilege by the 'right' people? Bonhoeffer may be thought to be ingenuous on that score. But he had a searing honesty which did not shrink from asking a more penetrating question of himself and his fellow-conspirators: 'Are *we* any use?' That is, those who were acting in a desperate attempt to salvage Germany's honour might find that the deceits and ethical compromises involved in the conspiracy might have so warped their outlook as to render them unfit for the shouldering of public responsibility in normal circumstances, where 'simplicity' was required. So Bonhoeffer was not indulging in special pleading either for himself or his associates. They might have to forfeit claims to a place among the elite. In the baptismal sermon, Bonhoeffer continues:

It will not be difficult for us *to renounce our privileges,* recognizing the justice of history. We may have to face events and changes that take no account of our wishes and our rights. But if so, we shall not give way to embittered and barren pride, but consciously submit to divine judgment, and so prove ourselves worthy to survive *by identifying ourselves generously and unselfishly with the life of the community and the sufferings of our fellowmen* . . . 'Seek the welfare of the city . . . and pray to the Lord on its behalf' (Jeremiah 29.7).[25]

(Emphases mine.)

This is a clear statement of a commitment to the community of the people in a way which transcends class perspective, and which does not exploit 'loyalty to country' as a camouflage for preserving the present order, or as a way of rationalizing and justifying one's own privileged status. It is a patriotism which focusses on the people, and not on some ideal apart from them. It has radical implications for the expression of national loyalty, for it means a movement of identification with one's neighbours, especially those who suffer, rather than a deference towards those who are 'above' by virtue of privilege or accidents of history. Its emphasis is on discovering a common humanity, not overlooking the differences or concealing the pain involved in coming to terms with the difference. It is an affirmation of an ethic of solidarity instead of the usual bourgeois assumptions about private virtue and self-improvement.

Bonhoeffer's prison fiction: ways of being German

It is not surprising, then, that while in prison Bonhoeffer should have devoted considerable time, amongst his other diverse intellectual pursuits, to relationships between people of different classes, and to the nature of the German community as a whole. But the means he chose to explore these themes was quite new to him: the writing of fiction. He produced three such items during the first few months of his imprisonment in 1943. These were a short story, 'Lance Corporal Berg'; a section of a play; and an unfinished novel (neither the play nor novel fragments were given a title).[26] The medium was entirely new as a form of self-expression for Bonhoeffer, and he experimented with it not out of any desire to cultivate his artistic talents as such, but as a means of coming to terms with his new situation in prison.

'Lance Corporal Berg' is a cameo of military prison life itself, and the experiences of Tegel are obviously the primary source material. It is a picture of the kind of petty tyranny which Bonhoeffer found most repugnant, and doubtless he put it on paper partly as a means of bringing it to judgment. Sergeant-Major Meier is coarse, brutal, dishonest and above all inwardly ridden by feelings of guilt at not serving on the front-line. Lance-Corporal Berg, horribly disfigured by his wounds received in Russia, reports for duty and greatly discomforts Meier not only by his appearance but by his assured yet modest courage. We may take this as a sketch by Bonhoeffer of his view that it is moral quality which confers the true right of command.

The drama and novel fragments are not only longer, but also betray psychological and intellectual complexities of a depth and personal intensity normally concealed in Bonhoeffer's writing, making clear just how unsettling was the impact of arrest and imprisonment. Cut off from the sustaining communities of his life, and facing the increased possibility of early death, fiction offered a way of recreating the past which he had known and loved (or dreamt of having), and of exploring the new insights into the future of Christianity and Germany which were germinating in his mind. The style is somewhat wooden, the characters tending to be mouthpieces of prescribed views rather than live personalities in their own right. But most readers of Bonhoeffer will be looking for what these pieces say about their author and what their author is trying to say through them, rather than artistry. Relevant to our study, three themes from the drama and novel deserve attention.

First, we find a return to Bonhoeffer's earlier concern with the fact of social difference and the attempt to communicate across the divide. In the drama the central character, Christoph, comes from an upper-class family, and is a war-veteran. He comes to know Heinrich, a young man of about the same age, and working-class. Heinrich has made a sacrificial attempt to remain with the urban poor in their poverty, 'to live in hell with God' as he puts it. Both men share a concern for social questions; but Heinrich feels bound to make clear that they are conditioned to behave in very different ways. One evening, Christoph decides to pay a call on Heinrich for the first time in his flat:

CHRISTOPH: You aren't surprised that I came?
HEINRICH: No, I knew you would. One of us had to make the first move, and
             because you are the aristocrat, you came first.
CHRISTOPH: What is that supposed to mean?
HEINRICH: Very simple. It didn't enter your head that you might lower
             yourself by coming first. People like us wonder a hundred times
             beforehand what kind of impression it makes, how it looks,
             whether it won't be misunderstood. You don't need to, you are too
             much sure of yourself for that. You simply come, and take it for
             granted the other will somehow put up with it; and if he does
             misunderstand that doesn't bother you at all. That's the way you
             aristocrats are. We others are more distrustful and we have our
             experiences. But after all, we don't know each other yet.
CHRISTOPH: That's exactly why I am here. We must get to know each other.[27]

Heinrich continues to protest that Christoph and his like just cannot see the problem. His aristocratic calmness and self-assurance are in fact 'an unbounded contempt for people, a means of disarming

people'. Christoph in turn objects that, like Heinrich and others of
'the common people' he himself spent four years in the trenches, and
now he has come to talk with him 'man to man'. Heinrich's reply is
cold and devastating:

Man to man – you always say that when you want to silence the voice of the masses, of
the common people, that lives in us. You dislike this voice; you want to rip us out of
the community in which alone we are something, and you know perfectly well that
you needn't fear us any longer once you confront us as individuals . . . Man to man?
Let us become men first, then we'll talk with you man to man.[28]

Through creating this dialogue, Bonhoeffer shows what it means
to take the other person seriously. For Christoph is clearly playing
the part of Bonhoeffer himself, and by introducing Heinrich in this
way, Bonhoeffer is putting himself in the position where he not only
meets the proletarian individual, but is challenged and threatened by
him. The search for the common ground involves no sentimental
filling-in of the gap between them, still less any patronizing gush
from the upper middle-class side (the sort which says 'Ruddy salt of
the earth, these dustmen . . .'). Christoph with 'ground under his
feet' in the form of values tried and tested by generations in his
tradition, and Heinrich with his perpetual suspicion ('We can't
afford to have trust. Our experiences are too bitter') meet not in
agreement, but at least in dawning recognition of each other, and of
why the other is as he is. It is a meeting in pain – especially the pain of
new self-discovery on Christoph's part. But it could be the pain
signifying that new birth is on the way, the birth of new community.

In the novel, social relationships are again dealt with, though this
time the discussion is between people of the same upper-class
background. Younger members of the Brake family are out on a
summer's walk in the forest. The central character is again called
Christoph, and again he is probably Bonhoeffer's self-portrait, with
his close friend Ulrich playing the role of Eberhard Bethge.
Christoph and Ulrich discuss the problems caused by the
'equalizing' effect of Christianity, in view of the required order and
structure of society. An unpleasant encounter with a uniformed
estate keeper introduces into the plot the unacceptable face of upper-
class life, namely, its vanity and arrogance. Christoph and Ulrich
agree that by 'aristocracy' and 'rabble' they do not mean matters of
birth and social position, but qualities of character. The balance is
more than redressed by the appearance on the scene of Major von
Bremer who owns the state, with his wife and daughter. Through
Bremer, Bonhoeffer enables the voice of traditional, chivalrous and
humane Germany to speak.

The second theme to be considered is the need for co-existence in
society, and it is von Bremer who contributes most of the wisdom on

this. In response to Christoph's brother Franz – an ardent socialist –
he says:

For me the main question for people and nations is whether or not they have learned to
live with other people and nations. To me that is more important than all their ideas,
thoughts and convictions. . . But I wouldn't say that the result of history and life is
compromise. Whoever puts it that way still has his mind set only on ideas and must
therefore resign himself again and again to the fact that no idea prevails in all its purity
in life; then he calls that a compromise and sees it as nothing but a sign of the
imperfection and wickedness of the world. I only consider man and his task of living
with other men and regard the successful completion of precisely this task as the
fulfilment of human life and history.[29]

We are back with Bonhoeffer's lifelong emphasis on community
as the centre of existence. As early as *Sanctorum Communio,* we have
seen, his interest in community was pushing out through the walls of
the church into the world. Now, it is truly out in the world. We are
back, too, with his emphasis on reality. In actual relationships, in all
their awkwardness and apparent limitations, not in the seeming
purity of ideas and abstractions, is life experienced. Not in the imposition of some common ideology, but in people acknowledging
each other and moving towards a deeper understanding of each other
– especially downwards from 'above' – can a genuine community of
'the people' arise.

The third theme closely parallels an idea with which those who
know *Letters and Papers from Prison* will be familiar already. There,
Bonhoeffer speaks of the need for a certain silence about the great
central words and concepts of Christian faith: 'a secret discipline
must be restored whereby the *mysteries* of the Christian faith are
protected against profanation'.[30] 'In the traditional words and acts
we suspect that there may be something quite new and
revolutionary, though we cannot as yet grasp or express it.'[31] We
saw earlier how the young Bonhoeffer foretold a non-bourgeois
church, though he felt unable to visualize just what it would be like.
To press for too much disclosure before the time would be
unseemly. Both in the drama and novel pieces, a similar thought
appears with regard to the *country* and its character. In the drama,
Christoph sets these thoughts down on paper:

I am speaking to you to protect from misuse the great words given to mankind . . .
Those who are guardians of genuine values with their lives, their work, and their
homes turn in disgust from the ringing rhetoric that is supposed to turn the masses
into prophets. What well-meaning person can still utter the degraded words *freedom,
brotherhood*, and even *Germany*? . . . Let us honour the great values by silence for a time,
let us learn to do what is just without words for a while. Then, around the quiet
sanctuary of the great values, a new nobility will form in our time.[32]

In the novel, Christoph's reflections on his country are prompted
by his conversation with the Major's young daughter Renate, with

whom he is clearly falling in love at first sight. Frau von Bremer is English-born, and Renate was in fact born in South Africa, which she still regards as her 'homeland'. Germany is still a mystery to her, indeed in some ways alien. 'One needs a long time,' she says. 'Most of all one probably has to meet people through whom one can understand the life, the fate of this country.'

The last remark gives Christoph cause for profound reflection, and he resolves to be Germany's interpreter for the girl. But how much did he himself know of his native land? He and Ulrich had hiked and camped among the most scenic and historic spots in Germany – yet that Germany was almost impossible to express in words. 'Renate would have to travel, to see Germany in order to love it.' Moreover, it was Ulrich's companionship which had made those places so significant – 'the country had opened itself to the friends only through the medium of the living soul of the other'.[33]

Christoph then takes account of the fact that 'the people' comprise many different sorts – from the unpleasant forester met earlier, to the large-hearted Major himself; Germany on the way down, and good, healthy Germany.

We have then in Bonhoeffer one who did take his country seriously, as the community of its actual people – *all* its people of whatever race or class or belief. It was, he knew, a community fractured by real and tragic social differences in which experiences had conditioned their victims to react to one another in certain ways. To love the country therefore involves taking the other, strange person with complete seriousness and learning of his background through him, letting him speak, letting him put the challenge of his own questions, letting him express his own pain, letting him challenge one's own presuppositions and prick one's own presumptions. That is the way in which one's own perspectives are truly relativized. Loving one's country means therefore a process of continual discovery of what the country is, as met in the actual lives of those who are part of it, and especially the lives of those who are at the worst end of it and who open up 'the view from below'. It means recognizing, too, that the country is something which any of us only partly know. Here is the paradox, of which Bonhoeffer was well aware in other dimensions of life, that the people and things which mean most to us, are not those about which we can speak glibly, or even find it easy to speak about at all. Really to know and love a friend means acknowledging the element of mystery in him or her, which eludes our exact comprehension. The acknowledgment of this mystery is an essential part of our loving, for love does not pretend to possess the other, but to allow the other to be himself or herself. It means loving the real, which we must try to discern, and not confuse with fantasies. But an element of reserve, and acknowledgement that we never fully know, is required in discerning the reality, for to pretend that we know everything completely about a person or community of persons, is a sure sign that we are substituting our ideas, ideals or ideologies for the real. To love the country means therefore an element of reserve, of agnosticism, about what the country finally is. It is more than we know of it. It is certainly not to be identified with our particular stereotyped image of it.

Loving Britain today

Incredible as it may seem, with something like four million unemployed, it is still possible to hear mannered voices in lounge-bars lamenting that Mrs Thatcher, for all her resolution, has still not solved the most important and perennial problem: how to make the British working man work. There is a social insulation in Britain which renders inequalities acceptable, an ignorance of others compounded with a moralizing contempt for the 'unsuccessful'. No-one, it is stated with conviction by the comfortable, is really poor in Britain today, or has any 'excuse' to be so. As for those blacks, always going around with chips on their shoulders . . . All such attitudes manifest an attempt to dis-own sections of the national community, rejecting their claim to belong to 'the people', and denying any claim on one's responsibility towards them. This is effectively an excision of people from the country, and is simply the obverse of equating the country with one's own particular experience, mores and aspirations. Social prejudices are then dressed in patriotic guise, and certain styles of life are labelled 'un-British'.

But the country is the people, all the people, and a genuine patriotism must be open to all the people. It requires an ethic of solidarity, or fraternity to use Halsey's term – and one which does not wait to be induced by some crisis or threat from outside. Those who really love their country will be those who, like Bonhoeffer, are prepared, at whatever discomfort to themselves, to find out about the others who are of 'the people', and what is happening to them. They will be prepared to be challenged by the otherness of their neighbours' experience – especially where it is the experience of suffering and deprivation – and by the anger of those who feel that no-one will really bother to listen to them, 'the people of England, that never has spoken yet'. In such people, they will recognize, the voice of Britain is to be heard, and so loving Britain means recognizing that the country is more than any of us comprehend at present.

True patriotism will not claim one's own picture of the essential Britain as the absolute truth. Like its theological equivalent of idolatry, such an attitude shows more reverence for our own prejudices and wishes than for the actual object of our devotion, whose reality will always be inviting further exploration by us in our encounters with others. In any case, a sense of history will prevent us from imagining that the present order must be the last word. Britain's history is still being made, even its character is in process, and as always, much diversity is going into the story. This fact alone should inhibit the mouthing of crude and glib slogans ('Britain *is* inequality of wealth' – said with pride) which tell us more about the speaker than the country. The speech of true love, even at its most ardent, is more respectful, knowing that there is always more to be discovered in the character of the loved one than is known or knowable at present. It is prepared to be silent at times, rather than prate and chatter about the virtues of the beloved. 'God, this *people* I have loved.'

9
True Ecumenism and
True Patriotism

What is ecumenism?

Most British Christians, if asked what they understood 'ecumenism' to be about, would probably say that it had to do with bringing the various denominations and traditions of the church closer together. They might have in mind the kind of scheme which juddered to a halt in the summer of 1982 with the failure of the Church of England to raise sufficient support in its synodical House of Clergy for entry into the Covenant with certain of the Free Churches. Or they might point to other 'ecumenical activities' such as observance of the annual Week of Prayer for Christian Unity, the work of local councils of churches, the British Council of Churches, Christian Aid and the like. Some will be aware of ventures at congregational or parish level, known as Local Ecumenical Projects. More vaguely, there may be mention of the World Council of Churches as a rather distant and sometimes controversial expression of ecumenism. By and large, however, 'ecumenism' will be understood as the 'coming together' of diverse Christian traditions at national or local level.

Yet one of the first things which a student of modern church history is told about the ecumenical movement, is that its modern inception is to be dated in 1910, with the *International* Missionary Conference in Edinburgh, chaired by the dynamic American J. R. Mott. The mission of the worldwide church to the whole world was its theme. Thereafter this global reference was kept to the fore in the three main strands of ecumenism which were fed into the eventual formation of the World Council of Churches: Faith and Order, Life and Work, and the International Missionary Council. 'Ecumenical' thus has a double reference, not only to the inter-relating of different traditions, but also to the manifestation of the universal church across the world of nations. Indeed many would say that the latter reference is if anything the more important. 'Ecumenical', it is pointed out, derives from the Greek *oikumene,* which both in the New Testament and its contemporary secular culture meant 'the world' or 'the inhabited world' or 'the world's inhabitants' or sometimes just 'the Roman Empire'. The great councils of the church which met during the early centuries and formulated the classic statements of orthodox Christian belief were called 'ecu-menical' councils because they comprised representatives of all churches in the *oikumene* or, put slightly differently, were representative of the one church throughout the *oikumene*. The true ecumenical vision is thus that which is conveyed in one of the scenes from the Book of Revelation:

After this I looked, and behold, a great multitude which no man could number, *from every nation, from all tribes and peoples and tongues,* standing before the throne and before the lamb, clothed in white robes, with palm branches in their hands, and crying out with a loud voice, 'Salvation belongs to our God and to the Lamb!' (7.9–10).

This dimension is no less present in the credal confession, 'I believe in one holy, catholic and apostolic church.' Christ is one, his body is one. Ecumenism is not an odd extra to the 'normal' worship, belief and practice of the churches, but is the working-out of that unity which is confessed on each occasion of worship.

On most Sundays in the year, somewhere in Britain at least one congregation is likely to be heard singing S. J. Stone's famous hymn on the unity of the church, 'The Church's one foundation', with its lines

> Elect from every nation,
> Yet one o'er all the earth,
> Her charter of salvation
> One Lord, one faith, one birth.

I leave aside for the moment the question of how real and immediate the sense of being part of a transnational church actually is, to most worshippers. But if it is the case that being a Christian is, *ipso facto,* to be part of the one body of Christ on earth, then clearly this must mean a qualification of national consciousness as far as Christians are concerned. How do those who are British and Christian identify themselves in the world? Primarily as British people, whose religion happens to be Christianity? Or first and foremost as Christians, members of the universal church who happen to be citizens of the United Kingdom? The questions may be over-simplified, but the most important questions in life are the very simple ones.

A Christianity faithful to the New Testament would seem to want the latter answer. Even the opening addresses of the epistles consist of the most emphatic assertions of the corporate existence of the total Christian fellowship: 'Peace and mercy be upon all who walk by this rule, upon the Israel of God' (Galatians 6.16). The First Epistle of Peter uses a highly significant phrase in its opening address: 'To the exiles of the Dispersion in Pontus, Galatia . . .' The 'dispersion' (*diaspora*) originally signified the emigration of Jews from their homeland after the exile, and particularly during the Greek empire. Whether voluntary or forced, such migration took Jews into far places in the Mediterranean world and the near east, and to a significant degree many of those who subsequently grew up in the gentile world assimilated much in Hellenistic culture. Yet a strong sense of Jewish identity was retained. 'The Jews who spread themselves abroad, left their hearts at home.'[1] Jerusalem remained the ultimate object of their earthly allegiance, and frequently of their pilgrimages also (cf Acts 2.5ff). The early Christian community, arising from within Judaism, came to see itself as a new *diaspora*. 'Home' for this *diaspora* was not so much a place – though note Paul's concerted efforts for the financial relief of the mother church in Jerusalem – as the person of Jesus Christ, crucified and glorified. Christians were encouraged to obey earthly rule and authority wherever they happened to be set in this world. 'For there is no authority except from God, and those that exist have been instituted by God' (Romans 13.2). But a faith founded on the confession 'Jesus is Lord' always implied dissent from the claims of certain forms of political lordship, especially when the ruler was elevated to the status of divinity. Should the issue be forced, then 'we must obey God rather than men'.

Once Christianity was adopted by Constantine as the favoured religion of Rome, the sense of being a *diaspora* among the peoples of the world was bound to lessen, and in its place grew a new, fused identity between national (or imperial) and Christian self-awareness. The religio-political concept of Christendom persisted through the middle-ages in the west, and even after the Reformation it was still possible to speak of 'the Christian world', especially in contra-distinction to the Moslem east. But the emergence of the nation-state and the national church now made unitary Christendom only a memory as the political and religious spheres both fragmented. The complexity was further heightened by the march of secularization, whereby the national identity of individual citizens and religious affiliation became detachable from each other. Hence, once again, the felt need for the Christian community to recover and express its oneness and universality throughout the *oikumene*.

British Christianity and the world church

Britain is peculiar among the European nations in having so much religious diversity so deeply embedded in its social fabric, a fact which impresses itself physically on the cross-channel traveller returning to England. Within minutes of driving off the boat, as likely as not one will have passed in quick succession a Methodist Chapel, a Salvation Army Hall and a Roman Catholic Church before even coming within sight of the Anglican parish church – and all these displaying in their architecture a confidence in their right to be there. The contrast with Cherbourg or Ostend or Hamburg could not be greater. This diversity is, as has been mentioned several times in this book, one of the enrichments of British life. But there is another side to the picture, suggested by the successive hesitations over visible unity in Britain. Denominationalism manifests a certain parochialism. Further, it has to be asked whether denominational introspection and self-satisfaction might not be related, much more deeply than has hitherto been acknowledged, to a low level of consciousness of the supranational dimension of Christianity.

At first sight these might seem to be quite unrelated issues. But the way in which a church or denomination sees its significance on a world scale does have a bearing on its attitude to other communions in its own country. In Britain, the self-understanding of the Church of England is crucial. Let me say at once that this is written by a Free Churchman who loves much in the Anglican inheritance and who owes an immense debt, intellectually and spiritually, to its life, worship and teaching. But I trust I may be forgiven for saying that in some Anglican quarters there is a vastly exaggerated opinion of Anglicanism's significance in the Christian world at large. Of course numbers are not everything, and statistics of total membership of the various Christian communions can be interpreted in very different ways. But they can help to bring one down from the clouds. Ought not the fact to register with the Church of England, that the total number of Anglican communicants worldwide is about half that of baptized members of Baptist churches? Anglicanism is also numerically outweighed by each in turn of the Lutheran, Reformed and Methodist communions, not to mention the Orthodox. In the total non-Roman cake, the Anglican slice looks relatively meagre. Yet the Anglican style sometimes gives the impression that world Christianity is holding its breath for the next epoch-making statement from Church House. Perhaps it is just another post-imperial survival, this time in religious dress, of the Anglocentric universe. But it does rebound on church relations within Britain itself, as well as cushioning Anglicans against the reality of the time.

This is not to say that other denominations are without reproach. All the major traditions in Britain have confessional links with corresponding communities across the most significant and dangerous divides of the modern world, but it is not clear how far world confessional organizations really enlarge the vision of the church in the *oikumene,* and how far they merely project a cosy denominationalism onto a wider canvas. Nevertheless it is very important, for instance, that British Baptists have close links with those in eastern Europe, that Roman Catholics now realize that their church is deeply involved in the struggle for justice in Latin America, and that all the British churches have links with churches in the Third World. Indeed it may be argued that the most crucial ecumenism today is that between churches in the rich north and the poor south. What does it mean for Christians in north and south to break one eucharistic bread, when those in the south are denied bread through economic exploitation by the north? How can unity in Christ be compatible with domination and deprivation? Then there is the question of what ecumenism means during and after actual conflict. The restraint of the British churches at the post-Falklands thanksgiving service at St Paul's must be given its due. But the really testing questions are only now emerging. Will the tragedy of conflict and violence be turned into an occasion for developing a clearer perception of Argentina, its people and its churches? Will the British churches make any real attempt to learn and convey how the world looks from a Latin American position? If not, it will be a failure in ecumenism as major as the failure of any unity scheme in Britain.

British Christians clearly need to break out of parochialism and insularity, into a deeper realization of belonging to the one holy, catholic and apostolic church of all times and places. But equally clearly, such an ecumenical loyalty is bound to generate tension between itself and national loyalty. Part of contemporary discipleship will be to learn to live with this tension and handle it creatively, for it is inevitable so long as the *oikumene* consists of diverse peoples, and so long as we insist on the universality of the church. The universality of the body of Christ will always present a challenge to the assumed rights of national sovereignty, for it is the clearest sign that the nation does *not* have an absolute and ultimate claim ('all earthly things above') on human allegiance. And a nation or state which does make such claims for itself will naturally see ecumenical loyalty as a threat to it, and in the ultimate perspective the 'threat' is real. The universal church is a pointer towards the final order of creation, the unity of the whole *oikumene* in Christ. On the other hand, an ecumenism which tried to ignore the present diversity, and divisions, within the *oikumene* would have no contact with reality. The end is not yet. So on the one hand, Christians cannot evade the challenge of searching for greater catholicity, by hiding within their own national and cultural refuges. On the other hand, they cannot, for the sake of an abstract universal Christianity which is nowhere anchored on earth, opt out of the particular tasks and responsibilities demanded by their home contexts.

Bonhoeffer: the one church

No-one understood this two-fold nature of ecumenical responsibility better than Dietrich Bonhoeffer, and so for the last time we turn to him for stimulus on this issue which concerns Christians specifically. Interestingly, in retrospect Bonhoeffer dated his first experience of 'ecumenical Christianity' from his year in Spain 1928–29, followed by his study year in America in 1930–31 – that is, ecumenism for him meant first of all relating to the church abroad. Not until his attendance at the Cambridge Conference of the World Alliance in the summer of 1931 was he actually involved in what would normally be called the 'ecumenical movement'. Indeed, prior to that conference he had been highly suspicious of such affairs. This was on account of his highly eschatological, Barthian perspective which viewed efforts at peace-building as worthy but misguided human attempts to erect the kingdom of God. The 'Life and Work' conference at Stockholm in 1925, under the leadership of Bishop Nathan Söderblom, was the most impressive – or dangerous, according to one's stance – manifestation of this approach so far. But Bonhoeffer's encounter with both social activism and the peace question in America had left its mark on him. The World Alliance was the least prepossessing of all the strands in the ecumenical movement, neither as professionally equipped with expertise as 'Life and Work' nor as scholarly as 'Faith and Order', but rather being a somewhat diffuse collection mainly of Europeans, British and Americans sharing a common desire for world peace and seeking the best means of bringing it about. It put great store on personal contacts and the passing of resolutions. Yet paradoxically, the young sophisticated product of the highest reaches of German academic theology entered into this movement with utmost seriousness. In fact he took it more seriously than it took itself.

'There is still no theology of the ecumenical movement.' So Bonhoeffer began his paper 'A Theological basis for the World Alliance?' at the Youth Peace Conference in Czechoslovakia in July 1932. He immediately dismissed the idea that a body like the World Alliance should leave theology to 'Faith and Order' and concentrate on practical tasks instead. Precisely by ignoring theology, its work was being undermined:

Because there is no theology of the ecumenical movement, ecumenical thought has become powerless and meaningless, especially among German youth, because of the political upsurge of nationalism. And the situation is scarcely different in other countries. There is no theological anchorage which holds while the waves dash in vain . . . *Anyone concerned in ecumenical work must suffer the charges of being unconcerned with the Fatherland and unconcerned with the truth,* and any attempt at an encounter is quickly cried down.[2]

The theology which can and must counter such nationalism is nothing other than a definite view of the church:

The church as the one community of the Lord Jesus Christ, who is Lord of the world, has the commission to say his Word to the whole world. Each individual church has geographical limits drawn to its own preaching, but the *one* church has no limits.[3]

Bonhoeffer continually startled his colleagues in the World Alliance by his assertion that the organization should regard itself as nothing less than a manifestation of that one church of Jesus Christ. Bonhoeffer did not see this view of the World Alliance as an exaltation of that body. It could only speak and act as the church through the confession of its own sins, and only in such humility could it be a sign of, and a witness to, international brotherhood.

This brotherhood is based on the peace which Christ brought to the world on the cross. – The new brotherhood is the community of those chosen by God, those who are humble under the cross, of those who wait, who believe, who are obedient, and the community of those to whom it is God's will to be gracious. This is of course something quite different from international friendship on the basis of the old world.[4]

In none of this is Bonhoeffer trying to be 'original' or revolutionary. He is simply wanting himself and his fellow-Christians to accept without compromise or evasion the theological truth of the *una sancta,* the one holy, catholic and apostolic church, gathered from and transcending all the peoples and nations, yet interceding for their peace. For him, the ecumenical movement was not to deliberate endlessly on the marks of the true church of Christ, but to *act* without reserve or delay *as* that church of Christ speaking to the nations. And Bonhoeffer took this view in face of the most threatening pressure at home to reject all ecumenism and other forms of 'internationalism' as by definition unpatriotic and even positively treacherous towards the Fatherland. His ecumenism was no bland or romantic lauding of idealized Christian brotherhood. It expressed a definite commitment against the tide of nationalist sentiment in Germany, and sought the taking of risks in concrete action by the movement itself. Parallel with 'costly discipleship', we may justly speak of 'costly ecumenism' in Bonhoeffer's eyes, especially in its challenge to national sentiment.

Bonhoeffer thus offered the ecumenical movement the opportunity of viewing itself with greater theological seriousness than ever. With the advent of the Church Struggle in Germany, he in turn made rigorous demands upon it. His friendship with George Bell and his co-optation onto the council of 'Life and Work' in August 1934 brought him much closer to the main stream of the ecumenical movement than was possible in the World Alliance alone. The work of the latter was crumbling as far as Germany was concerned, in any case. Now, Bonhoeffer saw the ecumenical movement as representing the universal church, and he saw the Confessing Church as *the* Evangelical Church in Germany. To him the logic was clear: the ecumenical movement, to be true to itself, must unequivocally declare its recognition of the Confessing Church as the true church of Germany by virtue of its upholding the one faith in Jesus Christ. The Confessing Church, by struggling for the true confession of faith, was fighting not just for Christianity in Germany, but on behalf of Christianity everywhere. The interest of the ecumenical movement and the Confessing Church in each other was therefore highly significant – or dangerous, depending on one's viewpoint:

It is offensive, because it is vexatious to the German nationalist for once to have to see his church from the outside and to have to allow it to be seen from the outside, because no one gladly shows his wounds to a stranger. But it is not only a remarkable and an offensive fact, it is still more a tremendously promising fact, because in this encounter the ecumenical movement and the Confessing Church ask each other the reason for their existence.[5]

Despite this 'tremendously promising fact', Bonhoeffer's hopes of the ecumenical movement were never realized. In 1934, at Fanö, 'Life and Work' resolved to recognize the Confessing Church as its partner in ecumenism, but a small loophole in the resolution later allowed the official Reich Church leaders to claim that they too had a right to representation in this wing of the ecumenical movement. Nevertheless George Bell continued to exert all his powers in support of the Confessing Church, and at the Oxford Conference on Church, Community and State in 1937 there were no Reich Church representatives present. Nor were there any from the Confessing Church, travel permission having been refused by the authorities, but at least their absence was an eloquent one. 'Faith and Order', on the other hand, remained determinedly neutral as far as the German situation went, a fact which deeply disillusioned Bonhoeffer who refused invitations to participate in its work because invitations were also being issued to Reich Church theologians. Bonhoeffer's interview with Leonard Hodgson, secretary of 'Faith and Order', at Oxford in March 1939, was one of the most painful confrontations of his career.[6]

Even after the passage of fifty years, to read Bonhoeffer's ecumenical papers and sermons from this period is an unnerving experience. In them, one meets a man for whom the universal church was as real as the ground beneath his feet, and to such an extent that one begins to feel that by comparison most of us do not offer more than lip-service to the idea, or regard it as an interesting diversion alongside more localized tasks. He brings us back to that simple question: primarily Christian, or British? To confess Jesus Christ as lord of lords qualifies all other claims to loyalty, not least of country, and signifies a bond with the *una sancta,* the universal community which exists among the nations and points to the new creation lying beyond them. Every time belief in the catholic church is confessed in the creed, every time we sing of the church being 'one o'er all the earth', patriotism is being put in its proper perspective, national sovereignty is being questioned, for we are stating where we most truly belong, and that here we have no abiding city. We are also committing ourselves to face the scandalous inequalities and divisions of our world more intimately than ever before, because these inequalities and divisions do not stop outside the church door. As we have already said, the north-south divide is an ecumenical issue, for it runs right through the church. And for Bonhoeffer, one of the strongest condemnations of modern warfare stemmed from the way in which it inevitably and quite literally rends the body of Christ. Can one really believe in the church universal, and countenance the slaughter of fellow-believers in the Soviet Union as part of the price of 'deterrence'?

Ecumenism for the country's sake

The charge that such a universalist concern is subversive of one's loyalty and duty to one's country must obviously be met. And the answer has to be given with integrity. It is not enough simply to point to this community which transcends the nation. For there *is* always the possibility that in the name of wider commitments, excuses can be sought for disengagement from humbler and less glamorous tasks at home. It is analogous with the domestic family scene where involvement in 'community' affairs can be at the expense of the community of one's spouse and children, and even many a vicarage and manse has echoed to the cry 'But you've never time for *us*.' It is one thing to say that one's own country is not the whole world, but quite another to detach oneself from it with a superior smile. Ecumenism, or any other form of internationalism, is false once it becomes a privilege, an escape.

It was this sudden realization which prompted Dietrich Bonhoeffer to return home from the United States in the summer of 1939.[7] He had had every reason for emigration, both on a personal level (to avoid military call-up) and in the interests of the wider church (to share the theological lessons of the Confessing Church with American Christians). His ecumenical contacts had made it almost too easy, through his friendships with Paul Lehmann and Reinhold Niebuhr. It could all be justified by his own doctrine of the *una sancta*. His very presence in the United States would soon have been hailed as a manifestation of the unbroken oneness of the church in time of war. It would all have been so secure – and it was precisely that which made Bonhoeffer so suspicious. It would have been a man-made security in contrast with the true security grounded in obedience to God. So too the 'freedom' so highly prized in America (and in Britain, come to that) was a largely external freedom, a matter of possibilities to opt for. It was not the true freedom which God gives to his church, the freedom to preach his word in obedience. '. . . Where thanks for institutional freedom must be rendered by the sacrifice of freedom of preaching, the church is in chains, even if it believes itself to be free.'[8] Bonhoeffer now knew, as was described in Chapter Two, that his loyalty to his church and his country required him to return home. Not the way of individual privilege via ecumenism, but the way of corporate solidarity in suffering and guilt, was to be the path of authentic discipleship. But in a sense, it was still in the service of ecumenism that he returned to Germany. It was as a servant of the universal church that he had to go back to the place where the church was apparently denied 'all possibilities' on a human level, and there to live in obedience in order to demonstrate what Christian freedom really means. As Eberhard Bethge puts it, 'Paradoxically, it is his final entrance into German particularism which has made him ecumenically so alive and effective today.'[9]

Bonhoeffer as a conspirator remained an ecumenist, although it was now an underground ecumenism. In fact it was his ecumenical knowledge which made him of service to the resistance. Through Geneva the threads of communication between the Confessing Church and the ecumenical community abroad were kept intact. Karl Barth, Visser't Hooft and of course George Bell were kept informed of what was happening. Nor was it only the immediate issue of the conspiracy that was communicated. Via the office of Hugh Martin at the SCM Press in London, a document compiled by Bonhoeffer and Visser't Hooft on the future of post-war Germany, was circulated for discussion in British church circles. The paper was a response to William Paton's *The Church and the New Order* and issues of the *Christian News Letter* edited by J. H. Oldham, in which the problems of reconstruction in Europe after the war were already being discussed. Supplied with such material by Visser't Hooft in Geneva, Bonhoeffer had at once seen that much of the thinking in the British churches was of a much more positive nature than the sheer assertion of 'unconditional surrender' being nightly broadcast to Germany by the BBC. 'The Church and the New Order in Europe'[10] therefore sought to respond to sympathetic circles in the Anglo-Saxon world by giving an accurate picture of Germany from a non-Nazi perspective, and of the kind of situation likely to be found after an allied victory. Above all it welcomed Paton's call for a clear statement from the allied leaders as to what, apart from the defeat of Germany, their war-aims were. The absence of such a clearly-stated policy was simply feeding the Nazi propaganda machine, and was clearly discouraging to the German army which was the only group which could act effectively against the regime. But the chief importance of the paper lay in its exposure of certain awkward factors in the current and future German situation which liberal British opinion was apt to miss.

The Anglo-Saxon world summarizes the struggle against the omnipotence of the State in the word 'freedom'. And Paton gives us a charter of human 'rights and liberties' which are to provide the norm of action by the State. But these expressions must, as Paton indicates, 'be translated into terms which relate them more closely to the life of other peoples'. For freedom is too negative a word to be used in a situation where *all* order has been destroyed.[11]

In a country lying in social and political chaos one could not speak of the rights of individuals as if these could subsist independently of a firm – and probably authoritarian – basis of order for a time. Meanwhile Britain's attitude towards Germany must bear in mind the need to retain the sympathy of anti-Nazi circles which, it was hoped, would eventually provide a new leadership of Germany in the world.

We do not deny that Great Britain has the right to demand safeguards against a return of National Socialism in one form or another, and that it may therefore have to take far-reaching military measures against Germany. But we feel that for the sake of the future these unavoidable measures must be counterbalanced by a positive policy. Now it is recognized in England and America that this time there must not be a repetition of the economic clauses of the Versailles treaty, and that is indeed an important insight. There remains the question as to how Germany may find its way back to a system of government which is acceptable to the Germans and also be an orderly member of the family of nations.[12]

Of course some of the thoughts expressed in this paper were overtaken by events. A divided Germany was not foreseen (though the paper did conclude with acknowledgment of the threat of Soviet totalitarianism). Nevertheless the paper stands as a classic illustration of what ecumenism can mean in the context of conflict. For Bonhoeffer the ecumenical movement had always been a place where one met others, not out of any desire to demean one's country but precisely in order to represent it before the wider community. Before the war, Bonhoeffer had never left his ecumenical contacts in any doubt that they had much to learn about Germany – not least the effects of the Versailles treaty as a factor in the rise of Nazism. So now, during the war, he was presenting to the ecumenical move- ment a picture of his country largely hidden under the exchange of propaganda from both sides. It was a picture of the country's needs which had to be recognized both for its own future's sake and the peace of Europe. Recognizing the justice of the allied case against Hitler, sharing in the desire for Hitler's downfall and being himself an accomplice to that end, he is still the friend and loyal servant of his country. He is aware of how it must be treated, even in defeat, if it is to return to sanity. In such a case, ecumenism and patriotism coincide.

Ecumenism and patriotism – the necessary partnership

The only way in which a nation can live, in the end, is with other nations. It needs both to understand and be understood by others. The church of the *oikumene* has a vital role here, for those who claim to be members of the one body of Christ should at least be able to converse with each other in openness, honesty, humility and trust. And because the church does not lead a life isolated from the context of the people, and because even Christian people are still people of their particular scene, the ecumenical movement has to be a matter of the interrelating of peoples, not just of churches and denominations. Ecumenism is a matter of Britain and Argentina, Britain and the Soviet Union, Britain and the Third World. In the end, the God in whom Christians believe has his eyes set on the total *oikumene,* and in the final, inclusive city of God, the new Jerusalem, the peoples of the world find their fulfilment as they offer themselves up to a community greater than themselves, and radiant with the light of God himself: 'By its light shall the nations walk; and the kings of the earth shall bring their glory into it . . . they shall bring into it the glory and the honour of the nations' (Revelation 21.22–26). Note that the glory and honour of the nations are not denied, nor are the peoples asked to repudiate that glory and honour. But they willingly offer up their best to that city in which God dwells with his *oikumene* and from which light irradiates to all people. Glory and honour are no longer possessions to be clung to and defended at all costs, but are returned in grateful worship to the Creator who is their source, that they may be shared with all.

That is a vision of the end, and the end is not yet. As yet the nations still live with the realities of power and self-interest, and it is dangerous romanticism to imagine that corporate entities like nations can behave like saints when even individual saints are hard to come by. But there are signs of the end, and the universal church is above all called to be one such sign. For that reason, loyalty to country and loyalty to the universal church cannot be set over against each other in sheer opposition, as though the former represented 'realism' and the latter 'idealism'. Ecumenism would then be an exotic extra to the 'real world'. But it is exactly as a means to discovering what the 'real world' is, that ecumenism is so important for a country. To use the analogy of personal life, in order to live effectively an individual not only needs a measure of confidence and self-respect, but a proper awareness of the world of other people, of how they feel and view things, and of how his behaviour affects them and theirs his. He needs it in his own interests, not simply as a matter of altruism. At some points his life must depend on others. Total self-sufficiency is an illusion, and to attempt to live solely for himself and out of himself will eventually wreak havoc with his own life as much as the lives of others. 'Self-interest' is therefore more complex than appears at first sight. Paradoxically, it is in our own interests to take others' interests into account, however utilitarian a philosophy this may sound. If our nation is but one part of the *oikumene*, if our life as a people is bound up with that of other peoples, then it is not as patriotic as it sounds to behave as though our first concerns were the only ones that mattered. Our country, for its own good, needs to know more about the world of which it is part, needs to know how things look from Argentina, and Zambia, and the German Democratic Republic. British people need to realize that the development of the Third World is, in the long run, not incidental or antithetical to British prosperity, but essential to it. Living as we do on earth, national acquisitiveness will ultimately prove destructive to all.

Britain today badly needs a public education in the realities of the world in which it is living. The empire may have gone, the maps in the atlases may have been re-coloured and re-named, but it is still an imperialist picture which dominates popular attitudes: a world which exists for Britain's benefit, or, if it cannot be made to work that way, to be ignored. The stark fact that for the majority of people on this earth life means poverty and hunger, hardly enters into that picture. In such a world, what does national greatness mean? To say that it means dispatching a fleet to the far end of the globe at the cost of several hundred lives and £700 million to rescue two thousand islanders from alien occupation, while being blind to the colossal misery already abounding in the southern hemisphere, is to say the least unreal. Britain has an almost obsessive desire to be admired by other countries. Only rarely does she ask what, in today's world, most of the world's people would admire her for. One day, we may hope, national greatness might be conceived in terms of making a determined contribution to an onslaught on the threats to the survival of the human race itself.

Britain therefore needs the internationalism of the ecumenical movement, through which churches and peoples represent themselves to each other. Ecumenism needs to be seen as a means whereby Britain herself can be better understood and helped by others, no less than other countries being better understood by Britain. At times, British church representatives in gatherings of the World Council of Churches have found it a painful experience to listen to Third World Christians condemning Britain's record on racism and related issues. The instinctive defence postures come into play. But they have found that the most effective way of serving their country's interests has been to continue to listen and to discern the truth in what is being said. Dietrich Bonhoeffer continues to be an exemplar of how, at certain points, love of the universal church and love of country coinhere under the forgiveness of sins. As his Major von Bremer says, 'For me the main question for people and nations is whether or not they have learned to live with other people and nations.' And as Bonhoeffer himself said in his last recorded words, the hurried message to be passed to George Bell, 'I believe in the principle of our universal Christian brotherhood which rises above all national interests, and that our victory is certain.'

10
A Patriotism for Today

This book began by examining a disorder in British self-awareness and self-esteem, underlying all the various crises in social and economic life which usually occupy the headlines. The disorder was likened to that of a man who is not only unsure of who he is and who he is meant to be, but is unwilling and perhaps even afraid of finding out; someone unwilling to take responsibility for himself in the real world of here and now, preferring to dream of the life he once enjoyed, or thinks he enjoyed; someone unable to accept himself as he is and the world as it is. It was called a crisis in patriotism. British people seem curiously indifferent to the actual state of their country in the world, thinking it unworthy of devotion or affection, and snatching at spurious demonstrations of 'greatness' which are irrelevant to a people seeking to survive with other peoples on the same earth.

In the first chapter we saw that there were certain objective factors in the uncertainties besetting what has traditionally been called 'patriotism' in Britain. Regionalism – in the 'regions' themselves if not in England – has somewhat eroded a 'British' consciousness. The multinationalism of modern life has made inroads on even British insularity. Yet the British still exist as a people and as a political entity. How the British people relate to and identify with their community is therefore still vital. And at present they feel reluctant to identify with their community as it is. The belief in 'decline' in so many areas of life manifests itself in an attachment to the supposed glories of yesteryear rather than commitment to the tasks of today. Britain today, many feel, just doesn't deserve to be loved as their fathers loved her in their time. The old patriotic language and symbolism no longer fit the reality, but instead of a search for a new meaning to patriotism, with a new language and symbolism, there is a half-hearted retention of the old which is suddenly jerked into life by a Falklands War. Spiritual emigrés suddenly return to see the fleet set sail.

In writing on this theme, pictures of Britain as seen through one's own eyes naturally come into view by turns, like transparencies on a screen. Yes, there are the calendar pictures, for Chatsworth, the Cambridge backs, half-timbered Cheshire villages and cobbled fishing ports are all part of the scenery. So too is the squat Durham mining village crouching under the east wind, and the urban mass of

Newham, not to mention the largely sad, silent steel works in the valley at Ebbw Vale. A true catalogue of Britain must do justice to the beauty and the grimness, the growth and the decay, the peace and the discontent. A true loyalty to Britain will neither pretend to be unmoved by the good and the lovely, nor will it flinch from the depressing and disturbing side of the picture.

The same is true if one focusses the lens on one's more immediate scene. 'A citizen of no mean city', is how the Apostle Paul described himself, with almost British understatement. Certainly I and my fellow-Bristolians often talk in such terms of our own city. 'Yes,' we nod to our envious friends, 'a good place to live in.' It is a city with a great tradition of trade and maritime exploration, of industry and manufacturing, from tobacco to Concorde; the city of Isambard Kingdom Brunel, whose suspension bridge spans the Clifton Gorge, a permanent monument to that blend of engineering and grace which is a form of genius; a city of natural and man-made beauty, of theatre and entertainment, of music and education and broadcasting . . . The list could go on. Yet it is a city which many of its citizens do not find so good, the city to produce the first of the recent urban riots in April 1980, with the St Paul's disturbances. It is a city of protest as well as pride, of misery as well as opportunity, two-sided as with so much else in the human story. The ambiguity is as deeply-rooted as the city's history. From the Bristol Channel (and how many other cities have given their name to such a large area of sea?), up the Avon, came the ships laden with sugar from the West Indies, source of so much of the prosperity by which the city made its mark. Yet that homeward voyage was but one side of the notorious triangle. There was also the middle passage of those same ships laden with their human cargoes, westwards. Past oppression is built into the fabric of the city – quite literally too in some instances, as in the church of which the magnificent mahogany screen originally furnished a slave ship. A city, like the country of which it is part, has an ambiguity about both its past and its present, which has to be recognized if responsibility for its future is to be accepted with integrity.

We have tried to enter into a dialogue with a man who belonged to another country. We cannot see Bonhoeffer's Germany exactly as he saw it. But no other nation this century has revealed its contrasts more starkly, and with such fateful consequences for the rest of Europe. Perhaps I may be permitted to describe how sharply some visual images of those contrasts are imprinted on my own mind. It was a bright winter's day a few years ago, when a small party of us from Britain, a study delegation from various churches visiting the German Democratic Republic, stopped in Weimar for lunch. We were entertained in a house which was once the home of Cranach, the great portrait painter of the sixteenth century. Indeed Weimar as a whole is a monument to the genius of German culture. Walking its elegant squares, one breathes the air breathed by J. S. Bach, Handel, Herder, Goethe and Lizst to name but a few. Then, only a few minutes in the coach brought us to a very different scene among the wooded hills: the site of Buchenwald concentration camp. Much of the site has been cleared, a desolate waste. The barbed wire fence remains, and the iron gates with their cynical motto *Jedem das Seine* – 'To each his due'. Likewise the guardhouse and adjoining cells, the cellar in which men were hanged or shot with brutal efficiency, and the ovens in which they were cremated. The visitor from the west may be irritated by the overt propaganda made out of the place by the East German authorities, but what is seen makes its own point regardless of ideological polemics. Here is what humanity at its worst is capable of doing, and almost unbearably close to Weimar, a symbol of humanity at one of its peaks.

Buchenwald, however, does not symbolize only depravity. It also witnesses to resistance, heroism, and the tragic glory of martyrdom. Among the cells that remain is that which was occupied by Paul Schneider, murdered there in 1939, the first pastor of the Confessing Church to be martyred. Just outside the gates are the houses built for prison staff, and it was in the cellar beneath one of these that Dietrich Bonhoeffer was kept for several weeks in early 1945, between his transfer from Gestapo headquarters in Berlin and the final journey south to Flossenbürg. Whether Bonhoeffer himself mused on the tragic juxtaposition of Buchenwald and Weimar we shall never know, but as we have seen repeatedly the capacity of his homeland for both splendour and shame was a tension he constantly bore. He refused to evade the tension by attending to only one of its poles. That is what many of his contemporaries did, by no means Nazis or fellow-travellers, but simply people who refused to believe that a country with so great a cultural heritage could behave criminally, and who did not *want* to know what was going on, for fear the beautiful image would be smashed for ever. Neither did he take the equally evasive stance of attending only to the other pole and, in reaction to the distasteful spectacle, disengage himself from his country altogether. Half a century earlier, that lonely genius Friedrich Nietzsche considered his countrymen to have sunk beneath contempt: 'I do not care to say what I think of the Germans.' 'They are *my* enemies . . . these Germans.'[1]

Nietzsche died an exile from his homeland, both literally and metaphorically. It is not simply that Bonhoeffer evaluated the cultural and Christian tradition of Germany differently from

Nietzsche, for in fact he too found questionable elements within the German heritage, and more than enough to repudiate in present manifestations of German character. But for Bonhoeffer repudiation did not mean disengagement. The recognition of guilt did not mean withdrawal, but even deeper involvement and identification to the point from which true confession, repentance and intercession could begin. In Thomas Mann's *Dr Faustus,* Serenus Zeitblom describes his lifelong friendship for the composer Adrian Leverkühn, who in his brilliant nihilism personifies his country: 'It was always a love full of fear and dread, yet eternally faithful to this German whose inscrutable guiltiness and awful end had no power to affect my feeling for him – such love it may be as is only a reflection of the everlasting mercy.' Mann has told a parable, but Bonhoeffer has actually lived out such love.[2]

Bonhoeffer illuminates what it means to love one's country in its ambiguity: to recognize and cherish its good; to acknowledge and confess its guilt; to search for a deeper appreciation of its character in the total life of its people; to identify the points at which it becomes a danger to itself and others, through searching for security by power alone; to look to the future, the continuation of the story for the next generation. These are the elements of true patriotism. It is these which make for a love which has both clarity and passion – clarity which sees what is really there, passion which says in effect 'I will never leave you.'

Weimar has been mentioned as a place which symbolizes Germany's cultural heritage. But the name of that town of course also stands for the republican period between Germany's defeat in 1918, and the advent of Nazi power. The reasons why Germany could not sustain a parliamentary democracy, and why it eventually fell at the feet of fascism, continue to be a matter of historical debate. Analysts from the left argue that only a resolute adoption of social-ism could have prevented Hitler from coming to power. Certainly Hitler exploited the fear of 'Bolshevism', and it was the apparent salvation from this bogey by which so many well-meaning people, not least in the churches, justified their welcome for Hitler. It might have helped if the parliamentary left had itself been more resolute, and more co-operative with other parties against the Nazis. But the biggest factor in the Nazis becoming the largest single party in the Reichstag in late 1932 and early 1933, was undoubtedly Hitler's eventual capture of both industrial financial support and middle-class votes. For a long time during the Weimar Republic, liberal democracy had been seen as a second-best option by many people, and at the end was viewed as failing to deliver the goods. Germany in a state of dilapidation and street violence was a somewhat distasteful place in which to live. Contemptuous both of the Socialists and the Nazis, too many people complacently assumed that these warring factions could be left to annihilate each other, leaving commonsense to pick up the pieces afterwards. At root, there was not enough commitment, not enough clarity or passion, to make the Weimar Republic work. Things eventually drifted to the point where extremism seemed the only way out, and the hitherto 'common-sensical' people took fright and threw in their lot with Hitler. The eagerness to grasp at a solution so attractive by its very simplicity stemmed from a failure in clarity, a failure to see realities for what they were, and a failure in passion, the passion to work hard at the social and economic building-bricks instead of dreaming of magical transformations.

It is important not to forget Weimar when trying to draw lessons from the historical episode of Nazism, and the resistance to the regime. The heroism and sacrifice of July 1944 need no exaggerating. But what, after all, should really engage our attention is not what a number of very brave people attempted to do in 1944, but what a lot of ordinary people did in 1933, in locking themselves out of democracy. This becomes especially important if we are to engage in the hazardous process of drawing parallels between the German situation and our own. Only the most lurid imagination could call Britain today fascist. But the resemblances with Weimar Germany may not be too remote: inflation, rising unemployment, racism and militaristic hankerings. True, there is not the deep resentment against democratic institutions. But there is now, as there was during Weimar, a tendency to disengagement, a reluctance to commit oneself to the country that actually *is*, however apparently mediocre.

'This eternally mediocre Switzerland will be loved as such', wrote Karl Barth to a friend, an army commander, in 1964.[3] For a relatively small nation like Switzerland which has been a kind of still centre in Europe during the upheavals of the past two centuries, its existence depending on its neutrality and its historical role being what Barth called 'one great compromise', the acceptance of 'mediocrity' in the world league table may be accepted with equanimity. It is much more difficult for a nation with a living memory of a 'great' past to accept mediocrity in the present. That was Germany's sudden problem after 1918. Less dramatically, it has been the problem of Britain throughout this century of 'decline', especially since the Second World War. To a great extent Britain was able to compensate for her decline as a world power by the post-war rise in standards of living, the welfare state, and seemingly sustainable economic growth. But the trials and tribulations of the seventies and eighties have largely drained these compensating factors. Not even North

Sea oil, at first hailed as the national saviour and the answer to the newly truculent Arab world, has made much discernible difference.

Honesty requires us to see that the kind of 'greatness' which the British have for the last century associated with themselves, greatness conceived in terms of power and domination, has gone for good. In the real world of today, that kind of prestige is futile. In terms of military strategy and human heroism the Falklands campaign was a splendid endeavour. In longer historical perspective, it has achieved nothing except to invest the South Atlantic with potentially still more explosive antagonisms between Britain and Latin America. If patriotism means rejoicing in this land of enterprise, it is an indulgence we can do without, and the sooner the better. It is not a true love of country which encourages such self-mutilation.

Love of country as it has been explored with the aid of Bonhoeffer, makes such 'patriotism' trivial by comparison. Of course at first sight the true patriotism appears less grand, especially since it is grounded in a view of the sole and ultimate sovereignty of God, before whom all human boasting is reduced to silence. Yet one of the basic insights of Christian tradition is that only in the light of the divine dimension do earthly realities appear in their true proportions. Only so are they saved from the trivialization which leads to decay, and from the exaggeration which brings about their self-destruction. Gratitude before the Creator and responsibility before his commands and his mercy form the basis of a true relationship to one's country, as to everything else. All Bonhoeffer's ethical thinking was an attempt to do justice to these basic affirmations. A strong echo from them was heard at the Oxford Conference on Church, Community and State in 1937, the ecumenical gathering of 'Life and Work' which Bonhoeffer and his Confessing Church associates were prevented from attending, yet which paid all the more attention to the truths being contended for in Nazi Germany. For its clarity, the section of the conference report on 'The Church and the National Community (*Volk*)' is still worth reading today:

The love of the Christian for his people should therefore be part of his gratitude to God for the riches which are his through the community into which he has been born . . .

As with every divine gift, the gift of national community has been and is being abused by men and made to serve sin. Any form of national egotism, whereby the love of one's own people leads to the suppression of other nationalities or national minorities, or the failure to respect and appreciate the gifts of other people, is sin and rebellion against God, who is the Creator and Lord of all peoples. Even more, to see in one's own nation the source and standard of saving revelation, or in any way to give the nation divine status, is sin.[4]

So then, from this Christian perspective, in summary, what will a patriotism for Britain today look like?

A patriotism for today will be deeply thankful for nationhood without making it an end in itself. It will not idolize the nation. Britain will be seen not as an order of creation, of eternal significance for the world, but as an historical phenomenon for preserving the life of the people who live here. Therefore love of Britain cannot be a 'love that asks no questions', but a love that is prepared to ask very hard and penetrating questions indeed. Like every other nation, theologically speaking, Britain exists not for itself but for the reception of the kingdom of God, which is righteousness and truth. We might adopt a phrase used by Christians in the German Democratic Republic, 'critical solidarity', to describe the kind of loyalty this implies. Citizenship means accepting that this is indeed the community where one lives, by which one is sustained in earthly existence and to which one owes work and responsibility in return. But there is a perspective, not derived from the nation itself, in terms of which the life of the nation is to be assessed. This transcendent perspective is the belief in the creative and redemptive work of God. True patriotism reserves the right to raise questions in the light of that perspective. It will continually ask whether the country is moving in the direction of a truly human society (it will not of course be so naive as to pretend that it has ever got there). A true love of Britain will not sweep under the carpet the issues of endemic racism, lengthening dole-queues and overcrowded prisons.

A patriotism for today will try to look at the country as it really is. It will not be, cannot be, non-political, for our commitments need some machinery if they are to relate to the community as a whole, and that is politics. But it will be aware that our frames of reference are always in danger of distorting the reality they claim to illuminate. Not an idealized Britain, but the Britain that actually is, must engage us. Not the ideology itself, but the actual people in whose interests that ideology is said to be effective, must primarily be loved. That means listening to what real people are saying to us. David Jenkins writes:

'The contemporary' has to be engaged in contestation and in testing as well as in acceptance. It may also be added . . . that it cannot be uncritically assumed that any form of politics authentically engages the contemporary either. Many of the current slogans of both Right and Left could easily be judged to be fantasies or superstitions with little authentic engagement into what is actually going on.[5]

A patriotism for today, as with all patriotisms that have enlivened their peoples, will have a sense of the past, of the heritage that has been bequeathed to the present. But as with all great stories, it has to be recognized that there is no one single plot. The British story is a complex and many-textured drama, and we have to decide which themes are the most significant for today and tomorrow. It is 'how the coming generation will live' that must determine how we draw upon, select and put to use the items from our tradition. And put them to *use* is what we must do, if Britain is not to become an island museum. The past cannot really survive if merely preserved to be enjoyed and admired. 'Tradition' usually signifies conservatism, the maintenance of a deferential social structure, and certain selective attitudes to the British past seek to reinforce this notion. (The story is perhaps apocryphal, of the public school which discretely tried to omit the Commonwealth period from its history courses.) Yet there is nothing more deeply embedded in British history than the radical stream of life and thought, that is, an outlook which questions the *status quo* in the light of its effects on real people, which regards life, health, liberty and fulfilment as more sacrosanct than order for order's sake, let alone privilege for privilege's sake. Never has it been more necessary than now to reiterate that government exists to serve ordinary people, not *vice versa*, that power must be made accountable, that access to power in the form of information on issues vital to their lives is a right – not a privilege – of citizens. And it has to be asked whether even Parliament iself today is truly in line with the democratic thrust of the British story, which is a story of the struggle for representation of the people, not a story of devising ever-increasing powers for the leader of the party which happens to gain most seats at a general election.

Inventiveness is also part of the British tradition, yet, as has often been pointed out, in the scientific and technological sphere the industrial and commercial exploitation of British discoveries and designs in the past few decades has time and time again been carried out overseas rather than in Britain itself. But today the need for invention, experiment and imagination arises from the basic questions society itself is facing. If indeed we are moving into a post-industrial society where paid employment as known hitherto is going to be much more restricted, then the most significant voices will not be those who offer instant cures for our economic difficulties on the basis of assumptions relevant only to the past, but those who are calling for a radical re-examination of the place of work itself in the life of the individual and the community. Perhaps Martin Wiener is right in saying that Britain never fully industrialized its outlook, and that we are paying the price for that reluctance today.[6] But perhaps he was wanting just a little more than Britain can afford to give without losing herself completely. It may sound like special pleading, but the most imaginative people rarely sell themselves to one idea to the exclusion of all else, certainly as regards the means of human fulfilment. They know that life consists of more than one level, and that there is a need for keeping options open. If it was inventiveness and imagination which brought in the industrial revolution in Britain, those same qualities could well have been part of the braking mechanism against a headlong dash into industrialism for its own sake. If the imaginative flame were to glow again, such a country might be the one to offer pointers towards human fulfilment which do not depend on unlimited economic growth and ravagement of the natural and human environment. Would not that be a matter for 'pride' at least as much as winning prizes in the economic league-table? The decline-syndrome has affected us all so much that it takes a real effort of mind to see the positive resources of Britain today. Britain has a highly diverse population, especially with the arrival of the ethnic minorities in recent years; a cautious but relaxed approach to affairs; a certain inventive, experimental cast of mind. Diversity, reflectiveness, inventiveness: these are the qualities often found in the most effective *teams* of people engaged in creative work, from producing television programmes to developing new techniques of surgery. A country with Britain's human and historical resources *could* occupy an important place in the western world as a kind of laboratory for the post-industrial age. Only, now it is on themselves that they will have to experiment, and the habit of wanting to organize and reform other peoples may still be hard to forego. Above all, to adopt this more modest image of themselves will require the British to drop, for good and all, that other image of power and glory. This in itself would be a liberation, because that image haunts our generation with the accusation of continued failure compared with the successes of our grandparents. We can surely admit that that particular theme, important for a relatively short period of our history, need have no permanent role in the story. Our identity as a nation is not bound up with it. It is now time to take up other threads in the story, less glamorous perhaps, but no less significant for being more modest; no less demanding for being less aggressive; no less adventurous for being concerned with transforming ourselves rather than others. Now, no less than during the headily jingoistic days of the Boer War when they were first uttered, G. K. Chesterton's remarks on the need for a 'renascence of a love of the native land' are apposite: 'We that have produced sages who could have spoken with Socrates and poets who could walk with Dante, talk as if we have never done anything more intelligent than found colonies and kick niggers.'[7]

True patriotism will serve this historical adjustment in national self-understanding, because it will not evade the question of the nation's guilt. It will know that where the nation has deliberately or negligently inflicted harm on other peoples, or on communities within its own society, it is in the nation's own true interests that the guilt be acknowledged, confessed and repented of. Guilt does not allow either the individual or the nation to face the future realistically or creatively, because it is always trying to forget the past and its lessons, or is always trying to re-live the past in self-justification. 'A nation consisting of citizens whose consciences are bruised, is itself broken in its national strength.'[8] The bruised consciences may not always be obvious. Sometimes guilt weaves a fantasy world around the conscience to prevent the bruising. Says one respected citizen, 'In general, the nation is stable. It doesn't go and get all flared up and have riots everywhere. You see, the riots we've been having are not of our own making. It's the incomers that are making them.'[9] Such complacency may require prising open with some pretty tough language which may provoke in turn the cry of 'Traitor!' A Christian patriotism, at any rate, will be less concerned to shout back, than to take the perceived wrong into its own prayer of confession and repentance, and take such steps as it can in reparation.

A patriotism for today will distance itself from the increasing identification of patriotism with militarism that has marked this century. It does not have to be pacifist in order to question the pursuit of security via the arms spiral. Precisely because of its concern for the country, such patriotism will insist that political considerations must determine military planning, not vice versa, and that those political considerations in turn must not be based on a paranoia which seems to *demand* that we have an enemy threatening us. To require such an enemy for our own self-definition and sense of identity means that we have come to the point where we think we have nothing instrinsically and positively distinctive in ourselves.

A patriotism for today will therefore seek out and appreciate the 'national character' in the people who actually make up the country. It will recognize that the character cannot be completely defined and is always being shaped in history. It will be an inclusive patriotism, recognizing diversity, perceiving that the long-term health of the society will owe more to newcomers being accepted, than to an increasingly casuistical attitude to 'nationality' such as we have seen in recent legislation. Whether Britain has 'institutional racism' or not is partly a matter of definition. The fact is that many in the ethnic minorities are prevented from playing the part they *want* to play in British society. True patriotism will declare racism wrong not just in an abstract moral sense. It will declare that Britain, for her own good, simply cannot afford racism, for a healthy nation can only be built if it is a fully participatory one.

Finally, today's patriotism will always try to see this people in the total context of other peoples, the *oikumene*. In an increasingly crowded and interdependent world, national loyalty and international responsibility, seeking the best for one's country and seeking a more just order in the world, steadily converge. The only safe future for Britain lies in a world of greater justice between north and south, and less antagonism between east and west. And one of Britain's own vital contributions to the peace of the world is so to order her life that she does not create aspirations and dreams incapable of fulfilment, resulting in frustrations unleashed in aggression on other peoples. Loving Britain means wanting her particular, fascinating and lovable story to continue for the next generation. But that story is sustainable only in a certain kind of world, and we can only love Britain in the context of a wider concern, which for the Christian is God's concern for the whole inhabited earth, the *oikumene*.

'Never was anything in this world loved too much,' said Thomas Traherne in the seventeenth century, 'but many things have been loved in a false way, and all in too short a measure.'[10] Britain cannot be loved too much, but it must be the appropriate kind of love. We have tried to follow the main contours of that love, from a Christian perspective, and in the company of one who died for his country as a result of the clarity and passion with which he viewed his people under God. As yet, we are at a disadvantage in trying to express and communicate this patriotism for today. We have had to discard the old language and symbolism as unreal. The new poetry, hymnody and ceremony have yet to arise. One day, if sufficient people tread this way, the new words and tunes and images will come. For the present, let us keep on walking.

Notes

Abbreviations

Works of Dietrich Bonhoeffer cited in the text are abbreviated in these notes as follows:-

SC   *Sanctorum Communio*, Collins 1963.
CT   *Creation and Temptation*, SCM 1966.
C   *Christology*, Collins Fontana 1971.
CD   *Cost of Discipleship*, SCM Press 1959.
LT   *Life Together*, SCM Press 1965.
E   *Ethics*, SCM Press 1971.
LPP   *Letters and Papers from Prison*, SCM Press 1971.
NRS *No Rusty Swords: Letters, Lectures and Notes 1928-36*, Collins 1965.
WTF *The Way to Freedom: Letters, Lectures and Notes 1935-39*, Collins 1972.
TP   *True Patriotism: Letters, Lectures and Notes 1939-45*, Collins 1973.
FFP   *Fiction from Prison: Gathering Up the Past*, © Fortress Press, Philadelphia 1981, used by permission.

The following studies on Bonhoeffer are also abbreviated, thus:

DB   Eberhard Bethge, *Dietrich Bonhoeffer*, Collins 1970.
IKDB W.-D. Zimmerman and R. Gregor Smith (eds), *I Knew Dietrich Bonhoeffer*, Collins Fontana 1973.
BEM Eberhard Bethge, *Bonhoeffer: Exile and Martyr*, Collins 1975.

Chapter 1

1   P. Kleinman and S. Fisher, 'It's the age of Patriotism', *Guardian* 23rd April 1982.
2   C. S. Lewis, *The Four Loves*, Geoffrey Bles 1960, p36f. The whole section on love of country, pp32–41, is still worth reading for its common sense.
3   Adam Smith, *The Wealth of Nations*, Penguin Books 1980, p519.
4   A. H. Birch, *Political Integration and Disintegration in the British Isles*, George Allen and Unwin, 1977, p28.
5   A. R. Booth, *Not Only Peace*, SCM Press 1967, p35f.
6   Norman Wisdom, interview in *Radio Times* 30th May–5th June 1981, p7.
7   *Essays on Duty and Discipline*, Cassell 1913.
8   Bernard N. Nossiter, *Britain: A Future that Works*, Andre Deutsch 1978, p45.
9   Hymn by J. Ellerton (1826–93).
10 Donald Horne, *God is an Englishman*, Angus and Robertson 1969, p15.
11 Dr Robert Runcie, address to the National Free Church Federal Council Congress, *Free Church Chronicle*, Summer 1981, p20.
12 Speech at Louth, 1963.
13 Enoch Powell, *Still to Decide*, Batsford 1972, p26.
14 Tom Nairn, *The Break-Up of Britain: Crisis and Neo-Nationalism*, New Left Books 1977, p79.
15 Trevor Beeson, *Britain Today and Tomorrow*, Collins Fount 1978.
16 Daniel Jenkins, *The British: Their Identity and Their Religion*, SCM Press 1975, pvii.
17 ibid., p18.

Chapter 2
1   *The Herries Chronicle*. LPP p189.
2   Bethge, DB, p552.
3   LPP, p158.
4   CD, p79.
5   Phrase used by A. R. Vidler as the title of Chapter 24, on the 1960s, in his *Church in An Age of Revolution*, Penguin Books 1971.
6   Though it should be noted that the American scholar J. A. Phillips wrote his study of Bonhoeffer's christology, *The Form of Christ in the world* (Collins 1967) as a doctoral thesis at Glasgow University under Ronald Gregor Smith.
7   Bethge, DB, pxix.
8   ibid., p791.
9   Cf TP. Also Mary Bosanquet, *Bonhoeffer: True Patriot*, Mowbrays 1983.
10 Bethge, DB, p86.
11 ibid., p4.
12 Sabine Leibholz, 'Childhood and Home', IKDB, p26.
13 Bethge, DB, p34.
14 ibid., p72.
15 Paul Lehmann, 'Paradox of Discipleship', IKDB, p41f.
16 Bethge, DB, p148.
17 For an overall assessment of the churches under Nazism, see J. S. Conway, *The Nazi Persecution of the Churches*, Weidenfeld and Nicolson 1968.
18 A complete version of the Barmen Statement may be found in E. H. Robertson, *Christians Against Hitler*, SCM Press 1963.
19 CD, p272.
20 LPP, p381.
21 WTF, p246.
22 Bethge, DB, p557. But see WTF, p230, for slightly different translation.

Chapter 3
1   Keith Robbins, 'Religion and Identity in Modern Britain', in S. Mews (ed), *Religion and National Identity*, Blackwells 1982, p466.
2   Cf Eric James, 'I Vow to Thee, My Country', *Hymn Society Bulletin* 153 (January 1982), pp1–4.
3   Reinhold Niebur, *Moral Man and Immoral Society*, SCM Press 1963, p91.
4   *Richard II*, Act II, Scene 1.
5   *The Last Years: Journals 1853-55* (ed R. Gregor Smith), Collins 1965, p241.
6   Niebuhr, op. cit., p83.
7   Speech at Queen's Hall, London, 19th September 1914.
8   *Guardian*, 17th May 1982.
9   Quoted in W. Shirer, *The Rise and Fall of the Third Reich*, Pan Books 1964, p111.
10 ibid., p114.
11 K. Barth, *Ethics*, T. and T. Clark 1981.
12 'Guiding Principles of the German Christians', in P. Matheson (ed), *The Third Reich and the Christian Churches*, T. and T. Clark 1981, p5.
13 CT, p9.
14 NRS, p179f.
15 ibid., p180.
16 ibid., p167.
17 Michael Alison MP, 'The Christian in the World', in *The Christian and Conservatism Conference*, Conservative Party Central Office 1983, p21. We might add that it is dubious exegesis to identify the modern 'nation' with the 'peoples' in this text – which in any case is fundamentally a statement about the essential unity of the (diverse) peoples as God's creation, rather than their diversity as such.

18 'Thy Kingdom Come on Earth: A Bonhoeffer Sermon of 1932', translated by E. H. Robertson, *Expository Times* 88 (February 1977), p148.
19 ibid.
20 op. cit., p18f.

Chapter 4
1 CD, p136.
2 E, p169f.
3 ibid., p177.
4 ibid., p3.
5 ibid., Chapter IV.
6 ibid., p102.
7 ibid., p103f.
8 ibid., p111.
9 Cf Chapter 3, above.
10 LT, p15.
11 ibid., p78.
12 E, p52f.
13 ibid., p65.
14 For the classic expression of this analysis, See Anders Nygren, *Agape and Eros,* SPCK 1953.
15 G. K. Chesterton, 'The Rolling English Road'.
16 Jenkins, op. cit, p137.
17 Burke, *Thoughts on the French Revolution,* Everyman Edition, J. M. Dent, p153.
18 ibid., p75.
19 Quoted in Humphrey Berkeley, *The Odyssey of Enoch. A Political Memoir,* Hamish Hamilton 1977, p62.
20 ibid., p32.
21 ibid., p127.
22 ibid., p126.
23 Tom Paine, *Rights of Man,* Penguin Books 1969, p165.
24 Penguin Books 1980.
25 Penguin Books 1981.
26 Paine, op. cit.
27 'The Secret People'.
28 E, p187.
29 ibid., p105.
30 ibid., p106.

Chapter 5
1 J. Marsh, *Edward Thomas: A Poet for his Country,* Paul Elek 1978, pix.
2 'Words', *Collected Poems,* Faber and Faber 1979, p94.
3 *The British Monarchy,* Hamish Hamilton 1977, p200.
4 'Medicine Man', *Guardian,* 8th January 1983.
5 *Culture and Society 1780-1950,* Penguin Books 1979, p311.
6 *Notes Towards the Definition of Culture,* Faber and Faber 1948, p31.
7 *The English Inheritance: An Historical Essay,* SCM Press, 1950, p174f.
8 Peter Calvacoressi, *The British Experience 1945-75,* Bodley Head 1978, p228.
9 op. cit., p64.
10 *English Culture and the Decline of the Industrial Spirit 1850-1980,* Cambridge University Press 1981.
11 ibid., p158.
12 Nossiter, op. cit., p89.

13 NRS, p78.
14 TP, p64f.
15 LPP, p211f.
16 TP, p136.
17 LPP, p295.
18 ibid., p227.
19 NRS, p29.
20 'After Ten Years', LPP, p7.
21 TP, p133.
22 ibid., p139.
23 E, p85f.

Chapter 6
1   Enoch Powell, op. cit., p30.
2   Lewis, op. cit., p38
3   F. A. Iremonger, *William Temple – Archbishop of Canterbury,* Oxford University Press 1948, p210.
4   Heidelberg Disputation, Thesis XXI, *Luther's Early Theological Works,* SCM Press 1962, p291f.
5   Commentary on Galatians, *Martin Luther, Selections from His Writings* (ed J. Dillenberger), New York, Archer Books 1961, p112.
6   NRS, pp50ff.
7   CT, p65.
8   ibid., p122.
9   C, p113.
10 LPP, p393.
11 SC, p83.
12 ibid.
13 NRS, p79f.
14 SC, p83f.
15 The Intercession Liturgy, Matheson, op. cit., p77f.
16 W.A. Visser't Hooft, *Memoirs,* SCM Press 1973, p192.
17 E, p92.
18 ibid., p93.
19 ibid., p95.
20 'After Ten Years', LPP, p16f.
21 E, p210.
22 LPP, p353.
23 ibid., p354.
24 B, p791.
25 'The Dilemma of Exile', BEM, pp97–116.
26 The Long Revolution, Chatto and Windus 1961, pp84–93.
27 See e.g. Max Hastings, *Bomber Command,* Pan Books 1981, pp410–416. The Strategic Air Offensive remains a subject of considerable military and moral dispute. Any 'guilt' is least of all to be borne solely by the airmen who carried out the raids with appalling casualty rates and who, at the end of the war, were denied a campaign medal by those who now sought to distance themselves from the policy they had sanctioned.
28 Cf *Diego Garcia: A contrast to the Falklands,* Minority Rights Group Report No. 54, 1982.
29 *God is an Englishman,* p267.
30 Rudyard Kipling, 'Recessional' (written on the occasion of the Diamond Jubilee, 1897).

Chapter 7
1   Hodder and Stoughton 1982. In February 1983 the Church of England Synod
    rejected the report's recommendation of British unilateral disarmament, while
    calling for repudiation of the 'first strike' use of nuclear weapons.
2   NRS, p289.
3   *Britain and Atomic Energy 1939-45,* Macmillan 1964.
4   DB, p112.
5   CD, p102.
6   'Gedenken für den Prediger am Volkstrauertag' and 'Kurzer Entwurf zum
    Volkstrauertag', *Gesammelte Schriften* Band IV, Munich: Chr. Kaiser Verlag
    1965, pp197-201.
7   ibid., p198.
8   E, p155.
9   ibid., p229.
10 CD, p98.
11 NRS, p163f.
12 ibid., p168f.
13 ibid., p169.
14 ibid., p169f.
15 ibid., p170.
16 ibid.
17 ibid., p290f.
18 Bethge, DB, p311.
19 LPP, p7.
20 E, p73.
21 Quoted in *The Church and the Bomb,* p146f.
22 Jeremiah 45.1-5. See LPP, pp369f.
23 SCM Press 1982.
24 *The Epistle to the Romans,* Oxford University Press 1933, p51.

Chapter 8
1   Horne, op. cit., p82f.
2   *The Lion and the Unicorn: Socialism and the English Genius.* First published 1941.
    Penguin Books 1982.
3   ibid., p115.
4   ibid., p36.
5   ibid., p122f.
6   Jenkins, op. cit., p4.
7   See Nairn, op. cit., for a widely acclaimed exposition of this view.
8   Horne, op. cit., p22f.
9   ibid., p262.
10 *The Binding of Leviathan: Conservatism and the Future,* Hamish Hamilton 1980.
11 ibid., p100.
12 *Change in British Society,* Oxford University Press 1978, p164.
13 E, p79f.
14 SC, p191.
15 ibid., p193.
16 ibid., p193f.
17 Richard Rother, 'A Confirmation Class in Wedding', IKDB, p57f.
18 NRS, p151.
19 BEM, p118.
20 NRS, p221-229.
21 LPP, p17.
22 ibid.

23 ibid., p167.
24 ibid., p299.
25 ibid.
26 Complete translations of these writings (including Bonhoeffer's preliminary drafts where altered, and a critical essay from a literary and psychological perspective by Ruth Zerner), are in FPP. A translation of 'Lance Corporal Berg' may also be found in LPP, pp253–260. Certain passages from the drama and novel fragments are included in TP.
27 FFP, p43.
28 FFP, p44.
29 FFP, p121.
30 LPP, p286.
31 ibid., p300.
32 FFP, p33f.
33 ibid., p92f.

Chapter 9
1 W. E. Barnes, *Hastings Dictionary of the Bible* Volume II, T. and T. Clark 1904, p515.
2 NRS, p159.
3 ibid., p161.
4 ibid., p188.
5 ibid., p328.
6 Bethge, DB, p545f.
7 See Chapter Two, pp.
8 'Protestantism Without Reformation', written in New York 1939. NRS p105.
9 Bethge, BEM, p79.
10 TP, pp108–117.
11 ibid., p113.
12 ibid., p114.

Chapter 10
1 Nietzsche, *The Anti-Christ,* Penguin Classics 1968, p185.
2 Thomas Munn, *Dr Faustus,* Secker and Warburg, 1949, p452.
3 Karl Barth, *Letters 1961-68,* T. and T. Clark 1981, p177.
4 *The Churches Survey Their Task.* Report of the Conference at Oxford, July 1937, on Church, Community and State, George Allen and Unwin 1937. p71f.
5 David Jenkins, 'Putting Theology to Work', in *Putting Theology to Work* (Report of the Fircroft Consultation 1980), Conference for World Mission, p89.
6 See Chapter Five, pp84f.
7 Dudley Barker, *G. K. Chesterton: A Biography,* Constable 1973, p90.
8 Abraham Kuyper, quoted by J. W. de Gruchy in 'Bonhoeffer, Calvinism and Christian Civil Disobedience in South Africa', *Scottish Journal of Theology* Volume 34 No. 3 (1981), p245.
9 Sir Vivien Fuchs, interview in *Guardian,* 11th December 1982.
10 Thomas Traherne *Poems, Centuries and Three Thanksgivings,* ed. A. Ridler, Oxford University Press, 1966, p244.

Index